# THUNDER
## ON THE
# TUNDRA
## FOOTBALL ABOVE THE ARCTIC CIRCLE

## LEW FREEDMAN

ALASKA NORTHWEST BOOKS®

Anchorage, Alaska • Portland, Oregon

**Library of Congress Cataloging-in-Publication Data**

Freedman, Lew.
 Thunder on the tundra : football above the Arctic Circle / by Lew Freedman.
    p. cm.
 ISBN 978-0-88240-742-5 (softbound)
 1. Barrow High School (Barrow, Alaska)—Football. I. Title.

 GV958.B36F73 2008
 796.332'62097987—c22

                                    2008017078

Alaska Northwest Books®
An imprint of Graphic Arts Center Publishing Co.
P.O. Box 10306
Portland, OR 97296-0306
(503) 226-2402 · www.gacpc.com

President: Charles M. Hopkins
General Manager: Douglas A. Pfeiffer
Associate Publisher, Alaska Northwest Books: Sara Juday
Editorial Staff: Timothy W. Frew, Kathy Howard, Jean Andrews, Jean Bond-Slaughter
Editor: David Abel
Design: Andrea Boven Nelson
Production Staff: Susan Dupèrè

Printed in the United States of America

# Contents

# Acknowledgments

I WOULD LIKE TO THANK North Slope Borough Schools Superintendent Trent Blankenship for his help, cooperation, and open-mindedness in allowing me to spend the 2007 football season with the Barrow High School team at home and on the road.

A special, deeply felt thank-you goes to head football coach Mark Voss, for his unfailing cooperation, his important observations, and his openness in allowing me to tail along all season and watch him and his staff at work teaching football and imparting life lessons to thirty-five teenaged players.

Also deserving of special gratitude for their continual assistance are assistant coaches Jeremy Arnhart, Brian Houston, and Brad Igou. They merely answered a couple of thousand questions, and were always generous with their time.

It is obvious that this project could not have been completed without the cooperation of the players who signed up to play football for the Barrow Whalers. The young men repeatedly offered valuable, humorous, and thoughtful comments, and graciously accepted me into their world.

The same is true for Fran Tate, operator of the world's northernmost Mexican restaurant, "Pepe's Top of the World," longtime Barrow philanthropist, and keeper of the Arctic Ocean Polar Bear Club archives, who provided many keen insights.

Thanks to my old friend, Big Bob Aiken, also known as "the world's largest Eskimo," who was a major presence on my visits to Barrow, serving as a go-between, introducing me to many people, and offering his thoughts and insights.

And above all, my appreciation goes to the people of Barrow: parents of players, other relatives, football fans, and even those who opposed the creation of a football team, for their hospitality, advice, suggestions, warmth, and acceptance.

# Introduction

THE MOMENT I HEARD that Barrow High School was going to start a football team I knew something special was in the works.

*Who are they going to play?* I thought.

*Where is the closest opponent?* I wondered.

*How will this predominantly Eskimo community embrace this quintessentially American Lower-48 sport?* I pondered.

Wow, how things have changed, I realized.

During my seventeen years in Alaska, between 1984 and 2001, all spent working in the sports department of the *Anchorage Daily News,* I had visited Barrow several times. And I had written about Alaska high school football's quirks and triumphs, from its earliest-in-the-nation start in mid-August to its earliest-in-the-nation conclusion by the third week of October, and its often freezing weather.

When I first arrived, Alaska's population was the smallest of the fifty states at around 500,000. By the time I moved away, it was up to forty-eighth and there were about 620,000 people. While undeniably still the Last Frontier, Alaska had become far more integrated into the mainstream life of the other forty-nine states. This manifested itself in many ways, not the least of which was better access to jet plane service, telephone communications, and cable TV. With connection and population growth came chain stores and chain restaurants, and parents and children with the same demands as their Lower-48 counterparts.

Alaska became much more like the rest of the nation than it had been, and that also meant unseemly influences on youth. There were drug and alcohol problems in villages and communities where it seemed impossible for drugs and alcohol to surface. Cultural changes were vast. Not only did residents of once-remote Alaskan communities know who the most popular singers of the day were and which were the hottest movies, they gained access to them—if not through their computers, at least through shopping trips to Fairbanks and Anchorage.

Concurrent with those changes were changes in the high school sports landscape. Basketball has always been king in the Alaska Bush, partially because many schools were too small to field other teams and you only need five to play hoops. As elsewhere, girls' sports proliferated. Whereas once the only high school football teams in the 570,000-square-mile state played in Anchorage, Fairbanks, the Mat-Su Valley, and the Kenai Peninsula, all situated on the limited highway system, population shifts meant towns of 4,500 people wanted their own football teams.

One by one, communities like Nikiski, Skyview, and Houston opened new high schools and sought a broad-based sports menu. Football spread. When Juneau—the isolated state capital, reachable only by boat or airplane—added football, new barriers were breached. Located in the Southeast corner of the state, adjacent to the Canadian border, Juneau is eight hundred miles south of Anchorage. Big bucks were required not only to outfit a team, but to travel.

Until Barrow suited up a team for a limited, nonconference schedule in 2006, Juneau was the standard-bearer for overcoming financial and logistical challenges. Barrow is the flip side, located eight hundred miles north of Anchorage, four hundred miles north of Fairbanks. It is the northernmost community in the United States.

And unlike Juneau, Barrow is culturally and historically quite different from many other Alaskan road-system communities. Barrow has been home to Iñupiat Eskimos for thousands of years. Residents remain strongly connected to a subsistence hunter-gatherer culture. Among the most powerful influences in a community with a sleek high school, and modern buildings and homes, are the annual bowhead whale hunts. The people are still very close to the land, aware that in a supremely harsh climate it remains imperative to rely upon one another.

The same outlook can be applied to football, sometimes regarded as the ultimate team game. With eleven moving parts on offense and eleven on defense, the players' reliance on one another for success usually transcends the individual. This posed a particular challenge in Barrow, where the basic exposure to football was confined to National Football League games on television. There were no youth leagues. There was no junior high feeder program. If you wanted to play high school football in Barrow you learned from scratch: These are the knee pads. These are the hip pads.

Whaling and football. Remoteness and journeys of a thousand miles. Costs and cash. In a place where gigantic crossed whale bones on the beach facing the Arctic Ocean defined the heartbeat of the town, it was fascinating to see how it would all work out.

Two-a-days—the twice-daily preseason practice regimen that coaches employ to drill their players, while they have their undivided attention before school starts—began on July 30 and continued through early August.

My same-day Alaska Airlines flight (people didn't think it was possible) chased the time zones westward, carrying me from Chicago to Seattle to Fairbanks to Barrow in about thirteen hours. On a day when the nation sweltered and the Chicago Bears leaked sweat in their own Illinois training camp, I was the only passenger carrying a full-fledged, hooded parka.

## CHAPTER 1

# *August Two-a-Days*

ALBERT GERKE'S HALF-MILE WALK in full football pads from Barrow High School to the Bobby Fischer practice field in the center of town took him past the community cemetery, past the boxy houses built to withstand ferocious winter weather, and across an uneven grassy landscape. His blue helmet swung loosely in his hand by his side.

Three little boys watched him approach and one said, "Do you play football?" The quarterback of the northernmost high school football team in the world said yes. Gerke is six-foot-one and weighs a slender 160 pounds, but to the kids about ten years old he was a giant.

"Can we touch it?" one youngster said. Gerke smiled, stopped, and held out his Whalers' football helmet. The boys admired it, stroked it, and looked at Gerke with awe in their eyes. To them he might as well have been Brett Favre.

In this remote city of 4,800 people, where the only neighbors are whales hunted by the Iñupiat Eskimos of the region for more than a thousand years, football has long been only a television program. National Football League games were beamed into the community best known to many as the place where famed aviator Wiley Post and entertainer Will Rogers died in a plane crash in 1935. Those popular football TV shows featured characters like Tom Brady and Peyton Manning, only slightly more real to the viewers than Tony Soprano and Gregory House.

For Gerke, something unfathomable only a year before was unfolding. He was a flesh-and-blood football player and, at least for this fleeting moment, he was a local hero. Gerke, only a sixteen-year-old sophomore, immediately grasped the significance of the brief encounter. They were boys, just like he had been a few years earlier, and he provided something to ignite their imaginations that he had never had. He was the TV football player come to life and he had become very much the role model just by slipping into uniform.

Football was new to everyone in Barrow: the elders whose lives were rooted in subsistence hunting and fishing culture, the Native corporation officials who saw the value in providing a new activity for teenagers' participation, the school officials who sought ways to keep students from dropping out, and the athletes themselves, who were trying to adapt years of long-distance football watching to on-field situations.

Gerke, like most of his teammates, understood the function they were serving. They were pioneers who knew they were the originators of something they hoped would last and inspire future generations.

The contrast between early August football in Barrow and early August football in the rest of the United States can be measured on the thermometer. A big worry for coaches in the Lower 48 is keeping their players hydrated during the demanding two-a-day preschool practice sessions, when the mercury might hit 95°F and the humidity creates steam in the air you can practically reach out and grab. In Barrow, the issue is whether or not a sweatshirt is needed for warmth.

The temperature might drop to 35°F, and with the wind whipping in over the flat tundra from the adjacent Arctic Ocean, the cooling breeze might well be a freezing breeze. There is no true summer in Barrow; not the way it is perceived in the rest of the country. If the temperature hits 70°F meteorologists check the records. A handful of days in the high 60s may arrive, sprinkled between June and August, though in these days of global warming volatility, nobody knows just what to expect.

Still, Barrow players were well supplied with drinking water, carried to practice each day in a beer-keg-sized container in the back of an old beige station wagon. They bought a few moments of respite from drills by filling small water cups and savoring the liquid. Once in a while, distracted by one or two four-wheelers filled with girls who stopped to watch practice, they might linger over one cup of water too long for the coaches' taste. Defensive back Dave Evikana, in full uniform, once even jumped on the back of a motor scooter parked by the station wagon, to get the feel for it.

High school football in Alaska was a long shot from the start a half century or so ago, representing transplanted mainlanders bringing their game north. But the permanent population grew when those transplants settled down after the Alaska Pipeline opened in 1976 and built more schools. The sport has spread as the population has expanded, but it remains very much at the mercy of the elements. Alaska high school football has always started earlier in the summer and ended earlier in the fall than in any other state. In Alaska, the climate dictates the football schedule.

Barrow football practice in 2007 started July 30. Unless the Whalers made the playoffs during their first season in the Greatland Conference, the games would be finished by October 1. The state championship game would be played in Anchorage the third week in October while the biggest sporting event going on in the rest of the country would be baseball's World Series. Even at that early date the participants would be darned lucky if they didn't have an icy field, see snow falling, or need space heaters the size of spaceships on the sidelines.

The gang that gathered thirty-five strong to represent Barrow during its first season of league play was weather toughened. Many of the players wore short sleeves. They were in their environment, anxious pupils for Coach Mark Voss and his trio of assistants Jeremy Arnhart, Brian Houston, and Brad Igou, men who had football on their resumes as players more than as coaches, and who had volunteered to lead when the North Slope Borough School District put out a call for coaches in 2006.

These were men who had years of teaching experience in the Arctic, and coaching backgrounds in other sports, as well: who wanted to build men as well as football players, but who knew that the squad they sought to shape was as raw as any team in the universe. Their boys did not grow up playing tackle football in the backyard—for one thing there was no grass—nor did they graduate from Pop Warner programs (none of that in Barrow) or junior high teams.

More than half a century ago, his fame still waiting in the wings, Red Auerbach, coach of the Boston Celtics, once began a practice with the most rudimentary comment of all. "This," he said, holding up a leather sphere, "is a basketball." Now that's going back to the fundamentals! But Barrow coaches also had to gently instruct in the art of dressing in football equipment. Where shoulder pads go may be self-evident, but the difference between a thigh pad, a hip pad, and an elbow pad can be more subtle.

Coaching a high school team requires sensitivity and balance, for teaching the sport and teaching life lessons. Coaches should be disciplinarians and father-confessors. There are rules for all, and then there are nuances for bringing the best out of certain individuals. Above all, fairness must rule, and the crowd of candidates must be molded into a unit.

All of this begins in preseason, when there are no fans, except for periodic drop-ins from parents, or wandering children yet to start school. And for Barrow the practice site was emblematic of the harshness of the terrain that has forever defined human life at the top of the world.

Bobby Fischer Field was once the town's softball complex. A seemingly abandoned red-and-white fire department trailer was parked at one corner of the grounds. The field is ringed by generally weatherbeaten and weatherproof buildings, and the airport is close enough that the periodic landing of jets can be noted.

The land is a slab of hard earth thickly inhabited by rocks, some embedded in the ground, some loose on the surface, all inconvenient obstacles to soft landings when football players are taken down. Barrow in general is not a place that harbors soft landings, but the open space was the best option for practice. From their first moments on the pockmarked field, the players adapted to a routine of tossing inch-size rocks off the field any time they saw one or fell on one. They went home from practice with bruises and scrapes every day, but they didn't complain. Each day they returned and when they came across a rock they bent down and discarded it, or climbed to their feet with a rock in hand and flung it away. There were many more rocks than hands available, so the job was never finished.

The field is about half a mile from the school. Barrow residents have grown used to the sight of players like John Wilson zipping past in uniform on his four-wheeler, wearing dark glasses. It is a slick look for him. Or of Zac Rohan, helmet in one hand, skirting around the town cemetery on foot, through a residential area, past the strange signs nailed to telephone poles noting the distance to the other planets, including "Neptune, 2,800,000,000 Miles From Sun." There are plenty of times during the year when the sun seems 2.8 billion miles from Barrow.

During two-on-one blocking drills, when one charging player made an attempt to rush an invisible quarterback, the dirt kicked up by the players' feet formed mini dust storms.

One morning, Voss watched his watch as the second hand inexorably announced the time as 9:00 A.M. About ten players were in sight, still jogging to the practice field.

"Line 'em up!" Voss yelled.

Team captains and assistant coaches formed rows of players to start calisthenics and other loosening-up exercises. Hats on. Players had their names written on tape on the front of their helmets.

Voss, forty-seven, who grew up in Arkansas, gauged the weather, predicted the temperature would reach 50°F and that remnants of morning fog would evaporate. Voss played college ball at a small school named Henderson State in Arkansas. He has broad shoulders, stands six-foot-four and weighed 190 pounds as a player, though there has since been some thickening around the middle. He has blondish hair, still thick, with blue eyes and a mustache, and it has even been suggested that he resembles Kevin Costner. But after twenty-three years in Alaska, some spent in villages like the even-more-remote Anaktuvuk Pass, and sixteen in Barrow, there is not a Hollywood bone in his body.

It is not impossible for it to snow in July in Barrow, so any day of comparative mildness is welcome. On a day the year before, the players had begun their hike from the high school to the practice field in clear skies. Abruptly, it clouded over, a heavy drizzle started, and high winds ripped across the field. "Within forty-five minutes we were shivering," Voss said. "I was thinking, 'We need to wrap this up.'"

The team broke up into small groups. Quarterbacks with receivers. Offensive and defensive linemen. Running backs and defensive backs. The assistant coaches put players through drills. Voss moved from group to group, sometimes hands-on, throwing passes to ends. Orange traffic cones marked spots on a field that had no yard markers.

To demonstrate what he wanted on a play out of the I formation that he favors from his own experience, Voss took a snap, faded back— and threw short. Hmm. He said he had to throw longer. The next snap he overthrew the receiver by yards.

"I did throw it farther," he said.

Listen to what I say, don't emulate what I do.

"I messed you up," Voss said to Gerke while affectionately giving him a push in the shoulder.

Brad Igou, a former lineman at Arizona State, oversaw some passing drills. The coaches all knew how sorely lacking in experience, in reps, even in practice, their players were. Even the best players in the world in every sport comprehend the value of repetition in making plays. That's why baseball players hit for hours in the batting cage. That's why an NBA player like Caron Butler can commit to an off-season regimen of taking one thousand jump shots daily— 100,000 during his team's seasonal break. Barrow football coaches knew there was no time for that much repetition, but they hoped to drum things into players' heads so hard that one day they would wake up and not think before acting, but act instinctively.

"Catch with your hands, not with your pads," Igou scolded.

Voss could hold a conversation and watch practice at the same time. When a player stopped a pass route and spun the wrong way, Voss blew his whistle. The player had interrupted the flow of the offense. Voss ran over and showed him the proper technique.

Back on the sideline, he said, "Sorry, I had a teachable moment there."

The coaches desperately wanted to make a football team out of their hopefuls. Once the games began, they didn't want to be overwhelmed by mistakes, by missteps that provoked officials into tossing yellow penalty flags like confetti. But they also wanted their guys to play hard, to harness and direct their energy into useful and meaningful assaults.

When the ball was hiked, the coaches wanted to see their linemen explode into the player across the line. They didn't always get what they wanted.

"Nice dancing, ladies," groaned Brian Houston, a former University of New Haven lineman who weighs more than 300 pounds.

A little bit later, Houston supervised the universal linemen drill of pushing heavy blocking sleds around the field. This is man's muscle against weighted inanimate object, five players at once seeking to cohesively power a metal monster downfield by blending their own brute strength. The drill mimics offensive linemen firing off the ball creating a hole for their ball carrier to burst through, and shoving defensive linemen backward so they can't make the tackle.

The five big boys who stepped in and manhandled the bulky sled for ten yards, twenty yards, brought a gleam to Houston's eyes. That is the type of unified effort that produces bonding. Oh, Houston adored what he saw.

"I love you!" he announced. "I want to see it again. You're going to move some people. There you go! Drive!"

There is beef on the line. Senior John Lambrecht, who weighs about 340 pounds, is called "Big John" as if it is his given name. Senior Denver Enoch stands six-foot-seven and his younger brother, Dane, is nearly as big. So is junior Trevor Litera. All flirt with the risk of breaking bathroom scales during weigh-ins. For a small school, this size is unusual and can become no small advantage if the green players smooth out their technique.

One difference between established high school programs and a freshly created one can be the mere appearance of players at the start of a season. In a school district where players have gone through youth programs, coaches have a pretty good idea about up-and-coming young talent. Voss had no idea who was going to show up. He never figured that Ganina Pili would be among his candidates for the defensive backfield.

A volleyball star and accomplished basketball player, the five-foot-four Pili was one of the top athletes at Barrow High, outstanding on state championship teams. But Pili was a she. In the spring, Pili asked Voss if she could try out. Taken aback, Voss said yes.

"I didn't expect it," Voss said of a girl wanting to play football. "I just have to deal with the issue of making sure she has a place to dress."

On the field, Pili blended. All of the players wore the same blue helmets protecting their heads and faces. They wore the same white practice jerseys. When passes came her way, Pili grabbed her share. When it was her turn to backpedal in coverage, Pili stuck with her man. If you didn't know, you wouldn't think she was a girl. She was a player. It was hard to know so early if the other players would be skittish about playing with a girl, but when Pili ran off the field for a breather she high-fived with another player. Just one of the boys.

In the middle of practice, an older Native man rode a bicycle onto the field and rode right up to Voss. He had an idea that would help the team with play calling, he said.

"They could count in Iñupiaq," the man said. "The other team won't have a clue what they're calling." The man repeated, "I just had an idea," and rode off.

The funny thing was that the year before, when things were just getting started, Voss actually did have the Whalers call some plays in

Iñupiaq. As the man rode away, Voss bent down, picked up a rock, and tossed it away from the playing area.

"Last year we had one that was the size of a melon," he said.

The loose rocks were rocks, not slivers of gravel or pebbles. Pebbles were part of the texture of the field.

Preseason is about hard work, getting ready, but you can't bring three dozen teenagers together and not expect moments of levity. It is neither realistic, nor should it be expected. Fun should be part of playing the game. It is just ill-advised for a player to make the wrong wisecrack when coaches are being serious.

During a punting drill, the ball floated against the half-gray, half-blue sky and wide receiver Jim Martin, standing on the sidelines, made his teammates chuckle with the silly observation, "Holy flying pigskin, Batman."

Sophomore tackle Mike Olson removed his helmet and displayed a new decoration in the back of his closely cropped hair. His number, 75, was carved into his hair. Why?

"I was bored," Olson said. "It's just for fun."

Receiver Justin Sanders, who exhibited a budding Afro, took one look at Olson's artwork and announced to everyone in earshot, "My hair is not being cut."

Once in a while a coach's shouted instruction was drowned out by a jet plane landing a couple of blocks away. Passenger service to Barrow is limited to a few flights a day, and Alaska Airlines is the main carrier. During practice at Bobby Fischer, a just-landed plane was visible in glimpses, the trademark smiling Eskimo on the tail playing peekaboo between houses as it pulled up to the outdoor gate.

Near the end of practice, Sanders, who foresees a future for himself catching passes in the NFL, hit the dirt after a play and unconsciously scooped up the closest rocks and threw them away.

"We're just in the habit," he said. "I sprained my left ankle on one last season. When the receivers are running our routes we don't see them on the ground. But when you fall you do."

With eleven-on-eleven drills, some players slouched off to the side, some chatted, and some sat on the ground. Igou noted the casual atmosphere and bellowed, "You guys are teammates. Get off your butts and cheer for them. They need to hear you."

At the end of practice, the team huddled in the middle of the field. At first the players were noisy. One muttered, "I didn't get a chance to hurt anybody today." Another player replied, "That's your fault." Apparently a dig at the other's lack of tackling vigor.

The players quieted as the coaches spoke. Each coach delivered a message about what he saw that day and what he thought the team needed to work on. Focus and fundamentals. That's what the Whalers still needed to improve on. This sport was still so new to them.

As the players and coaches scattered, Arnhart, thirty-three—like Voss from Arkansas originally, but the offspring of a family of Bush Alaska educators—mused that one good thing about this point in the practice schedule was the pleasantly warm 50-ish weather.

"I haven't had to wear gloves yet," he said.

## CHAPTER 2

# *This Is Barrow*

ON A MID-AUGUST NIGHT in 1935, a world that had never heard of Barrow, Alaska, received a geographical education even as it devolved into mourning. A small plane flown by swashbuckling, one-eyed pioneer aviator Wiley Post, carrying as sole passenger Will Rogers (perhaps the most famous man in America), crashed nose first into the mud on the outskirts of town, killing both men.

More than seventy years later, the accident remains a defining incident in Barrow history, and the root of most knowledge about the community for those who live thousands of miles away.

Post was known as a prominent pilot, chiefly admired for becoming the first solo flyer to circumnavigate the globe, a remarkable feat in the early era of flight. But the fame of Rogers crossed many lines. He was a radio star, a newspaper columnist, a Wild West show performer, a vaudeville star, and was breaking into the movies. Part Cherokee Indian, Rogers gained his first notoriety for dazzling audiences with rope tricks.

Rogers was an accomplished writer and humorist, beloved in all corners of the country for his homespun commentaries and for being possibly the most down-to-earth celebrity in the world. He made pithy comments that made politicians seem foolish, and identified with the masses of the public that couldn't speak for themselves. Rogers's most famous homily was the statement, "I never met a man I didn't like."

Both men were adventurous travelers. Rogers came to Alaska to interview aging survivors of the gold rush. Post wanted to explore a new air route between Alaska and Russia. Given their personalities, it seemed likely Post and Rogers were just itching for an excuse to fly north and check out new territory, and they might have gone on a whim as likely as for a tangible reason.

They flew north, with stops in Juneau, Anchorage, and Fairbanks, and Rogers wrote newspaper columns along the way on a small type-writer, the laptop of its day. Undaunted by a forbidding weather report that called for snow, Post steered his plane to Barrow. Through declin-ing visibility, Post guided the plane to the Walakpa Lagoon, sixteen miles from Barrow.

Post landed at a fish camp belonging to Clair Okpeaha and his wife, and asked directions to Barrow, as one might by pulling over a car at a gas station. Post and Rogers waved, the plane took off, and promptly spun out of control, its engine dead, and crashed into the lagoon nose first. The plane then flipped over on its back. Okpeaha ran to administer first aid, but both men died on impact.

Okpeaha had no idea who the occupants of the plane were, but he realized he must report the accident. The terrain between the lagoon and the city is mostly squishy tundra, and is uneven with tussocks. Okpeaha ran the distance back to town—much like Pheidippedes in ancient Greece, delivering news of battle by running the twenty-six miles from Marathon to Athens. According to myth, Pheidippedes (who apparently had not done his interval work) dropped dead after telling authorities that the Greeks had defeated the Persians.

It took Okpeaha five hours, and if he suffered more than a blister, history does not record it. A rescue party was organized, but from the first it was in actuality a body retrieval party. The word of the deaths of the two famous men was transmitted from Barrow after their bodies were taken into the community. Later, Barrow named its fire station after Okpeaha, though as a monument it is certainly less visited than the Post–Rogers memorial.

Visitors who fly to Barrow land at the Wiley Post–Will Rogers Memorial Airport. Across the street stands a memorial that provides biographies of the men and the story of the crash, adjacent to cross-roads signs featuring arrows and mileage points from the street corner to cities around the world. Some of the places highlighted: the North Pole, 1,131 miles thisaway; the South Pole, 11,109 miles thataway; Greenland, 1,520 miles; Chicago, 3,000 miles; and Iron Ranch, Oklahoma, the birthplace of Will Rogers, 3,246 miles.

Barrow is located roughly three hundred miles above the Arctic Circle, and has been described as being about equidistant between Juneau and the North Pole. That would mean the North Pole directional sign's distance proclamation is considerably exaggerated. The city is named after Sir John Barrow, a member of the British Admiralty who, in the 1800s, sent expeditions into the Arctic seeking the elusive Northwest Passage. In 1826, to honor Barrow the man, mapmakers affixed his name to Point Barrow, currently on the outskirts of town. The permanent settlement followed.

Much of Barrow's well-being is linked to the discovery of oil on the North Slope of Alaska. As the oil companies made plans to develop the famed Alaska Pipeline between Deadhorse in the north and its terminus at Valdez in the south, negotiations were conducted to protect Alaska's native peoples. The Alaska Natives Claims Settlement Act was shepherded through Congress, and President Richard Nixon signed the agreement into law on December 18, 1971. It provided for 44 million acres of land to be divided by Alaska Natives, $962 million in cash, and for the disbursements to be managed by thirteen Native corporations. The Arctic Slope Regional Corporation is the major corporation that supervises the land, investments made with the cash, and dividends paid to shareholders for the Iñupiat people of the area.

There are a handful of hotels, but the best known is the Top of the World Hotel. Sometimes while visitors are waiting to check in they are treated to a snack: the bite-sized, pink and black squares on the plate are muktuk, or whale meat. Muktuk is very chewy and takes as much mastication as bubble gum, though it is meant for swallowing. Locals always perk up, waiting for the reaction of the initiate who partakes of the delicacy, which is also often quite salty. It is fair to say that muktuk is an acquired taste.

Skittish visitors have been spied spitting out the remnants of their snacks when they think no one is looking. Residents do not seem to mind—at least the newcomers tried. Tasting muktuk is a reach across a divide.

So is jumping into the Arctic Ocean. Barrow is situated where the Beaufort and Chukchi seas merge and become the Arctic Ocean. In a normal summer (or at least before global warming made inroads in the Arctic), the water across the street from the Top of the World is ice free for only about ten weeks. The sun is above the horizon twenty-four hours a day for much of this stretch. This is the respite, the flip side of the dark of winter. For sixty-seven days between mid-November and mid-January, wrapped around the winter solstice, the sun does not rise above the horizon in Barrow. Streetlights downtown are on at noon.

During the open-water period, those with a sense of adventure, those with a sense of curiosity, or those simply with a screw loose, are invited to become members of the Polar Bear Club. This is definitely a place for a Polar Bear Club. When author Peter Jenkins moved to Alaska temporarily to explore the state and write of the essence of being Alaskan, he discovered that Barrow averages 322 days a year on which the temperature does not exceed 32°F, or freezing, so if you are looking for warm water, forget it. Fran Tate is the keeper of the Polar Bear Club records. People are requested to check in at her restaurant, pay a $10 fee, and then every afternoon at 5:00 P.M., Tate, or her son Joe, supervises the plunge. To make it an official jump, swimmers must go in over their heads.

There are bad days to try this, and there are slightly better days to try this. When the water temperature warms to the 40s because of an intense sun, it feels almost like cheating. But on the days when the water temperature is in the 30s, and it is overcast and windy, jumpers can't wrap towels around themselves and dash the one block to get back indoors fast enough.

The reward, besides the shivers, is a story to tell, and a souvenir patch and certificate that Tate mails weeks later when she has time. Anyone who observes this daily phenomenon long enough detects a pattern. The jumpers are usually tourists, or local teenagers—such as football players demonstrating their toughness. Adult Eskimos—who are wary of the changing ice conditions in other seasons, and are all too familiar with the most frigid wintry elements—are only seen in the neighborhood fully clothed and chuckling.

At no time is the hilarity greater than on teachers day. Yes, admitted Big Bob Aiken, a lifelong resident, locals do think the jumpers are nuts. He was not about to strip down and participate.

At the end of the first day of teacher orientation for the North Slope Borough School District, a yellow school bus pulled up to the beach across the street from the Top of the World and disgorged a gaggle of jumpers. In one of his other roles, besides being the founder of football, Trent Blankenship had spoken to his new teachers earlier in the day, welcoming them before they were deployed to the villages. Offhandedly, with a tongue-in-cheek tone, he informed them that it was a tradition for newcomers to dive into the Arctic Ocean as a sort of homage to their new surroundings. Good thing Big Bob and his friends didn't hear that one. They would have gagged holding back laughter. Oh yeah, and they charge ten bucks, too. How funny is that?

It wasn't clear to the new teachers if they were being put on, the dunk was mandatory, or by participating they would just curry favor with the boss.

The bus arrived and out poured three dozen pale, white-skinned imports from the Lower 48, who had fallen for the spiel. They were lucky enough to catch a sunny day, with an air temperature of 49°F, albeit windy. The school personnel were joined by a few tourists with recklessness in their souls.

"You only live once," said Scott Leighton, thirty-five, of Warwick, Rhode Island, who was in Barrow on business to inspect water tanks. "I'm doing it just to do it. Do you have hot drinks here?"

Clearly, he was a man thinking ahead, if not thinking clearly.

The scene very much resembled something Fellini would have dreamed up for one of his movies. Yep, here we are, forty people frolicking on the sandy beach in Barrow, Alaska, trying to avoid stepping on whale bones. As a cold breeze raked the shore, people parked their coats on the sand, took off shoes, shirts, and pants. Men were bare-chested in bathing suits or shorts. Women wore T-shirts or swimsuits. The water temperature was 37°F—heck, practically a heat wave.

"No toe-tipping," Tate announced.

The run-up to the water was a bit less organized than a pistol being fired at the start of the Olympic 100-meter dash: more of a "ready, set, go" thing. Jumpers jumped in groups or singly, shouted as the cold water assaulted their flesh, then ran out of the ocean as fast as they could, hoping to avoid a jellyfish sting, an unexpected obstacle.

"My legs are a little cold," announced Julianna Shields, a thirty-year-old medical student from Anchorage in Barrow temporarily. "It was cold underwater. It was definitely cold. But no regrets."

Craig Crebar, fifty, came to Barrow to become an assistant principal. His wife, Claire, fifty, came to Barrow to become a kindergarten teacher. Kelly Crebar, seventeen, came to Barrow to become a high school junior and because her parents were quirky enough to move from Knoxville, Tennessee, before she could graduate. The family that swims together, stays together. Actually, the Crebars said they were not under intense pressure to go jump in the big pond during this break in orientation action.

"We could go home and chill out," Mrs. said.

"Or we could come here and chill out," Mr. said.

"I'm doing it once and that's it," proclaimed Mrs., thinking ahead to her tenure in Barrow.

The trio ran across the sand and jumped into the Arctic Ocean. Pretty fast, they were back, drying off as quickly as their hands could move those towels.

"I thought it would be colder," Mr. said.

"It was colder than I thought it would be," Miss said.

"It was refreshing," Mrs. said. "It feels like I'm part of the community now."

In a demonstration of solidarity with his new teachers and administrators, Blankenship appeared on the beach, fully clothed, wearing a sport coat and tie. Blankenship had a mischievous look in his eye when he said these teachers knew they should do the jump to butter up the boss.

Then, all of a sudden, apparently caught up in the mood of the moment, Blankenship ran into the ocean. There were screams. There was laughter. He was still wearing that sport coat and tie when he emerged from the deep soaking wet.

"Yeah, it's team spirit," Blankenship yelled.

Practically open-mouthed, Darrell Richard, an assistant principal for Point Hope, surveyed Blankenship's dripping form and said, "I can't believe you jumped in with your clothes on. You one-upped us."

Teachers day was the biggest jump-in day of the season, but there were almost always customers. The Polar Bear Club is one extreme indication that people in Barrow can go a little bit cuckoo. The event represented a minor hullabaloo, but in the seventy-two years following the Wiley Post–Will Rogers fatal crash, there had been only one other occasion when things turned nearly so wild in Barrow.

In October 1988, three gray whales, late departing the area for their seasonal migration, became trapped in the rapidly closing off-shore Arctic Ocean ice. They needed holes in the ice to gain air, but the water was freezing around them. At least initially, the adult Eskimos of Barrow were content to apply the same outlook to the whales' situation as they brought to the polar bear jumpers—watch from a distance as things sorted themselves out.

For the hardened Eskimos who survived on their wits against the harshness of the land and climate, the forty-foot-long whales seemed to be examples of the process of natural selection. Meaning, if you mess up, you die. However, the whales became an international cause célèbre, and for love or money, the Natives of Barrow became heavily invested in aiding the escape of the trapped whales.

Scientists from Alaska and elsewhere became involved. Governments took time off from raising taxes and making wars to cooperate and free the whales. A Russian icebreaker arrived, offering reinforcements. The whales were given names and schoolchildren watched from afar praying that their favorites would survive and escape to southern climes. Small fortunes were made by locals who ferried rescue personnel and television and newspaper teams onto the ice. But then seasoned whalers became caught up in the effort and lent their know-how to the cause. The entire epic made *Free Willy* look like a cartoon short subject.

Barrow was in the international spotlight in a manner it had not been since the 1935 plane crash. There was considerable mixed feeling about the event, though. Many felt it a waste of time and resources to try to save whales that hadn't been smart enough to save themselves, in a whaling community to boot—where, as Big Bob joked, some looked at the gray whales and thought, "Dinner." (But really, they were the wrong species for whaling.) Others believed it was a noble cause, softening the hearts of the rugged Northerners.

In the end, through the cooperative efforts of Barrow whaling captains, Barrow and North Slope Borough resources, American and Russian ships, oil companies, and even Greenpeace, two of the three whales were last seen swimming to freedom beyond the ice pack. The third submerged and never surfaced again. The humans involved in the effort had no way of knowing if the two set free survived, if they were strong enough to reach their off-season destinations, or if they ever returned to Barrow. The story ended in mystery.

After a couple of weeks, everyone packed up their chain saws, their cameras, and decamped. Barrow settled into another long, cold winter out of the limelight.

There is enough of a fascination with Barrow's position on the map, the dot at the top of the country, to bring visitors to town to see what it's all about. They nearly all come in the summer, never the winter. There are limits to curiosity.

Daniel Lum, a heavyset man in his thirties wearing an ivory necklace, operates Northernmost Tours.

"The crash in 1935 put us on the map," Lum said. "To this day we get historians who want to see the place."

More recently, Lum, who is six-foot-two and weighs 320 pounds, hears more about football than he ever thought possible. Oh yes, he definitely would have played if the game had been available at Barrow High when he was a student, about fifteen years earlier. Football made an impact in the community almost immediately, Lum said.

"I'm starting to hear the young guys around the team talking about college," he said. "And I'm starting to see the junior high kids scrimmaging on the beach."

Lum, who has obligations to other visitors this day, turns over a small tour group to an assistant driver, Mike Toovak, thirty-eight, but not before asking the passengers to sign a release form for the thirty-two-mile, round-trip drive, acknowledging that it's "inherently dangerous." It is not clear if the danger lies in poor roads or the possibility of polar bear attack, but everyone laughs and no one asks questions.

The dirt road winds out of town, leaving the boxy homes and businesses behind quickly. The ocean is on the right and the waves lap at the shore, eroding the land in some places. At times the road is pitted, mandating slow, 5-mph progress in Toovak's Nissan Titan truck. The spongy tundra is on the left, sometimes ending in small cliffs perhaps a dozen feet above the road.

Some of the soil is exposed, the land chewed up, turned over. What had once been perpetually frozen was softening.

"There is a lot of erosion on the tundra," Toovak said. "Global warming."

A decapitated walrus lay on the side of the road. The head was missing. Someone had apparently sawed it off to keep the tusks.

"That's illegal," Toovak said. "Me, I harvest the meat and give it to the elders."

Eskimo mores demand respect for elders and the elderly. It is understood that years of experience produce acquired wisdom. Toovak said his father, Dr. Kenneth Toovak, Sr., eighty-four, remembers the Wiley Post–Will Rogers crash. People are born, live, and die in Barrow. Generations stay and go on, adapting to modernization, but adhering to the old ways as well. Hunting and fishing remain staples of Native life.

The porcupine caribou herd, some 123,000 strong, passes this way, cutting across the Arctic National Wildlife Refuge (where many politicians want to drill for oil) on its annual migrations between Alaska and Canada in the spring and fall. For hundreds, perhaps a thousand years, the indigenous people of the area built sod huts with cellars constructed in the permafrost to keep meat fresh, before there was refrigeration or freezer capability. The cellars are still in use by many, but in the surest sign of global warming that needs no scientific interpretation, the permafrost is disintegrating.

"They're really thawing," Toovak said. "I threw away a bunch of meat from last year's harvest. I'd rather live off the land, hunting ducks and geese."

Toovak said tourists always ask him what muktuk tastes like and he tells them it's just like sushi. But, he confides, that's not really true, just the best analogy he can come up with.

"I can't stand the smell of sushi," he said. "Muktuk is different from sushi. The texture's the same, but not the taste."

The waves broke on shore to the right as Toovak's truck forced its way down a road that did not want to be traversed. At one point he pulled it up a hill and stopped in front of some dilapidated sod houses. They had been used as "authentic" props when Hollywood came to town decades earlier. (The Walt Disney Company filmed the movie *Track of the Giant Snow Bear* on location here in 1969.) Underfoot there were spent rifle shells. Hunters used the area to spot and shoot at waterfowl.

Part of the Eskimo diet is ptarmigan, the Alaska state bird (contrary to sarcastic humor, it is not the mosquito), the bird that turns brown in summer and white in winter to blend with its environment. Toovak compared the taste to quail, but then he said, "The meat is really tough."

After an hour's drive, the road narrowed some more and the stone obelisk that was erected as the original memorial to Post and Rogers came into view. The stone was faded and any inscription had been weathered off by the violent winds, lashing rain, and powerful snowfalls that pounded the area.

"This is all history right here," Toovak said.

➡ ⬅

The Alaska Commercial Store is a modern grocery store, and the key reason everything is so expensive is that all of the goods are shipped in. However, the Eskimos who live in Barrow invariably supplement their diet with the foods their ancestors ate, which also provide cultural ties. Caribou meat is popular. The waterfowl harvested makes its way to the dinner table. One whale is divided between not only the whaling captain and his family and the crew members, but those in the community no longer able to go on the hunt or who are not even physically able to carve up the monster after it is towed to shore. Big Bob's mother, Martha, makes a mean seal stew that can't be found on restaurant menus, mixing the meat of an *ugruk,* or bearded seal, into a pot with carrots and boiled potatoes. It is very much like beef stew, only the meat is saltier.

On cold but sunny winter days, seals sun themselves on the ice. Extremely wary (especially about the possible approach of polar bears, who love seal for a main course) the animals hover close to openings in the ice so they can swiftly plunge into the water at the approach of perceived danger. Human hunters must sneak up stealthily, quietly aim their rifle, and fire unnoticed. If the shot is not perfectly placed, the seal will dive into the hole and disappear into the Arctic Ocean and the meat will be lost.

Barrow may have the modern conveniences of automobiles and trucks, television, and a high school fielding a football team, but the people live very close to the land. The same treats their Iñupiat predecessors devoured are staples of their own diets.

On the road leading north out of Barrow, the street also narrows. This is a much better maintained road, but in places there is water on both sides. On a sunny afternoon, Clancy Itta, the city fire chief, was fishing on the Beaufort Sea side for whitefish, Arctic char, and king salmon with his wife, Marie, and other family members, not with a fishing pole, but with a net.

The four-and-a-half-inch mesh net was one hundred feet long and six feet wide. Marie Itta, wearing calf-high rubber boots, tended the net in a small dory. Son Addison, twelve, and nephew Simeon Ahkivgak, four, played near their vehicle.

Once the fish swam into the net, they got tangled. They are too big to swim through the holes, they are not good at backing up, and they can't extricate themselves.

"The kings just catch their teeth in it and spin," said Itta, whose cousin is the mayor.

Marie slithered into a wet suit—a necessary precaution, even for a twenty-foot row to the end of the net, so that she will not risk hypothermia if the boat capsizes and she falls in. She checked the net and brought in a twenty-inch-long whitefish. It was a handsome fish, and worthy of a night's dinner.

Itta is the former basketball coach at Barrow High. He spent nine years running the squad, so he thinks he understands the students and the excitement with football, and he thinks he understands any longtime Barrow residents' hesitation in fully embracing it. They don't want to give their hearts to something that might not last, Itta said.

"When there is anything new for the North Slope," Itta said, "there is an apprehension. At first there was an attitude, 'Right, it ain't gonna happen.' A little bit of it was the financial part. But I do believe it's going to be around for a while. I'm glad to let the kids have that little bit of discipline. I think it's well worth it. It's good for the community. It's good for the kids."

Itta, forty-nine, said he remembers what it was like being a basketball player in 1974 and having little kids look up to him. He heard them say, "I want to be Clancy."

Only the night before, around midnight, with the sun still out, but fading, Itta saw about thirty boys running up and down on the sand. In the dim light, he was pretty sure they were playing football.

CHAPTER 3

# *Beginnings*

WHEN TRENT BLANKENSHIP ACCEPTED the job as superintendent of schools of the North Slope Borough in 2005, he was trading a position on an Indian reservation on the Rocky Mountain plateau in Wyoming for a vast district on the tundra, encompassing 89,000 square miles.

It is the largest school district in America and you can't drive anywhere. Unconnected by roads, but by a flat, featureless, frozen tundra devoid of trees, the villages of the North Slope Borough are primarily populated by Eskimo Natives. Some villages have only a few hundred residents. The primary mode of travel between the communities is small airplane, or in the case of individuals in winter, snowmachine.

The region is located mostly north of the Brooks Range, a barrier of mountains separating it from the southern three-fourths of Alaska, and the hub of activity is Barrow, where the district's offices are located. A burly man standing about six-foot-three, with black hair containing gray streaks and a black beard, Blankenship, forty-eight, has an outgoing manner.

However, he was appalled upon arriving in the north country to learn that Barrow High School, with its annual enrollment of about 250 students, rather than turning out assembly-line graduates was hemorrhaging teenagers. The dropout rate was catastrophically high. In a four-year school, about forty students per class dropped out before graduation, Blankenship said. The abuse of drugs and alcohol was depressing, even in a place where there were no bars and alcohol was not sold in stores. Over the years, through votes of the inhabitants, Barrow has shifted between being a dry community, with no alcohol permitted, and a damp community, where individuals' possession of alcohol is allowed.

Not long before, a teenager had shot a taxi driver in a robbery, bringing big-city violence to Barrow. In a scandal, two high school teachers were indicted for selling meth. Although they were not convicted, they departed the North Slope with hard feelings all around.

"People were less than enthused about what role models the teachers were," Blankenship said.

Barrow has no movie theater. It has a limited number of restaurants. It has no dance clubs, no professional sports franchises, it is dark twenty-four hours a day for nearly two months of winter, and the temperature dips to a forbidding –20°F or lower frequently.

"There is not a lot to do in the northernmost community in America," Jim Martin, a Barrow High football player, said wryly.

Reversing the negative trends, which many would expect only of a big, impersonal city, was one of Blankenship's first goals. He was hardly alone in his concerns. Key figures in the community watched as their children squandered futures.

Barrow has its own allure, and once in a while celebrities of one stripe or another would drop in for the novelty of saying they had visited the top of the world and seen the Arctic Ocean. Invariably, they stopped by Pepe's North of the Border Restaurant for some Mexican food, and often had their picture taken with Fran Tate, the seventy-nine-year-old proprietor.

Tate is a singular community booster, who takes it upon herself to send out thousands of Christmas cards every year (sometimes not completing the task until July), and who personally funds community fireworks exhibitions and donates to many causes. Years ago she appeared as a guest on *The Tonight Show* and there is a framed photograph of Tate, on the set with Johnny Carson, on a wall near the front door of the restaurant. She greets people warmly at the northernmost Mexican restaurant in the world, and often sits at their tables. She has a glass case on display of Alaskan knick-knacks and another glass case containing sports-only memorabilia. One of her souvenirs is a photograph of her posing with Hall of Fame linebacker Dick Butkus.

Little did Tate or Blankenship realize how important a visit from a different former National Football League star would be. Larry Csonka, the bruising fullback on the Miami Dolphins' undefeated Super Bowl championship team of 1972, lives in Alaska, where he hosts an outdoors television show.

In early 2006, Csonka made a guest appearance in Barrow, speaking to high school students on the value of education, working together, having goals and striving for them, and believing in themselves. The six-foot-three Csonka played football at 240 pounds, and was elected to the Hall of Fame in 1987. He also fishes and hunts. All of these were sound credentials in an imposing man. Whether it was the delivery or the message, something Csonka said struck a chord with the kids.

Concurrently, North Slope Borough mayor Ed Itta spearheaded an areawide "War on Drugs" program. The initiative brought together concerned officials from local and regional governments and school systems to vote on grants to groups throughout the Borough. Among other activities funded have been Eskimo dance lessons and Iñupiaq language lessons in Point Hope, Anaktuvuk Pass, and elsewhere.

"We pass on the traditions," said Itta, a fourth-generation whaling captain wearing wire-rimmed glasses and sitting with his feet up on a drawer pulled out from his office desk beneath a painting of a polar bear.

Whatever wealth Barrow has stems from the discovery of oil, and the taxes from its production as it slithers southward down the Pipeline from Deadhorse to Valdez. Although none of the streets are paved, there is a network of roads for the community's 4,800 people, a population that is now about 65 percent Eskimo, Itta estimated. Although four-wheelers are relied on for some travel, there are plenty of cars and trucks and homes have satellite television. Houses are not fancy on the outside by Lower 48 standards, but they exude warmth on the inside. The Borough is the source of many jobs, from heavy equipment operators who keep the roads clear of snow, to office workers who keep recreation, sanitation, and construction departments humming. Many jobs pay in the six figures.

"The majority of the services started here came from North Slope Borough taxes through oil money," Itta said.

As someone who lived for thirteen years in Denver and Seattle (starting in junior high school) before returning to Barrow years ago, Itta is quite familiar with football. He just never expected the sport to play any role in his hometown.

"It has value," Itta said. "These were kids who did not play basketball. And Barrow has been in the media as the first team on the North Slope. That has surprised me."

Itta realized the sport was becoming an educational tool, one that could tell the world a little bit about Barrow, and attract more curious tourists who will want to see the Far North community in person. On their short visits, he figured, they will absorb the culture, develop an understanding, and spend a little money on hotels, food, and souvenirs. Maybe next time they see a news report about Barrow they will relate to its people, not just think they must be crazy to live there without malls, and without the sun for a couple of months in the winter.

Football is more important to Itta as a vehicle for change than as a sport recording wins and losses. When he sees a game he roots for Barrow to win, naturally, but he is more focused on counting the number of boys dressed out—who are involved in an activity that will keep them in school, and force them to study to stay eligible. To that end, the coaches do grade checks year-round. They don't want any surprises from classroom casualties.

Itta's primary interest is in saving a generation from itself.

Blankenship understood the hunger in the teenagers for something extra, something different, in their lives. They wanted more to do. They wanted to break out of ruts. Students were asked to fill out a survey that listed numerous choices for activities schools could add to the extracurricular offerings. Football was an option, as were riflery, music programs, chorus. More Native games rooted in the subsistence culture and contested annually in the World Eskimo-Indian Olympics were also among the choices.

Football won. Handily.

"It was the number one thing that came back from Barrow, and it was not even close," Blankenship said.

The vote of the students seemed to represent a yearning for something fresh, and for something that would better connect them to the Lower 48. Many adults were taken aback by the results. It was a foolish answer, they concluded: impractical, too costly, it provided an activity for boys only, rather than boys and girls, and seemed like a wacko pipe dream given that the closest schools also participating in the sport were located in the Fairbanks area, about four hundred miles south. The transportation costs alone would be monstrous. Then there would be the cost of food, and hotels, and rental cars. There was a transitory feeling of wistfulness when Blankenship received the results.

*Wouldn't this be great if we could?* he thought.

Others suggested substitutes—let's give them something else, like soccer. But once the vote carried, by golly, Blankenship became determined to make the Barrow High School Whaler athletes into football players.

"The first thing that happened," said Blankenship, sitting behind his desk at the school district offices in "downtown" Barrow near the police station, "was that two ladies came in and they said, 'It's a horrible idea. It's a waste of money.' People said a lot of teachers didn't like it, but I've never had a teacher tell me they didn't like it—not to my face. The school board was supportive."

The money issue was a flashing neon light. There had just been a contract settlement with teachers that called for raises of 1.5 percent for three years straight instead of the 5 percent they had fought for.

There were some teacher layoffs due to declining enrollment. But instantly the link was made: "You're lowballing teachers, you're firing teachers, but you can afford football?"

In Texas, Ohio, Pennsylvania, and across sections of the South, it's likely that some high school football teams make money. There is no such thing as a profit-making sport in Barrow, Alaska.

Around the same time the football debate heated up, Barrow received a state grant of $3 million for the purchase of computers and other materials to keep up educationally. But in some ways the grant had no strings attached. Blankenship earmarked a chunk of the money for the start-up cost of football.

"I knew it would be expensive," he said. "It's just the cost of living here."

The cost of living in Barrow must factor into the import of all goods and services. On the same day Blankenship was musing about the high price of everything in the city, a man with a full cart was cashing out a grocery expenditure of $307.70 at the Alaska Commercial Store. A gallon of milk sold for $8.99. A sixty-four-ounce carton of no-pulp Tropicana orange juice sold for $9.99. A fourteen-ounce box of Cap'n Crunch peanut butter cereal cost $7.89. And an eight-ounce jar of Folger's Classic Decaffeinated coffee cost $9.55.

A full Mexican dinner at Pepe's—the portions are plentiful—costs about $20. A room at the adjacent Top of the World Hotel ("ocean view" it reads on the registration card if your window faces the water) is $180 a night.

There would be $300 spent for each new uniform, and of course there would be travel. The Barrow boys basketball team, committed to twenty-three games, had a budget of $200,000 for the 2005–6 school year.

"Basketball is king," Blankenship noted, an indisputable fact in Alaska, particularly outside of the largest cities.

Football came in at $178,000 that season. Blankenship felt it was worth it. The kids voted for it. A few dozen boys would participate. It might energize the community. It was worth a try. He wanted one more sign from the student body that football was the right choice.

An assembly was called at the high school in the spring, and fifty-one boys expressed interest in signing up. They didn't know what would come of the meeting. They had trouble imagining that Barrow High would start such a team. But many of them knew that if the team became a reality, they wanted to be part of it. Football in Barrow. Wow.

*Let it be true,* thought Tim Barr, then a junior, who loved football and was a long distance New England Patriots fan, who had never had an outlet to release his jones for the game.

"I've always wanted to play football, my whole life," said Barr, who became a linebacker. "I had no experience at all."

The boys liked what they heard, but they didn't know if, come the next school year, they would really have a team. Albert Gerke, the sophomore quarterback who had already made an impact on the basketball team as a freshman, has a cannon arm. His dad, David, from Wisconsin, molded him into a Green Bay Packer fan as a youngster, but even after the assembly the younger Gerke found it difficult to believe there was going to be Whaler football.

"I was kind of surprised and happy they were really going to do it," Gerke said. "I was in shock."

Not everyone in the community thought football would become a reality.

"Some people were saying, 'You can never pull it off,'" Blankenship said.

Tate, in her thirty-seventh year living in Barrow after growing up in Auburn, Washington, is an enthusiastic woman who has never met a visitor she didn't like or a civic cause she wouldn't embrace. She said she had mixed emotions about the addition of football to the school's sports menu, but philosophically Tate backed it and has hosted team-related functions at her restaurant.

"The cost is horrendous," Tate said, "but it's great for the kids. This gives them an opportunity they otherwise would have to leave town to have. Other places have all of these things to do. If it's for the kids' advancement, it's OK."

In Wyoming, Blankenship had become a fan of the Denver Broncos. He was about to develop a new football allegiance. On May 13, 2006, he sent out an e-mail districtwide, asking if there were any sports coaches or teachers working in the North Slope School District who might be interested in coaching a Barrow High football team.

Mark Voss—then teaching at the junior high—won the sweepstakes. Granted, with about a dozen applicants, the competition to be hired was less fierce than the one to replace retiring Michigan coach Lloyd Carr. Voss may still have a bit of Arkansas in his voice, but he had spent most of his adult life in the Arctic, twenty-three years, raising three sons with his wife, Terri, so he had the credibility that longevity brings in the North. And he had a sports background.

During his sixteen years teaching computer skills at Eben Hopson Memorial Middle School, Voss had taught some of the players, or their relatives. He had played football, and briefly coached it as an assistant at a high school near Glenwood, Arkansas: a start-up program, to boot. He also sounded the part. To listen to Voss shout on the field is to hear the perfect deep-throated pitch necessary to catch teenagers' attention. The assistants he added were perfect, offering a mix of Arctic, football, and coaching experience.

"Those guys that are running that program are the right guys," Blankenship said. "Mark is calm, cool, and collected. He's been in the Arctic forever. They're all just right."

Voss had coached basketball, cross-country running, and volleyball in Alaska, but had not envisioned a new sport requiring large equipment expenditures and an expansive travel budget, a sport that called for a few dozen athletes, being added to the curriculum. "I'm thinking, 'Football?'" Voss said.

Football in Barrow meant buying helmets and shoes and pads. Football in Barrow meant figuring out the minimum number of players needed to compete. Football in Barrow meant trying to book maybe twenty-five people into a hotel. Football in Barrow meant trying to squeeze the best travel deal out of Alaska Airlines or Frontier Airlines, with its fleet of prop planes out of Fairbanks.

"I just hope Dutch Harbor doesn't start a team," Voss joked.

Dutch Harbor is a commercial fishing hub that is part of Unalaska and its 4,300 people at the tip of the Aleutian Islands, about eight hundred miles west of Anchorage. Dutch Harbor is so far out there in the Pacific Ocean that it makes Barrow seem a puddle-jump from the rest of the state. After accepting the job as coach, Voss didn't care about all of that. He decided his focus had to be on Xs and Os, not logistics. Let other school officials tell him how much he had to spend and he would work with it. He wanted to think football and teach football and make sure Barrow was respectable in football.

At the introductory assembly, Voss decided the Whalers had the numbers for a team, but he fretted about the lack of experience and admitted, "This can be a heartbreaking endeavor. You can get beat 50–0 every week."

In fact, years before, when Nikiski High on the Kenai Peninsula was starting its football program as a young school, the Bulldogs had the misfortune of facing the established Soldotna Stars. The final score was 89–0. Voss grimaced at the memory of hearing about the game. There is nothing to be gained by either team in a game that ends like that, he said.

It became Voss's job to make sure that nothing like that happened to the Barrow Whalers.

CHAPTER 4

# *Practice Makes Perfect*

BACKUP QUARTERBACK DANIEL THOMAS may have watched too much NFL on TV, at least the highlight shows with Terrell Owens and other players with the same dance-on-their-graves celebratory tendencies.

Drill after drill, all day long, that was the Barrow Whalers' early August schedule. When Coach Jeremy Arnhart asked if there were any questions after one set of plays, Thomas raised his hand.

"Can we practice a touchdown celebration?" Thomas asked.

Arnhart didn't know whether to laugh or cry.

"No, no, no," he said, deciding to answer seriously.

Goofy kids. Discipline is part of the regimen. Coach Brian Houston knows about discipline. Voss and the other assistants work at the school; Brian is a juvenile probation worker, so he comes into contact with the community's kids who have crossed the line. Houston, forty, is a big dude, with you-do-not-want-to-mess-with-me size and an I-can't-believe-you-said-that scowl.

He grew up in New Bedford, Massachusetts, and is a longtime New England Patriots fan. Periodically, at practice, he can be seen wearing a Tom Brady T-shirt, homage to the great Patriots quarterback. Houston had a successful career as a lineman at the University of New Haven, an NCAA Division II school, and played for a national title.

He raised his eyebrows when he heard that Barrow High was thinking of starting a football team. It was definitely thinking out of the box, given the remoteness of the city, and what it might do to help teenagers at risk.

"I thought, 'Really?'" he said. "'I'm in. Count me in.'"

Albert Gerke is the main man at quarterback, but Thomas, fifteen, takes some snaps and runs the scout team imitating the next opponent. On one play, Thomas scrambled around in the backfield eluding first-team defenders until he was open and completed a long pass.

Voss loved it. "You looked like Fran Tarkenton back there!" he shouted. "Minus the $5 million," he said more softly.

There was only one problem: Thomas had no idea he was being complimented. He had a better chance of recognizing the name Francis Scott Key than the long-retired Hall of Fame quarterback.

On the next play, Thomas bobbled the ball and Voss chimed in, "You looked more like Ryan Leaf on that one." Not that Thomas knew much about the unfortunate bust of a career Leaf had as an NFL quarterback, either: a generation gap on player names.

Thomas's situation with regard to Barrow football was unique. He was an active, enthusiastic member of the team, friends with all the players, the number two quarterback and the number one punter and place-kicker. He loves the game, and like Houston, is a Patriots fan. However, his father, Bob, the city recreation director, was one of the most vociferous opponents of the creation of Barrow High football.

"My dad doesn't want to have anything to do with it," Daniel Thomas said.

What about the permission slips and signed forms for physicals, and all of those other details required to suit up?

"My mom [Gwen] signs all the papers," he said. "When I come home my mom and I talk about how practice was and how I'm doing. My father made appearances at the school board with petitions."

Bob Thomas, fifty-seven, has long hair, looks like he fit in well in the 1960s hippie era, and has no grudge against football. He was born in California, describes himself as a service brat who moved around, and has lived in Barrow since 1979. Thomas has been one of the foremost opponents of introducing the sport at the expense of other potential activities that he feels will benefit more kids. To him it is a political football, not merely an innocent addition to the curriculum.

"It's a selfish waste of money for so many reasons," he said. "It helps thirty kids, but there are 1,000 kids on the North Slope who have no spring sports. We have no girls' sports to coincide with football. We could be doing baseball, softball, cross-country, biathlon. Football just doesn't make sense. There are very few kids that football is reaching that are not being reached by other sports. In the villages they have nothing."

Besides sports themselves, Thomas said the North Slope Borough School District would be better served by using the money to hire more library aides, and by introducing more comprehensive science programs, especially since Barrow is a hub of scientific study on global warming and other climate and environmental issues.

"You'll see the novelty wear off," he said. "What else is there to do on a Friday night? I'm against the waste of money it represents."

The Thomases' situation of 2007 was analogous to the Carrolls' situation of 2006. Quin Carroll, running back, scored the first touchdown in Whaler history. Bob Carroll, father, was skeptical of the start-up of football. Carroll, a state Department of Fish & Game area wildlife biologist with a 56,000-square-mile territory, outsized as so many things are in Alaska, said his son had a good experience. Bob Carroll was a passionate high school football player growing up in Sheridan, Wyoming. And he still goes to games. But he isn't sure the district did the right thing.

"In 2006, the word was that the school district was real short on money," Carroll said. "It kind of struck me that football was a pretty extreme extravagance. I expressed my opposition. My son was all excited about it. He did really well and had a great time at it. To me, it is like Iraq. Once you're in, you've got to support the troops. I enjoyed the football immensely.

"I'm a firm believer in the great value of sports for kids. There are a lot worse things they could be doing. But we had cutbacks in science and social studies. We had good, long-term teachers and we had good principals. We were passing all of the tests for the No Child Left Behind criteria. I think we got our priorities backwards."

Blankenship has heard all of the arguments, but he long ago decided the addition of football was worthwhile for Barrow. He said he is trying to spread the athletic wealth. He planned to add eight-man football teams to smaller villages around the district for the 2008 season. Once a year they could fly into Barrow and hold a jamboree. Blankenship believes football will help keep kids in school. In the preceding two years, with that goal as a focus, Blankenship said the dropouts per class had already declined from forty to about fifteen.

"It's still a battle," he said.

Thomas is torn. He is passionate in his opposition, but one of his talents lies in broadcasting. The first thrown-together season in 2006 with a handful of games began with Blankenship in the radio booth. He was neither unbiased, nor accomplished in play-by-play; broadcasting was definitely not one of his strengths. Thomas volunteered to step in, though he declined any involvement in 2007.

When Daniel had the chance to make an out-of-state trip with the team Thomas supported that, but felt badly about the cost.

"My son went on the trip and had a great time," Thomas said. "You can't blame kids that age for wanting to play."

He admitted that being one of the faces of the loyal opposition and having a player living under the same roof could be awkward, but said, "The awkwardness started before football. Discipline could also be accomplished by doing your chores."

That sounded more like an intramural discussion point.

The players knew that not everyone in the community loved the idea of football, but *they* did, and they knew that many of the citizens favored the competition. Barrow is a community that cares deeply about its children and was alarmed over the preceding few years that it was losing them.

Football became a symbolic rallying point, but the talking points receded into the background during two-a-days when the players were living the sport. Most of their waking hours during the days leading up to the start of school were controlled by Voss's schedule, and most of their time was spent blocking and tackling till their bodies ached.

They were well aware that their practice field—which had no lines, no yard markers, and was a waiting dust storm on windy days— might be compared to a hazardous waste site by many well-to-do programs in the Lower 48. The rocks were ever present, and so were the minor scrapes and bruises caused by falling on them, but players and coaches alike ran through drills attentive to their business. They unconsciously removed rocks during the course of instructions or after a tackle.

They could pick rocks on that field until doomsday and not clear it.

Some of the players on the sidelines waiting to sub into drills periodically bent down and threw rocks far away, performing a public service, even as they chatted about the latest PlayStation–type games featuring scary movie scenes. "Did you see the one that had the zombies?" Zac Rohan said to Joe Burke. Burke said he had. It was definitely a teenage boy conversation, not for adults, and it wasn't about football, either, unless Brian Urlacher separate-the-head-from-the-body hits came up a little later.

It was 53°F—a heat wave—with the sun shining as two-a-days approached completion shortly before the scheduled beginning of the season: a home game against Ketchikan. The coaches warned, though, that the game might not come off. Ketchikan, located 1,600 miles away in Southeast Alaska, was having trouble pulling together a team so far in advance of classes, and might not get in the number of practices required by the Alaska High School Activities Association.

Privately, there was some suspicion that Ketchikan didn't really want to make the trip to the northernmost town in America. All the coaches could do was practice, and try to make sure the Whalers were ready to play whenever the games counted for real.

Bobby Fischer Field was semi-cloistered, but one end was near a road and periodically a parent would drive a car up close to the end zone just to watch for a while. Or someone would pull an ATV right up behind Voss's station wagon, open in the back with the tanks of water and stacks of paper cups.

A girl zipped past on a four-wheeler and three players waved. "My ex-, ex-, ex-girlfriend, like in seventh grade," said sophomore halfback Anthony Edwards.

The 205-pound Edwards seemed as if he could be the Whalers' secret weapon. He had the hugely muscular thighs and wide bottom that provide the low center of gravity and power a back can employ to distinguish himself. He had an uncle who had played college football, and—given the experience that could only be acquired in game action, something so sorely lacking among the Whalers—possibly the tools for stardom. Edwards was a big fan of San Diego Chargers' back LaDainian Tomlinson—there are worse role models—but illustrating just how raw Edwards was, he noted that watching football on TV was how he developed his ball-carrying moves.

Unlike many of his teammates, Edwards was not even enrolled in school when Barrow announced the creation of the team. He became a freshman the following August, and said Voss practically dragooned him into playing.

"Mr. Voss nearly ran me down in the middle of the street," Edwards said, "and asked me, 'What's your size?'"

Three girls sharing one four-wheeler buzzed up to the station wagon and dismounted, hanging out and talking to the guys. Players dripping sweat, with their helmets off, hovered at the reviving water hole, chatting with the girls. Justin Sanders, the end with NFL aspirations, who is regarded as one of the team's hardest workers, couldn't abide the scene. He lectured his teammates for not paying attention to what the coaches were saying.

"We can hear from here," retorted freshman Adrian Paniego.

But shortly afterwards the malingerers moved back the twenty-five yards toward the practice area. Clearly, these boys hadn't seen the original *Rocky* movie, in which trainer Burgess Meredith warned Sylvester Stallone, "Women weaken legs."

Voss, who either was committed to fooling himself into believing it really was summer weather, or was showing off to the boys that weather was no bother, wore a T-shirt and black shorts. Bare arms, bare legs, open to the periodic breeze that lowered the temperature. He eyed the guys returning to the field, fully aware that they had been flirting as much as replenishing bodily fluids.

"My coach used to have this thing that if he caught you out on roller skates, you wouldn't believe the punishment you got," he mused.

Players' eyes rolled. They looked perplexed. Roller skates?

"OK, I dated myself," Voss said.

There were drop-by visitors from all around town. Children either too young for school, or still getting ready for its start, wandered near the practice field. Curious adults pulled in and watched, fascinated by the goings on.

Big Bob Aiken, fifty-four, a six-foot-four man known as the world's largest Eskimo—who once weighed 500 pounds, but who has slimmed down considerably—rode up on an ATV. Aiken is a respected community figure, seemingly related to everyone in town—quarterback Gerke is his nephew. He has worked tirelessly to preserve Native traditions and culture. Yet it was easy to picture Big Bob as a devastating tackle in his high school years.

Aiken did not watch the NFL, and said football generally bored him, but he admitted that it was probably a good thing for the current teenagers.

"I thought the community was trying out something that would never really materialize," Aiken said. "We tried soccer, but it disappeared. No interest. We've got some people in there with football with the right attitude, people making a commitment. Kids wouldn't be in school if it was not for football. I think it's really benefiting these boys. They'd rather be partying, but they get in shape to be part of the first-ever football team up here.

"In our community, football always came to us on TV. We thought it belonged on TV. Now it's coming to us in our high school. It's different."

Not being a follower of the sport, Aiken, who starred for many years in the annual World Eskimo-Indian Olympics strength events, did not know football rules. He was like many of the older members of the community, whose lives were geographically far removed from the rest of the country and culturally removed from mainstream American sports.

"I was watching it and trying to figure out what they were doing," Aiken said. "It was mass chaos to me with everybody tackling everybody. Our boys didn't know what to do at first."

Aiken was surprised that his mother, Martha, and his aunts took to the sport. In his half century of life he had seen many significant changes come to Barrow. When he was a youngster there were hardly any vehicles, but now they were everywhere. There had been dog teams and now there were none, with a strong reliance on snowmobiles.

Aiken said that when he was young and his late father, Robert, bought a snowmachine, "we were the envy of the whole town."

And now there was football. Progress, or simply change, he didn't know for sure.

"It's like somebody else's vision materializing," he said.

Big Bob did think he would have been just like today's teenagers, hungry to play in 1971 if the Whalers had had a team, swept up in the enthusiasm and competing for something to do. And for sure, whoever the coach might have been, the sight of a gigantic student in the hallways or walking down the street would have sent him running in the same manner Voss captured Edwards.

➡ ⬅

School was about to start for the year, and that meant practice would be relegated to once daily, starting at 4:00 P.M. Math, social studies, socializing, things besides football would compete for players' attentions. Voss was pleased at how sharp his players looked compared to the year before when guys barely knew the difference between a handoff and a kickoff.

"We're not going to be ready for our first game," he said, "but I've got kids who can play cornerback and know what that means. We had athletes last year. A school can go out and get some things down due to just physical ability. Now they know a little bit more."

Still, for every player with a touch of seasoning, there were incoming players who never had a chance to boot a ball before.

A newcomer with televised football as his main background was one that Voss awed with his skimpy attire. Cody Gleason, Jr., was more into sweatshirts at 50°F. A sophomore whose aunt thought Barrow might be better fit for him, Gleason had moved north from a Navajo Nation reservation in Arizona where he was used to 115°F in August.

"It's a big change," Gleason said, in a comment that could win him understatement of the year honors in a national competition.

About six feet tall and weighing 180 pounds, Gleason had no football experience to speak of and was still finding himself in the sport. But he had toughness in his background. His dad, Casey, had been a heavyweight boxer, and Cody Gleason had gone 3–2 in amateur fights before embarking for Barrow. When he thought of newness he thought of many things, from new surroundings to new sports to "new wardrobe," he said.

Soon after, it became official that there would be no Ketchikan game. The season opener was moved back to August 17, a Friday, against Seward. Still a home game.

The opener was going to be a very special occasion, one that was going to attract some special out-of-town guests, including one that just might make people who believe that Barrow is right next door to the North Pole also think Santa Claus is real.

That someone demonstrated Santa Claus imitators don't all dress in a red suit and have a white beard. The first game of the 2007 Barrow High football season was scheduled to mark the first game played on the bright, flashy, new $800,000 artificial blue-and-yellow field brought to the northernmost town in North America by a slightly built, blonde, fund-raising football fanatic dynamo from Jacksonville, Florida.

It was completely, thoroughly, jaw-droppingly true. The Whalers were the recipients of the perfect gift and they discovered it was possible, even appropriate, to celebrate Christmas in August.

No more rocks.

CHAPTER 5

# *Are You Ready for Some Football?*

THE CALENDAR READ AUGUST, but the air felt like December on the third Saturday of the month in 2006, when the conjured-up-from-imagination Barrow High football team made its official debut, a scant three months after Trent Blankenship sent out his coach-recruiting e-mail missive.

The key lyric in the National Football League's *Monday Night Football* theme song, sung by country star Hank Williams, Jr., is "Are you ready for some football?" There was a commitment from forty-four students—a potpourri of nationalities as it turned out, from Eskimos, to Asian-Americans, Caucasians, Samoans, and Tongans, much like the town—but it was hard to argue that the Whalers were ready, since the team members barely knew how to dress in a full-scale football uniform. Since the coaches' playbook was by necessity thinner than the Barrow shopping guide. Since there had barely been time to throw together a suitable schedule of six games and figure out how to cover the costs of teams flying in and Barrow flying out. Since the field was going to be only a marginal upgrade over rocky Bobby Fischer Field.

Forget grass. Not in the cards. The challenge was to find a patch of land big enough to double as a playing field that could accommodate fans at all.

The Ukpeavig Iñupiat Corporation stepped up. Ukpeavig is the Iñupiat word for Barrow; it means "the place where people hunt snowy owls." Indeed, snowy owls may not proliferate to the degree of ducks and geese, but they are another staple of the Native diet. The corporation leased the North Slope Borough School District a chunk of land located along the road by the Arctic Ocean for $1.

After that it was up to the district to make it playable, if not hospitable. Neither the local Department of Transportation, nor any other construction or building department, had a ready supply of chalk to put down yard markers, out-of-bounds lines, or goal lines. As has often been the case in daily life in the Arctic, Barrow improvised. The necessary lines were drawn on the field with flour. Sometimes a gust of wind blew and created a mini-faux snowstorm. Sometimes seagulls dropped down for a nibble. But it worked. Workers made the hard-dirt field look pretty spiffy.

"It was remarkable how hard a field that was," Coach Voss said. "You could play basketball on it. But we were out there and we were lucky to be playing football."

Another preparation unique to Barrow had to be made. Security had to be on hand, not to keep a lid on raucous fans so much as to keep an eye out for an invasive polar bear. Polar bears, often when hungry, do appear on the beach and sometimes wander into town. There is a particular risk to humans when whales are hauled to shore for butchering. Once, Big Bob Aiken served as a polar bear guard and had to turn a shotgun on a threatening bear only yards away. The bear's whitish-yellowish fur was matted from the water, forming a protective armor. When Aiken fired, he didn't think he even harmed the animal, but simply drove it backward into the water through the force of the shot.

"Polar Bears" would have been as apt a name for the high school sports teams in Barrow as Whalers. However, the University of Alaska Fairbanks, an NCAA Division II sports-playing school, calls their team the Nanooks, the Native word for polar bear, and that's hard to compete with.

The first opponent in Barrow football history was Delta Junction, a small community located on the Alaska Highway about a hundred miles from Fairbanks. Barrow residents knew nothing about Delta's sports history, and many didn't have any knowledge of football terminology. Yet more than three thousand fans turned out for the game, lining the sides of the field, beating on skin drums and chanting in Iñupiaq.

"That was kind of cool and unexpected," said linebacker Jarid Hope of the turnout.

Seating of any type was at a premium, and the game marked the debut of Price Brower's legendary chair. He had the foresight to show up bringing his own furniture—a comfy, cushioned armchair. Brower is a member of one of Barrow's most famous families. The Browers have been accomplished whalers for generations; a Brower was the first to receive the news about the demise of Wiley Post and Will Rogers; there is a section of town called Browerville; and Charles Brower, the present patriarch of the clan, has served on numerous community boards and is a respected elder. For an outsider to sort out the relationships between all of the Browers would require intensive family tree instruction, or the aid of the FBI. It suffices to hear the phrase, "He's a Brower" to know that the subject is a person of stature in Barrow.

On August 17, opening day, Barrow lived up to its reputation as a place with fearsome weather. Windblown snow beat against the players' helmets and many of the supportive fans chose to create their own vantage point, watching the foreign game unfold from the warmth of their cars, less than one hundred yards across the street from the Arctic Ocean.

The cheerleaders painted their faces in blue and yellow school colors, but were not to be seen in bare-midriff and short-skirt outfits. They wore heavy jackets and gloves.

Media outlets from across the state, from the *Anchorage Daily News* to the *Fairbanks Daily News-Miner,* and from elsewhere, like ESPN, showed up to chronicle the event. The atmosphere was festive. Fans realized they were watching history unfold. The players had a sense of occasion. The simple existence of the game represented an against-the-odds milestone. The sport and team had moved from conceptual drawing board to on-the-field reality since May. No one in attendance could quite believe that reality.

Lineman John Wilson, fifteen at the time, said he had been about to ask his mother if he could move to Anchorage and live with relatives for high school, so he could play football. Then football came to him.

"I always wanted to play football," he said. "I didn't think it was going to happen. I was so happy. It was new to everyone. I think the whole town was there."

Of course, reality came calling with more harshness than the weather once the kickoff soared into the Arctic sky. Delta Junction dominated the game and thumped the Whalers, 34–0. Barrow fumbled six times. Voss admitted that when practice began only weeks before just four of the forty-four players had owned up to having any football experience. For one day, given the magnitude of the event, and even though the coaches would hate to admit such a thing, the results were secondary. The game was definitely the thing.

It was hard to top the comment made by spectator Billy Aiken, who compared the wintry atmosphere of Barrow to the often-described conditions faced by the Green Bay Packers in northern Wisconsin.

"Green Bay says they've got the frozen tundra," Aiken said. "Well, we've got the real frozen tundra."

What do you say to that, Vince Lombardi?

The subhead on the game story from the Barrow–Delta game in the *News-Miner* the next day called it "Northern Exposure."

A Delta Junction linebacker, Craig Cummings, was as enthused as possible about the experience (it probably helped that the Huskies won) when he called the excursion "Awesome." He couldn't get over playing football next door to the Arctic Ocean, with "icebergs floating all over the place. It's not something everybody gets to see."

You must hand it to the residents of Barrow that they know their weather. An effort was made to schedule home games early in the season in order to avoid playing in −20°F weather and a blizzard.

During one game, however, spectators' attention was diverted to the ocean. Three gray whales swam past within ten yards of shore, scraping barnacles off their skins.

A week after the opener, Barrow lost to Valdez, 33–0. Growing pains. The lack of experience showed every time the Whalers walked up to the line of scrimmage. They were more likely to collect a penalty than a first down on offense. They were more likely to react slowly and miss a tackle than throw a ball carrier for a loss on defense. With games against Nikiski and twice against Sitka, with a junior varsity opponent sprinkled in, Voss had to worry briefly about whether or not his team would (a) score, (b) avoid those 50–0, or 89–0 debacles he feared, or (c) might somehow actually win one.

That occasion came to pass at the end of September, in the season's final game, when the Whalers outlasted Sitka, 28–22, for the first football triumph in school history in a 1–5 truncated season. Halfback Quin Carroll scored the first, go-ahead touchdown on a short run.

Though the weather was far from hospitable, the joy was so great that the players ran across the field, weaving in and out of celebrating fans, to take the plunge into the Arctic Ocean in uniform. It was a Barrow Whalers football team special edition of Polar Bear Club jump-in. Even Voss went in over his head. There are times when the body's emotions are warmer than the body's skin.

When Voss reflected on the blur of a first season, when simply sorting things out was a major task, he decided it had gone, "wonderfully. It was a great experience."

Voss winked and said he didn't really jump into the water with his guys voluntarily.

"My wife pushed me in," he said.

Only Terri happened to be standing next to him when he said that.

"No, I did not," she said.

The water was 35°F that day.

"We don't do Gatorade," Voss said of the typical end-of-game dousings NFL championship coaches receive from their players. "We jump in the Arctic Ocean. I think there were some icebergs in the distance. It [the cold] sucks your breath right out of your body."

He was wearing a blue and white windbreaker, not exactly stream-lined swimwear, and that drew the water in like a sponge. Voss had to dog paddle back to shore. He thawed out by Christmas, or at least it felt that way.

The team gave Voss the game ball, which he keeps in his home within easy reach.

"You know," he said, "I'm not going to win any more first games in Barrow."

What amazed Voss about the start-up of Barrow football was the attention it garnered, not only throughout Alaska, but from all over the nation. He received e-mails and letters (one from a coach with the Minnesota Vikings) wishing him well, trying to fathom the extremes of Barrow, and the costs. The mystique of Alaska still carries weight with Americans, and they imagine Barrow as a suburb of the North Pole. Trent Blankenship said he too was astonished at the level of feed-back from media outlets and football fans smitten with the notion of football in the Far North.

"It's actually kind of surprising people are even interested," Blankenship said. "But it's gratifying. It is unique. We're way the hell up there."

Voss said he tried to stay out of the politics and for the most part, away from the budget makers, as well.

"I don't ask where the money comes from," he said. "They tell me what I can't do. I'm a fairly thrifty person. I like to make sure we're get-ting value for the dollar."

Voss had no illusions that he was building an instant winner. He agreed with the philosophy behind the creation of the high school football team, which was about harnessing the good in teenagers who might otherwise be at risk.

"I was trying to coach to the level of what you can do," Voss said. "I was hoping they were going to see some success and take pride in it. I'd like for them twenty years later to say, 'I played football in high school.' That it was an experience they were glad they all had."

For Barrow players, it was having the chance that counterparts in the Lower 48 had. For people in the Lower 48, it was fascinating that such a strange place was trying to provide football normalcy. For them it was casting against type; news outlets ran stories that readers found intriguing. ESPN gave the story a wider audience. And for one woman in Florida, the fact that Barrow High School was playing football above the Arctic Circle, and was working so hard through a consortium of parents, coaches, and teachers to provide life lessons through football, proved to be an epiphany.

Cathy Parker of Jacksonville, Florida, whose husband, Carl, was the offensive coordinator at Bartram Trail High, and who had sons playing high school football, was moved to tears by what she learned on ESPN. Moved to the point that she did not merely allow the story to take hold of her emotions, but to the point where she decided to move mountains to help Barrow through its challenges. What she couldn't believe, above all, was that all of those people were trying to take care of their kids and steer them onto life's righteous path, yet they still had to play tackle football on a field laden with rocks. Rocks! Can you believe that? Everyone was trying to do right by those boys, but they had to practice on rocks, play games on rocks, had to endure bruises and cuts because of rocks polluting their fields.

There was only so far the money could stretch. Building a stadium was a laughable notion. Installing an artificial turf field—and it would have to be artificial turf, since grass does not grow in tundra—was about as far-fetched. Rural Alaska has always embraced a can-do and make-do outlook. Barrow had done the best it could. No one could better appreciate the need for a better field than Blankenship, whose son Colton, a sophomore lineman, had to make regular chiropractic visits for hip alignment.

One day, soon after Barrow began playing football and its story was being disseminated, Blankenship was in his office, and his secretary informed him he had a telephone call from a woman in Florida who wanted to talk to him about the football team. Blankenship picked up the phone and listened to a feminine yet high-octane southern drawl explain how his life was about to change. He blinked. He nodded to the empty room and eventually he stammered, "Well, yes, ma'am." Blankenship was speaking to the Good Fairy. This woman in Florida was going to grant him wishes left and right.

Cathy Parker had just told Blankenship she was going to build him a football field, an artificial turf football field, worth about $800,000, and it was his just for the asking. Heck, he didn't even have to ask, she was providing. No, not out of her own pocket. She wasn't that kind of wealthy. She was going to raise the money for Barrow football to have its own state-of-the-art football field in time for the 2007 season.

"Put yourself in my shoes," Blankenship said.

That would involve pinching oneself. That would involve a drop-by visit to a psychiatrist for a sanity check and a hurry-up appointment with an ear doctor for a hearing check-up.

"Think about it," Blankenship said. "What amazing, extraordinary generosity."

When Parker told her three sons she was going to raise the money to buy Barrow a football field, they laughed at her. When Blankenship heard her say the same thing, he was dumbfounded.

Parker worked for a bank. She didn't own the bank.

"I was just so touched by what those people were trying to do for their children," Parker said.

As the mother of three teenage boys, as a faith-driven churchgoer who also believed in the discipline, responsibility, and teamwork values of football, she wanted to reach out to Barrow. She began talking up what she had learned, to her family, to her church members.

She thought Barrow was on to something important and wanted to support it.

"What attracted me was that football could absolutely change that community and give those boys some hope," Parker said. "We don't have a drug problem. I couldn't get it out of my mind. We knew it would work. Teach them about football and character concurrently."

Parker made it her mission to be the conduit between football in the Lower 48 and football on the Last Frontier. She thought about it and felt that bringing a field to Barrow was the best method for the madness. She told her family, "I've got an announcement to make." And her kids responded with, "Mom, that is so ridiculous. That is impossible."

Parker made a list and checked it twice. She thought of people she knew in the business world who had money and who had been impacted by athletics. She felt it important to ride the wave of momentum from the start-up and get the field installed pronto. Many times Parker got discouraged and felt she wasn't qualified to be a fund-raiser on such a grand scale. Then she got back to work. Parker picked up $5,000 here and $5,000 there. She went public with her idea. Golf tournament fund-raisers took place. Car washes.

"We just asked and asked and asked," Parker said.

And then she asked Blankenship if he would like to bring the team to Jacksonville, mix with the Bartram Trail kids for spring workouts, and hang out with the Jacksonville Jaguars pro team. A combination fund-raising effort was set into motion for that experience that tied together Whaler players attending football camps in the Lower 48 during the early part of the summer.

Something like that had been on Blankenship's mind. He hoped a large number of players would be able to attend camps in Tennessee and Nebraska, where details were being worked out, "so they could learn football." The Whalers desperately needed to absorb fundamentals, and simply the experience of taking more snaps in gamelike situations would help.

Blankenship's reaction to Parker for the Florida invitation? "I think you're an angel sent from God," he said.

A generation or so earlier, Barrow residents were not travelers. There was no jet service and residents had little money. They were isolated and insulated. With the influx of oil money and regular passenger service, it became much easier to visit Anchorage or Fairbanks, the state's two largest cities, and to travel on for vacations in the Lower 48. A very popular destination for Barrow citizens around Christmas is Hawaii.

With the addition of sports teams that made parents proud, high school students began traveling to games by plane routinely. Still, hardly every child came from a family well off enough to travel Outside. And some had hardly ever been to a state farther away than Washington prior to the late spring Florida trip.

As Parker revved up the field fund-raising, calling it "Project Alaska," about twenty-five Barrow players made the trip to Florida. They were put up in private homes, staying with Parker, her friends, and volunteers. Barrow coaches went over plays with Bartram Trail coaches. Then Barrow coaches and players lunched and mingled with Jaguars coach Jack Del Rio, his assistants, and players.

"That had to be the hands-down best lunch I've ever had," said receiver Jim Martin, who wasn't talking about the food, but the company. "Having lunch with professional football players. I definitely did not think I'd ever be having lunch with a professional team. I don't think that's something any of us will forget."

One by-product of Outside travel that Alaskan kids always face when they hook up with teams from other states is a blizzard of questions. Stereotypes usually prevail. For sure, Alaskans are going to be asked if they live in igloos and drive dog teams to school.

"We got lots of questions," Martin said. "There's always the igloo question. Someone asked if there are no trees in Barrow, how do you get oxygen? It was a shocking question. I personally didn't have an answer for that question."

Junior lineman Trevor Litera, a 300-pounder, said he found some of the Bartram players' questions amusing, too. Like how do the players even survive in frigid Barrow?

"I said, 'Hmm, try it,'" Litera said. "We'd see how they would survive."

Of course the flip side of the question was valid, too. How would Barrow players make out in 100°F temperatures with 90 percent humidity? Given how they guzzle water and exclaim over the heat when it reaches 60°F in Barrow, it seemed obvious a group meltdown would have occurred in those conditions.

For Barrow, the entire trip was like filling out an entry blank and winning a contest for you and twenty-five of your closest friends to bask in 80°F weather in Florida while it was still in the 20s at home. Barrow and Jacksonville aren't even on the same page in an atlas. Moving so many players, coaches, and chaperones so they could end up in the same place at about the same time was like moving the Third Army. Two routes were used. Some players flew from Barrow to Fairbanks to Anchorage to Salt Lake City to Cincinnati to Atlanta, and then took a bus. Other players flew from Barrow to Prudhoe Bay to Anchorage to Seattle to Houston to Atlanta, and then bused. Great opportunity for collectors of frequent flyer miles.

The hospitality of the southern city for the northern city kids from more than 4,000 miles away was overwhelming. Much of it was due to Parker's power of persuasion. She talked a Jacksonville chain restaurant into providing free meals for the Barrow kids, and she made the contacts with the Jaguars. Clearly, Parker had missed her calling. She should either be a legislator who could buttonhole others for their votes, or a presidential campaign fund-raiser who could twist arms for millions of dollars.

"She is an amazing woman," Barrow assistant coach Brian Houston said.

During a break from football in Florida, the Whalers went sightseeing. Of course, they went to Disney World. And they visited nearby St. Augustine, the oldest city in the United States. The players also liked the sight of girls wearing bikinis, not a common thing at home. The Atlantic Ocean felt like bath water compared to the Arctic Ocean.

Linebacker Tim Barr said he particularly enjoyed the visit to an alligator farm, and stopovers at beaches. But as someone who was rawer than uncooked steak as a football player, with no experience at all, he liked the bonding between Barrow and Bartram Trail players and the patience of the school's coaches.

"It was an awesome trip," he said.

At the end of the Bartram Trail spring game in Jacksonville, the Barrow players chanted Cathy Parker's name, dragged her onto the field, and gave her a group hug.

Voss admitted to being a little awestruck himself, sharing football gab with Jack Del Rio, who later guided the Jaguars into the NFL play-offs. He said he had tears in his eyes when the Whalers boarded the bus leaving their Jacksonville hosts behind because of the closeness gained in only a handful of days. And he was stupefied to learn about the level of Cathy Parker's devotion to providing a new football field for Barrow.

During the brief, dizzying, start-up year, Voss and the assistant coaches used to make jokes about the rough-edged practice and playing fields with all of their rocks. Their favorite joke was imagining how some rich benefactor would hear about the situation, swoop down, give a donation and presto, they would have an artificial turf field.

"Our joke was that we would play on artificial turf up here some day," Voss said. "This (Parker) is an amazing person. I'm just a heathen. There's no way I'm going to be as good a person as these people in Florida are to us. That community just bent over backwards for me and my kids down there."

The fund-raising was about $100,000 short for the field by the time the Whalers left Jacksonville. Long after the Whalers came and went, the Cathy Parker–driven fund-raising continued. The ProGrass materials, freight, and labor added up to $800,000, in cash and in-kind services. And it was a rush job. Barrow's 2007 season opener was in mid-August. Would the goods be ready? Would the money be there?

The field was to be manufactured in Dalton, Georgia, and the 300,000 pounds of materials shipped to Barrow in segments, where it would be laid in time for the first game. For anyone who wondered if the turf would hold up during a –50°F cold snap in Barrow, company officials said they had installed the product in Wisconsin and Canada.

Besides, for years there had been an artificial turf surface at Anchorage Football Stadium where most of the city's games were played, and a couple of individual high schools in the community were installing them, too.

An artificial turf football field for Barrow, Alaska. Was it a dream come true for Voss?

"Oh, it is," he said. "It's an extremely bizarre dream."

## CHAPTER 6

# *Football on the Last Frontier*

WHEN ROCKY KLEVER RECALLS his high school football career in Anchorage, the first thing that comes to mind about the conditions is the mud. It rains a lot in Anchorage in August and September, and by the end of September and beginning of October, the temperatures flirt with freezing.

The field where all of the local schools played their games was dirt long past the time when Klever graduated from West High in 1977, and continued his football education at the University of Montana.

"The field turned to mud and then it froze," Klever said. "It was like razor blades. That hurt more than anything."

Barrow did not invent football in Alaska. The history of high school football in the forty-ninth state does not run as deep as it does in Pennsylvania, Ohio, or Texas, where there are some who consider Fridays holy days on the order of Sunday churchgoing. But it has been around long enough, and played at a high enough level, that talented young people can realistically aspire to being sought after by colleges dangling scholarships, and even legitimately dream of a professional career.

Klever was the first to make the National Football League. A six-foot-three, 230-pound tight end, he emerged from Montana and the Big Sky Conference much more famous than when he enrolled. The New York Jets made him a ninth-round draft pick in 1982, and in a career that lasted through 1987, Klever played in sixty-five National Football League games, caught 46 passes, and averaged 11.2 yards per grab.

He was a national novelty at the time for sportscasters commenting about his Alaskan roots. "Everything I did, it was the first by an Alaskan," Klever said. "I was the first Alaskan to jump offsides. I was the first Alaskan to hold Lawrence Taylor. It was great. I loved it."

Klever, who will turn fifty next year, and lives in Linwood, New Jersey, near the South Jersey shore, said he was shocked to hear about the start-up of football in Barrow. "Who would you play?" he said was his first thought. "The travel schedule has got to be unbelievable."

When it comes to Alaskans and the NFL, Klever, who in 2006 was elected to the state's new high school sports hall of fame, is the pioneer. But pioneer days of high school football in the state predate him. In the 1950s, Anchorage had only two high schools, East and West. That's all the population demanded.

By 1969, when Tom Huffer began coaching at Chugiak High, things were still a bit rough around the edges, but were just beginning to take a form present-day fans might recognize. Huffer, the first coach selected for the high school hall of fame, spent twenty years coaching high school ball in the state, and has remained active on the periphery of school sports since, including a return to the sidelines to coach in the recently established girls high school flag football league.

When Huffer took over leadership of the program at Chugiak High nearly forty years ago, there were four Anchorage public high schools playing football—East, West, Chugiak, and Dimond. The Anchorage military bases, Fort Richardson and Elmendorf Air Force Base, had their own schools and teams competing. Now there are eight public high schools in Anchorage playing football, and a collection of private schools, most of which focus on basketball.

"With TV the way it is in Alaska," Huffer said, "and with football the number one sport in the country, I think it's just going to grow."

The quality of Alaska football has improved steadily. Klever was an exception. He achieved ahead of his time, even receiving a congratulatory note from then-Governor Jay Hammond when he reached the NFL.

Klever was a conversation piece, not in the forefront of a fad. However, he represented the hope to Alaskan athletes with first-rate talent that they could be noticed, and he made college coaches think about recruiting the state. At first the attention came from the Big Sky Conference, whose schools are situated in rugged locations in Idaho, Utah, Montana and the like. A former Weber State coach, who had half a dozen Alaskans on his roster at one time at his school based in Ogden, Utah, said he liked the toughness of "those northern-bred players."

Toughness seemed to be the qualities sought when Fairbanks linemen Tom Neville and Shane Bonham grew their way into the NFL, and Kenai's Travis Hall followed. Reggie Tongue, another Fairbanks athlete, who played at Oregon State, became a prominent defensive back. No one, however, could match the achievements of Mark Schlereth, a star for Service High in Anchorage. Schlereth won All-Pro honors, and won three Super Bowl rings—two with the Denver Broncos and one with the Washington Redskins. He is now a nationally known sports broadcaster.

Schlereth once described his Super Bowl ring from the 1992 Redskins triumph as being "big and gaudy and [it] has lots of diamonds." Schlereth, who is six-foot-three, seemed almost as wide as a Winnebago when he played guard at 285 pounds. Yet that is now considered small for an NFL offensive lineman. He paid a heavy price with his body, as well, undergoing a possible league record twenty-nine surgeries on his knees and elbows between 1989 and 2001.

When he retired at age thirty-five, Schlereth said he had no regrets, but did have some aches. "I'm in the position that I did the best I could possibly do," he said. "And I got as much out of my body as I could."

With each slice of the surgeon's knife, Schlereth's career was on the line, and with each hospital visit it became less and less likely he could bounce back. But Schlereth displayed remarkable resilience. In an against-the-odds situation, Schlereth's Broncos faced Tongue's Kansas City Chiefs in a playoff game in 1998. Two Alaskans on the same field at the same time was not the same as having two Californians face one another.

"It's kind of neat trivia," Schlereth said.

Tongue, who attended Lathrop High in Fairbanks and was also an adept punt returner, said, "That's cool."

Earlier that year in the off-season, Schlereth, who made his home in Colorado, had returned to Anchorage for a visit and to have his Service high school uniform jersey retired. He addressed the student body in an assembly, and then wandered around the hallways until he found his junior year and senior year lockers.

Schlereth recalled that when he was twelve, his dad, Herb, urged him to write down ten things he hoped to accomplish in life. He included on his list playing pro football and making All-Pro.

"They were fairly ridiculous goals," Schlereth said.

But he made them all come true. Schlereth's message to another generation of Service High students was that he was a regular guy who worked hard to achieve his goals. That's easy to believe when it is noted that he only weighed 205 pounds as a high school player.

During a public autograph signing, where some little boys were not wise enough to divest of Oakland Raiders, Seattle Seahawks, or Kansas City Chiefs' gear, Schlereth was asked, "Do you know John Elway?"

Know him? Schlereth was paid play-by-play to keep the Hall of Fame quarterback from being buried under 1,000 pounds of defensive beef. Among the visitors that day were Brandon Drumm and Phil Locker, two Service High players who were headed to Division I college schools.

"It's not often you get to see a pro football player in Alaska," said Drumm in explanation of why he showed up.

The autograph line stretched for quite a distance, though not as far as the Denver Broncos' season-ticket wait list, and Schlereth laughed when someone asked if he was ever requested to sign women's bras. Only big stars get groupies like that, he said.

"Me, it would be signing a pork rind or something," he said.

Schlereth, who in 2007 was voted into the new Alaska Sports Hall of Fame for his football achievements, is a regular on ESPN pregame, postgame, and game-day TV shows, and in a part-time job he probably couldn't have imagined when he was making out that to-do list at age twelve, has a regular role as a detective–crime novelist on the soap opera *Guiding Light.*

Schlereth's TV character was going to be named Rock Hoover, but cyber squatters claimed the domain name rockhoover.com and wanted $6,000 from Schlereth to give it up. He offered $1,000 and not a penny more. Then he changed the character's name to Roc. He scored the domain site for rochoover.com instead.

"We secured it for $9," Schlereth said.

As a state small in numbers—48th in the nation in population—Alaska does not mass-produce either NCAA Division I college players, or those who can compete at any level professionally. Yohance Humphrey, a Chugiak graduate who broke many of Klever's old records at Montana, played some Arena League ball. North Pole High's Derrick Beatty was a defensive back for the Edmonton Eskimos of the Canadian Football League, and Delvin Myles, formerly of Bartlett, an Anchorage school, also played in the Arena Football League.

Cole Magner, out of Colony High in the Mat-Su Valley, off the highway north of Anchorage, caught 99 passes in a season for Bowling Green, and twice was a late cut of the Atlanta Falcons. He stuck for a while with the Baltimore Ravens' practice squad. Dietrich Moore was a starting defensive back at Oregon and a slew of Alaskans, from James Price to Phil Locker, made their marks at Washington State.

For an Alaskan player, merely receiving recruiting mail from major schools seen on TV is a milestone. If the nation's most coveted prospects see it as their due, Alaskan kids are still in a little bit of awe when they hear from big-time football programs. They understand just how much of a leap it is from their living room, where the television shows these same coaches stalking the sidelines to their being able to stand next to them during a game.

Moore, who did play in the Pac-10, remembered his first piece of recruiting mail. It came from the University of Washington and he said it looked like a Christmas card. Moore said his "eyes were wide."

Humphrey, a five-foot-nine, 180-pound running back, who set rushing and scoring records for Division I-AA Montana, was a pen pal of then-Nebraska legendary coach Tom Osborne, who wrote, "If you take care of business, all good things will follow." Humphrey did, and they did, just not for the Cornhuskers. It turned out that Osborne's handwriting was quite a bit messier than John Hancock's on the Declaration of Independence, but then Osborne was probably writing his name two hundred times a day to teenagers he might never meet, and Hancock was writing for posterity. Still, Humphrey was suitably impressed.

"Like, wow," he said.

One of those most struck by the onfield NFL playoff matchup between Schlereth and Tongue (who also played for the Seahawks, Raiders, and New York Jets, and once scored a Chiefs touchdown on a lateral following a teammate's interception) was the late Buck Nystrom. Nystrom was a legendary Alaska coach, most notably at Eielson High, on an Air Force Base south of Fairbanks. Thinking of all the years of watching kids slog through the mud, being short on coaching wisdom and facilities, and forced into long road trips, Nystrom had perspective on what an Alaska player had to do to survive, thrive, and advance.

"That's amazing," said Nystrom, who died at age sixty-five in 2006. "A couple of guys in the NFL playoffs."

Coaches like Nystrom, Bruce Shearer at East and Chugiak, Byron Wilson at Service, and Huffer at Chugiak, frequently turned out winners and state champions, coached players into playing beyond their expected limits, and tried to develop boys into men.

One of the greatest high school players in state history was Brandon Drumm, who rushed for 2,241 yards and scored 27 touchdowns for Wilson at Service one year, and then played four years of fullback for

Colorado University. The Buffaloes wanted to make Drumm into a line-backer, but he wanted to stay in the backfield.

Service won the state title in 1997 and Drumm was the most heavily recruited football player in state history at the time. He received more mail than Santa Claus, from about as many places. His choice came down to Big 12 schools Colorado or Nebraska. Those were the type of football schools that demanded respect, were on TV as often as *Law and Order,* and played in front of 70,000 or so roaring fans. It was head-turning stuff for an Alaskan whose live audience might have topped 3,500 once or twice in a career.

Drumm was a bruising back at six-foot-two and 215 pounds, with more power than flat-out speed, so the biggest schools saw him as a guy who could bulk up, block, and deliver punishment. Even though Drumm missed cradling the ball and rumbling across goal lines, he played out his four years and had a couple of shots at the NFL, most notably with the Detroit Lions, who drafted him in the seventh round, in their training camp, and with the Tennessee Titans' practice squad.

"At least I've got my foot in the door," Drumm said.

The lesson was out there for all Alaskans who thought that just because barriers had come down it would be easier to make it to the top. If someone as good as Drumm had trouble cracking a roster, there would be no gifts. The door was open, but just a crack.

Seven years after Drumm completed his high school career at the school with the largest enrollment in the state (over 2,000), a smaller player from a smaller school came along to break his single-season rushing record. Although not endowed with the same physical attributes as Drumm, Perry Monzulla dashed for 2,860 yards during the 2004 season for North Pole. Incredibly, Monzulla averaged 9.5 yards per rush.

In some quarters, Monzulla, who led the North Pole Patriots to their only state championship, was nicknamed "The Patriot Missile." Nystrom, who in 1992 led Eielson, with its three-hundred-person student body, to the state championship, had retired, returned, and was again a head coach as North Pole finished 10–1 by upsetting West High, 44–13, in the title game.

"We did the impossible today," said Monzulla, who attended Eastern Arizona Junior College after high school. "We had the heart today." Nystrom, who became the winningest Alaska coach with 150 victories before he died, seemed shocked to win a second title with a different school. "I can't believe I'm back here again and we win again," Nystrom said. "Why am I so blessed?"

The triumph meant that Nystrom joined Shearer, who left the state to coach in Washington, north of Seattle, as the only Alaska football coaches to win state championships at two schools.

Nystrom was one of the pivotal figures in the development of Alaska football. He was born in Two Harbors, Minnesota—his given name was David—where his father, uncles, and grandfather toiled in the mines harvesting iron ore and displayed a work ethic he felt worth emulating. Nystrom played linebacker for the University of Minnesota-Duluth before he moved north in 1965, motivated by Alaska's reputation as an outdoors paradise. He was a hunter and a fisherman, and even shot a polar bear when it was still legal. Nystrom was so revered at Eielson, where he taught and coached, that the team's field was named for him while he was still active.

While he believed in discipline, Nystrom was popular among fellow coaches and other football observers for his compassion and humor. At a school filled with Air Force kids, during twenty-five seasons as head man, Nystrom also showed that the odds did not have to be in your favor to succeed. For years Eielson competed against the largest schools in the state and advanced to the title game in 1991 and won it 1992, the smallest school to do so.

Huffer, a good friend, said Nystrom was a superb motivator. "He had a special gift," Huffer said. "He had those kids believing they could whip the world. Some people think it's all about Xs and Os, and it ain't."

Eventually, as more small schools began playing interscholastic football, Eielson surrendered its permanent position of tilting at windmills, and banded together with similarly sized schools to form the Greatland Conference, the league Barrow joined in 2007.

Although he has mellowed at sixty, Huffer, who retired young from coaching, is a walking encyclopedia of Alaska football history. He actually grew up in Wisconsin and saw his first Green Bay Packer game when he was about six. The family moved to the Chicago area when Huffer was in eighth grade, but like any good Alaskan might, he played football at Montana, setting eighteen school records as a Big Sky star quarterback.

Huffer developed one of his trademarks as a quarterback. He always licked his fingers before he got the ball. But he kept up the habit long after he stopped being an active player. On the sidelines, before his Chugiak team hiked the ball, he used to lick them just as if the snap was coming to him and he had to be certain to handle the ball carefully.

When he was coaching, Huffer, who could be gruff in his commands, even if he was a sentimentalist at heart, would say things like, "Football, it's a war. It's a one-hundred-yard war." Huffer didn't mind at all cultivating an image of a general, with his bark stiffer than his bite. At one time cheerleaders had a chant that went like this: "You've got to be tough to play for Huff!"

Huffer, who had two sons play the game—Tom, Jr., and John Paul, in high school in Alaska and at small colleges—loves football. He follows it at all levels. For years after retirement he was as likely to be seen in the stands at Anchorage games as he was to be seen coaching on the sidelines for so long. He took an annual pilgrimage Outside to visit college friends and watch their small-college teams play.

Good enough as a six-foot, 185-pound thrower to attract nine scholarship offers, Huffer chose Montana because he had an uncle who was a rodeo cowboy. And as anyone who has spent time in both places will tell you, Montana is Alaska with a better road system, so it was no surprise to see him gravitate farther north after a stint in the Army, and a period in 1968 attached to presidential security details during the election season. Huffer said he talked football with Richard Nixon.

Huffer, this guy with short hair, bad eyesight, and a raspy voice, started the football program at Chugiak High. Starting a high school program from scratch means grabbing kids out of the hallways because they look like they might be football players. It means putting in long hours of fundamentally oriented practices. In other words, Chugiak was Barrow without the travel logistics, four decades earlier. The Mustangs went 0–6. The second year the Mustangs finished 0–7, though Huffer was in Montana working on a master's degree. He returned to Alaska, took over the program again and started 0–5. Chugiak lost its first eighteen games before winning one.

Huffer had one assistant coach, the late Harry McDonald, who was revered as a local hockey coach. When the Mustangs won their first game in 1971, deep into the third season, they hugged and cried. If they'd had an ocean nearby to jump into for celebrating, they probably would have done it.

Before Huffer was finished coaching at Chugiak High, he coached one son—Tom, Jr., was all-state on offense, defense, and as a kicker—and enjoyed an undefeated state championship season. He knows what it's like to put the time into building something, and he knows how much sweat it takes. He is happy to see schools like Barrow start football teams.

"That's a pretty neat deal," Huffer said.

He's also a man who knows from personal experience with his own start-up losing streak, and from watching around the state, that Voss was exactly right to warn about the threat of losing 50–0 in the early stages of development.

In 1973, West High defeated first-year Lathrop of Fairbanks, 74–0. In 1988, Soldotna defeated first-year Nikiski, its newest rival on the Kenai Peninsula, 89–0. While Soldotna coach Bob Boudreaux said he played every kid he had, and did everything but forbid them from advancing the ball, Nikiski coach Ward Romans was bitter. A month into the season, Soldotna had outscored foes 190–8 and Nikiski had two players on the roster who had never played the game before that season.

"For a powerhouse to come in here and totally embarrass us, it hurts a little," Romans said. "He accomplished his mission and that was to humiliate us."

There is always a danger that the schedule will catch up to a new program, and Barrow was especially careful to avoid that during its thrown-together season before joining a league. At the same time that Barrow was becoming the latest school to add football in 2006, another new dimension was added to Alaska high school football in Anchorage. And Tom Huffer was in the thick of it.

Partially in response to the demands of Title IX federal legislation that requires equal opportunities for girls, Anchorage schools started girls' flag football. Huffer was one of the organizers, and was called "Commissioner Tom."

Just as occurred in Barrow, a survey was circulated in the eight Anchorage high schools asking for student feedback on what activities they might most enjoy. The winner for girls was flag football. Some parents protested the addition of the game instead of a different sport that could lead to scholarship opportunities.

"But the kids voted that the number one thing they wanted was to start flag football," said Huffer, who also coached. "The girls themselves voted. We don't ever have enough girls going out for athletics. You know what? I played a lot of flag football in the Army. Great game."

Huffer said he gave introductory talks to girls who wanted to play, letting them know there was no end-of-the-rainbow goal to reach for like a scholarship.

"I said, 'It's not going to do you a bit of good,'" Huffer said, "'except when you go to college you'll be able to play intramural flag football and have a great time.'"

And the girls still chose flag football.

"We had a bunch of tough girls out there and they just had a great time," Huffer said. "Imagine. They just wanted to play for fun."

Compared to other states where football has been an institution for a hundred years, the sport is still young in Alaska. Smaller communities along the limited road system like Nikiski, Houston, and Valdez and others have added football along the way. And a few towns located off the road system, Sitka and Ketchikan, did so as well. But the situation most analagous to Barrow's took place in Juneau, the state capital.

Juneau is located eight hundred miles south of Anchorage, compared to Barrow's eight hundred miles north. There are no highways into Juneau, either. It is a larger city, with more than 30,000 people, but its primary athletic tradition, like Barrow's, was in basketball.

In 1990, the people of Juneau decided they wanted to add football to the high school curriculum. There was no groundswell of financial support, however, and all funds were raised through creative efforts such as marathon car washes ($10,000 worth of scrubbing went into that), the commitment of the nonscholastic Juneau Youth Football Program, and ticket receipts.

Just like Barrow, if the Juneau-Douglas Crimson Bears wanted an opposing team to play, they had to pay to fly the team in. The practice and game field was an old gravel patch spruced up for the occasion. A couple of years after things got rolling, NFL Films showed up to document a story on the team and its willingness to play on such a hardscrabble field.

The Crimson Bears spent $13,000 for its first-ever game against a Paonia, Colorado, team on August 31 that year, in front of 3,000 Juneau fans. Then they met Wasilla for their first-ever Alaska game in September.

Eventually, even though the geographic considerations were absurd, Juneau became a member of the Cook Inlet Football Conference—the Anchorage league—and fought the large schools on even footing. Later, the Crimson Bears shifted into the Railbelt Conference with Fairbanks teams. The program was founded by Coach Dave Raynie and nurtured by Coach Reilly Richey, who died in March of 2005. Richey led the team to a 37–25 record and into the playoffs four times.

Seven months after Richey's death, Juneau-Douglas was the number one ranked team in Alaska, with its players vowing to win the Crimson Bears' first state title to honor Richey. Juneau defeated North Pole in the first round of the playoffs, 39–7, and then beat Anchorage's East High, 21–3, in the semifinals. That game was dedicated to Richey.

"He made this program for us," said Juneau defensive end Faifo Levale. "We want to carry on his legacy and go all the way for him."

Richey had instituted some traditions that lingered. Each player slapped a sticker on his helmet with the letters "RIENG—Respect Is Earned, Not Given." And each season players wore dog tags with a special message. That season the message read, "Remember Reilly."

A week later, Juneau-Douglas finished the job of going all the way for Richey, besting Palmer High in the championship game, 49–29. Senior running back Tres Saldivar, who had promised at his former coach's funeral that the team would win the state title for him, rushed for 351 yards on just ten carries.

It took fifteen years for Juneau-Douglas football to come full circle, to grow from a fledgling program playing on a gravel field, being supported solely by the good will of citizens, into a state championship team that was second to none in Alaska regardless of size.

For good mention, the Crimson Bears did it again in 2007, winning a second title. The championships proved that neither distance nor humble beginnings were obstacles to success.

When Rocky Klever was a rookie on the New York Jets in 1982, a player on another NFL team came up to him after skimming his biography reading "Anchorage, AL," and asked, "Where the hell is Anchorage, Alabama?"

Klever did his part to put Alaska on the football map, but even he is astonished that there are teams playing in small communities all over the state, from Ketchikan in Southeast, to Nikiski on the Kenai Peninsula, to Barrow on the North Slope.

"I am very surprised," Klever said. "It's unbelievable."

CHAPTER 7

# *Field of Dreams*

WHEN THE CARGO PLANE carrying the first 62,000 pounds of materials landed in Barrow in early August 2007, word spread. Yes, the pipe dream was real. Yes, the largesse of a hard-charging, focused, devoted woman in Florida was real. The gift had arrived. Some called the field the "million-dollar baby," though it only approached that amount. Still, $800,000 worth of cash and in-kind services was raised in months so that the vision of one person could benefit many.

If they hurried up with the work, if the weather cooperated, if the experts could make it fit, the brand-spanking-new artificial turf football field would be installed for the Seward game, August 17, opening day of the season.

The land where the surface would be laid was a few miles out of town, just past some warehouses, a mile or so beyond the old, lumpy, rocky field played on in 2006. It was across the street from the Arctic Ocean, about a hundred yards away, but the temporary orange hurricane fencing on the visitors' side was only about five yards from Freshwater Lake. A wild overthrow, or an errant punt caught by a wind gust, might deposit the pigskin in the water.

Local workers smoothed the ground with many of the tools used for flattening the roads. Sets of bleachers were installed on both sides of the field. A hurry-up construction team built a press box that included electrical capability. There were two viewing boxes, actually. One was for media and the other for community elders, so on blustery days they might stay a tiny bit warmer than they would be in the open air. A small, horizontal sign was nailed to the outside of the boxes: "Top of the World, Barrow, Alaska." Day after day, residents drove by the site, parked for a few minutes, gazed at the progress of the work being made under conveniently sunny skies. It seemed like the last-second preparations for a nation about to host the Olympics.

That was all prep work. The turf, an incredibly dark, bright blue that would make the New York Giants jealous, waited in the wings, waiting for the experts to fly in from the Lower 48 and supervise its precise installation. When everything was set, the men arrived, and now Voss, the assistant coaches, and players were among those who dropped by, eagerly watching the first roll of turf unloaded and spread out.

To them the carpet was beautiful. The bright blue and yellow of the school colors shone brilliantly. Christmas was coming early and this present definitely wasn't going to be under the tree.

Sometimes Voss simply shook his head at the thought of it. The days of rocky fields were dwindling to single digits. The turf was going in at a rapid rate. It was easy to measure progress. The work began in an end zone and marched its way downfield, past the 10-yard line, the 20, the 30, beyond midfield. It was like a team driving to a touchdown, one first down after another.

At the end of practice each day, Voss told the players they were welcome, indeed, encouraged, to help the workers. Periodically, small groups drove out to the site and volunteered. They lifted. They carried. They unrolled. They were participants in the making of their own field. One end zone was blue with the word "Barrow" stenciled in the turf. The other end zone was yellow with the word "Whalers" inset in the turf. There was a big yellow school logo in the center of the field.

As the days ticked by leading up to the opener, the workers looked upon their labor with satisfaction. Everything was going according to plan. Everything was on time. One worker from Outside speculated about the advisability of installing the dark blue field so close to the lake. It was said that one such field of this color, installed near Atlanta, was mistaken for water by geese and ducks and several perished upon making unexpectedly hard landings. The story sounded like an urban legend, but who really knew how the birds of the North Slope would behave?

People had tons of questions about whether the field would hold up in the harsh winter weather, but that was not the true topic of the day. Was it going to be ready for the game? That's what everyone cared about.

It was ready. The field was finished. A day before the game, the Whalers boarded a bus and took the few-mile ride from the school to the field to practice there for the first time. Sophomore Robert Vigo could not contain his glee. He dashed onto the field and ran past the 10, the 20, the 30.

"I just want to make this clear," Vigo announced to his teammates. "I was the first one to run up and down the field."

Senior Mike Gonzales had an instant retort.

"Who cares?" he said.

Boys will be boys.

It was hard to digest, the sight and feel of the majestic field. It was not concrete-hard like some of the earliest artificial turf fields. It was not as soft as real grass, but the inch-long strands of synthetic material looked and felt enough like grass to pass. Except that they were blue. The only blue field just about anyone in Barrow had ever seen was the Boise State field in Idaho, via television. From above, those who had taken short flights in small planes assured others, the field was even more impressive, a splash of color in an otherwise gray landscape.

No more rocks, for sure.

On the first day of practice at the new field (and the last day before the season opener against the Seward Seahawks) Voss tried to keep his players' minds on football. He talked about players being flexible, about needing to be ready to play offense and defense and play more than one position.

Voss startled sophomore Luke George.

"Luke?" he said. "How many positions are you playing on offense?"

George's primary offensive deployment was at fullback, but Voss ticked off three spots that he could be used at and then added, "And you're the fourth-string quarterback."

"I am?" George said.

There was probably no reason to warm up his arm. Teams do not get to the fourth-string quarterback in a single game unless there is an epidemic of injuries or they are ahead 100–0 and trying to hold the score down. Heck, in the NFL, the emergency quarterback is the third stringer.

Barrow was about to embark on its first season as a member of the Greatland Conference, where the top two teams were guaranteed a spot in the small schools postseason playoffs. A lot had happened in a year. Even though Barrow did not have its own locker room at the school—players dressed in an empty classroom partially converted into an office for the coaches—the Whalers did know how to put on their uniforms without a guidebook. They did know how to line up in various formations without committing illegal procedure penalties.

The Whalers had ricocheted through a partial season, they had actually won a game, they had practiced football in Florida, and participated in summer camps in other states.

"They're a lot more seasoned," Voss said.

There was optimism among the players, not from blind positive thinking, but from more confidence that they knew what they were doing when the ball was snapped. They were still woefully short on game experience, but that didn't mean they didn't believe they could win all of their games.

"We weren't that organized," runner Anthony Edwards said of the year before. "We're a million times stronger."

There was a morning Alaska Airlines jet and an afternoon Alaska Airlines jet, and over the course of two days, passengers from Jacksonville, Florida, arrived in town. They were visitors from another planet, guests invited for some payback hospitality for the way they treated Barrow's boys in the spring. Bartram Trail principal Brennan

Asplen made the four-thousand-mile journey. Tom Ryan, a sportscaster from Pennsylvania, enthralled by the Barrow story, volunteered to call play-by-play for an Internet audience on the Black Diamond Sports Network, and showed up with his partner Phil Shamokin. However, no one was more profusely welcomed than the sainted Cathy Parker.

You did not have to be a football player, coach, or parent in Barrow to feel grateful to Cathy Parker. Daniel Lum, who donated a free tour to the Florida visitors in thanks, said, "That's honorable what she did. She's a stranger to us."

No more.

Barrow threw a welcome-to-town reception at the Iñupiat Heritage Center, a gleaming building that is part museum and part community center. This was the true thank-you event for Parker, more formal than telephone thank-yous. In a room decorated with glorious oil paintings of Arctic scenes, including whaling, by esteemed artist Rusty Heurlin, there was no stage, but a podium for speakers to lean on for the occasion.

"We are here to express our gratitude to so many people who have been so kind to us," said Trent Blankenship, who wore a hand-sewn Native top over his office clothes.

"Without this person here," he said, gesturing to Parker sitting in the front row, "none of this would have happened. She had a vision."

More than that, Parker had a schedule. Not only did she believe the momentum on the fund-raising must be maintained and the field be ready to go for the new season, she said she didn't have any more time to devote to raising money.

"I have a job," she said.

It was a day of friendship, of the mingling of cultures from the beach-oriented, warm-weather south, and the whaling-oriented, cold-weather north. Football has changed things in the area, observed Barrow city mayor, Nathaniel Olemaun.

Olemaun told a story about what was going on in his own household. His foster son, Dave Evikana, was a traditionalist in that he enjoyed hunting and fishing and spending time at hunting camp in the late summer and early fall. Evikana was a junior defensive back on the team.

"This year he had to make a choice between camp and football," Olemaun said. "He said, 'I have to hang around here.'"

It was a telling story, emblematic of what some of the Eskimo teens on the team were going through. They had been to camp for years with their families and they could always return to camp later, and they still could indulge in spring hunting, but football meant enough to them to sacrifice for the moment.

Susan Hope, mother of linebacker Jarid—who unfortunately had broken his left leg in practice three days before the opener—had undertaken a special project. Parker was called to the front of the room. Hope, the secretary of the North Slope Borough School District board, unveiled a spectacular, handmade blue parka with a white fur collar and presented it to a stunned and smiling Parker, who wrapped herself into it.

"We've been cold since we got here," she said, cracking up the listeners and recalling the 90°F Jacksonville temperature left behind. "This is awesome."

Over her first two days in Barrow, Parker had been swarmed by well-wishers. The thank-yous stacked up higher than winter firewood. She was a bit overwhelmed by the attention. But what touched her heart the most was when elders—some of whom just knew her as the philanthropic woman from Florida—stopped her to talk. The encounters reinforced for her that she had done the right thing, had thrown herself into a worthy cause.

"The most priceless thing to me is when parents or grandparents come up to me with tears in their eyes and say thank-you," Parker said.

Susan Hope was one of those enthusiastic parents who had sensed positive changes in her son since he threw himself into football. He had a focus, was part of a team, and had something productive to do with his time.

"We're so appreciative that our children are active," she said.

For the most part, the mood was one of frivolity, but with intermissions that offered a reminder that the start-up of football was not all fun and games. Dexter Rexford, fifty-two, project manager for the Ukpeagvik Iñupiat Corporation that had provided the land for the field and supervised installation, reflected on the origins of Barrow football.

He talked about the tough times young people were going through, how they made poor choices to drink and take drugs and drop out of school, and how they wandered away from the path of honor of Iñupiat ways. The people of the Far North have always been resilient, he said, and they have always "adapted to changes" over centuries. Usually, those had been environmental and climatic, more pertinent to physical adjustment. What was being faced now was more of a spiritual assault, an erosion of values.

By embracing football, the community was not merely adding an amusement, a sport, a game, but using it as a tool.

"We are taking a step forward into a new arena," Rexford said. "To strengthen our children's character. We are putting it in place to combat the many social ills that do damage. The elders cried for help for our youth. Today is an historical day for the Iñupiat people. A field of dreams . . . is now in use due to the remarkable Cathy Parker.

"It is not simply a football field, but a field of dreams to inspire our children."

Rexford then switched to Iñupiaq and continued, "When we work together, we can accomplish anything."

Of all the elements of the ceremony, Rexford's powerful speech touched people most deeply. The applause was mighty and sustained.

"Well said," Blankenship noted. "Well said."

The field was ready, the turf in place. The Whalers were taking a walk-through as a rehearsal to make sure they remembered all of the plays. Hope stopped by and watched for a moment. The Barrow kids she had seen grow up were decked out in football gear, running drills and plays, though her son was stuck on crutches. The ground was not dirt or gravel, but under the sun the artificial turf with its bright colors seemed like a mirage.

"I watched them running around on the field," she said. "It felt like I was watching TV. I had to remind myself that this was real."

It was real all right. There were carpenters nailing the final nails. Banners with advertising were being hung on the elders' box. Some of the older women wore their kuspusks, the fancy, colorful outer dresslike outfits generally worn for special occasions. Young people painted their faces. Some fans carried homemade signs reading, "God Bless Our Whalers" or "We Love Our Whalers." Defensive back Cody Romine's parents held a banner reading "Cody Is My Hero." Benefactors from Florida were pulling on layers so they could comfortably watch their first game above the Arctic Circle.

There was only one thing left to do—play a football game inaugurating the 2007 season and a shiny new football field.

"Life is good today," Blankenship said.

CHAPTER 8

# *Do You Believe in Miracles?*

IT WAS HALF AN HOUR to kickoff, and Coach Mark Voss seemed a little bit dazed. Fans created a minor traffic jam outside the makeshift fencing that passed for the walls of a stadium. The metal bleachers, a few rows deep, filled early with players' family members and community elders, all bundled in parkas and blankets against the harsh wind blowing in across the water.

There was nothing to break the wind, no structures around the field besides that hastily erected press box. But it's not as if the people of Barrow were going to stay home because it was too cold. Ha! These folks knew how to dress for the weather. The sky was gray and the wind was nasty, but people sensed that one day it was going to mean something to say that you were there on the day the Whalers played their first game on the new artificial turf football field. Still, a spitting drizzle did not make the experience any cozier.

Cathy Parker, who had turned forty-two during her fund-raising efforts, and had left her three boys in the care of her husband to journey above the Arctic Circle with her thirteen-year-old daughter, was struck by the splash of color the field represented. "It looks like God stamped the top of the world with a hundred yards of the most beautiful blue and gold you've ever seen."

Project Alaska was here in the flesh, and so were the Floridians who had put their muscle behind making it a reality.

The limited seating capacity reached overflowing rapidly. Fans filled the bleachers, lined up around the fencing behind both end zones, staked out areas on the visitors' side by the lake, or pulled their cars as close as they could to the action in a bold effort to simultaneously position themselves for the action and to stay warm. Makeshift food stands were erected and coffee and hot chocolate seemed to be the hottest sellers.

After their initial calisthenics, the teams retreated to their portable game locker rooms—yellow school buses. That was their shelter from the elements.

As game time approached against the Seward Seahawks (same name as the Seattle Seahawks, even if no one really knew what a seahawk was), a burly man with a powerful build and graying hair sticking out from under a baseball cap took Voss aside and passed on a few words of soothing advice.

That put the slightly awed look on Voss's face. He walked over to a familiar out-of-state visitor and said, "I was just talking to Larry Csonka." He didn't say it as a boast, but with a "what-will-happen-next" tone.

Csonka, whose catalytic speech had unexpectedly helped launch football in Barrow, traveled the eight hundred miles from Anchorage to see the new field and watch the opener. Some of the younger fans in the bleachers recognized Csonka from his previous trip and started a "Lar-ry! Lar-ry!" chant.

Csonka said he always thought Eskimos, who had cooperated in survival forever, would be able to play football well because the sport relies so heavily on cooperation. At twenty-two, there are by far more starting players in a football game than in hockey (six), basketball (five), or baseball (nine).

"They've always had a rich tradition of working together," Csonka said. "You can't bring in a whale without it, and they've been doing that for eight thousand years. The important thing is that they're playing and not drinking or doing drugs."

No admission was charged and no seats were numbered, so the crowd estimate of about two thousand was the best anyone could do.

A year after it made its sideline debut, Price Brower's cushioned swivel chair was back, with his bottom comfortably ensconced in it.

Brower once again was the only one smart enough to import his own furniture to a game, and he was the only fan who came wearing polar bear pants. The big, fluffy leggings resembled chaps with fur, though much thicker, and the polar bear Brower hunted years earlier donated its coat to a worthy cause—him.

Brower, fifty-four, is the grandson of Charles Brower, the author of the famed Barrow book, *Fifty Years Below Zero*. Besides his snazzy pants, Brower wore a "Whalers" football hat, a parka made of ground squirrel fur with a ruff of polar bear fur, and carried a blue megaphone. There was little doubt he was the warmest, most comfortable guy at the game.

"It was salvage from a dumpster at hunting camp," Brower said of his chair treasure redeemed from trash. "It swivels. It's soft."

Brower was toastier than Cathy Parker, anyway. Somewhere along the way in the dressing process, she had lost track of the number of sweaters and sweatshirts she layered on.

"A lot," she said. "I feel like the Michelin man."

As everyone stood, the pledge of allegiance was recited in Iñupiaq. It was showtime. Little kids, four-year-olds with parents, had come to watch big brother play; kids eight, nine, and ten had come to watch the first football game of their lives in person.

"You know," said linebacker John Wilson, "kids get a lot more footballs for Christmas now. They'll get more interested and they'll want to play."

At that moment, Barrow wanted to play.

Seward, located 120 miles from Anchorage at the terminus of the majestic Seward Highway (a National Scenic Byway decorated with mountains and waterways, perhaps the most beautiful road in America) was the first Greatland Conference opponent ever for Barrow. The Seahawks were not a league powerhouse, but figured to be a middle-of-the-pack team in 2007. Barrow didn't know enough about itself to determine whether it should be the favorite or the underdog.

Barrow kicked off. Seward received, but recorded only limited advances on offense. It went back and forth like that during the first quarter, trading possessions, but no scoring breakthroughs. The highlight for the Whalers was an interception by Anthony Edwards in the defensive backfield. Voss counted on several players to play both sides of the line of scrimmage. He had thirty-five players, but the talent was not equally distributed. Two-platoon football, the rule in the NFL and commonplace at most levels of the game, did not apply so strictly in high school. There is a vast difference in ability on high school teams, from the kids who just want to suit up and the kids who are hoping for college scholarships.

The first quarter ended 0–0, but that was something you had to know by paying attention because there was no scoreboard. Also, the temporary clock hanging out the window of the media booth was very difficult to read. A lot of it depended on the distance and angle of the observer and if the sun hit it in just the right way.

It was not long before public address announcer Dino Olemaun took to periodically informing the crowd of time remaining.

Neither team mounted a sustained drive. Players had trouble hanging on to the ball. Passes were off-target. Sophomore Albert Gerke did not start at quarterback, but soon enough assumed the job, one he would keep for the entire season. Officials, imported from Anchorage, blew their whistles as frequently as players made gains. It was sloppy football. Voss was right in saying the Whalers weren't ready. They were not exactly a smooth running machine.

Midway through the second quarter, Gerke took the snap from center Mike Gonzales, handed off to Edwards, and watched as his halfback scooted around the left side two yards into the end zone for a touchdown and a 6–0 lead. Fans jumped up and down and clapped— both effective methods for warming up—and yelled "Aarigaa!" The common Iñupiaq expression can be used to mean "good," or "great," or even "go for it."

The Whalers went for the extra point, but the hike for the kick was fumbled. The milestone of the first-ever Barrow Greatland Conference touchdown was registered at five minutes, twenty-one seconds of the second quarter.

Other than the fact that the crowd kept growing with latecomers, who squeezed in next to friends on those cold metal bleachers or edged their bodies into narrow spaces along the fences, that was the Barrow high point for a while.

Just a minute and a half later, Gerke was on the run in his own end zone, trying to slither away from the charging Seahawks when senior defender Justin Coon took him down. The safety gave Seward two points. And then with forty-four seconds left in the half, Coon burst free for a nineteen-yard touchdown run. It was 9–6 Seward at halftime.

The Seahawks liked the new field as much as the Whalers did.

"It's awesome," said tailback Andrew Ferkinhoff. "It's soft, like walking on a bathroom carpet."

Ferkinhoff was just one of the Seward players awed by the spectacle of the glistening new field. Except on July 4, when Seward hosts the state's most raucous Independence Day celebration in conjunction with its nearly century-old Mount Marathon race, Seward is no bigger than Barrow. And cities that size, especially in a remote place like Alaska, do not ante up for artificial turf fields.

"Our field is just this giant mud pit," lineman Ryan Dunno said.

It is a no-brainer to realize that Alaska is one place that artificial turf is a key tool for improving the quality of the game, but it is also a no-bucks answer if the issue is broached. Not everyone has a benefactor like Parker.

At the game, the field was at least as much of an attraction as the play. Ukpeagvik Iñupiat Corporation officials announced that the imported marvel would henceforth be called "Cathy Parker Field."

At halftime, Voss was encouraging, but the coaches firmly instructed the players to tighten their play. They were making too many mistakes. There were so many penalties one would think the Oakland Raiders had taken the field. Barrow exhibited a lack of precision that was glaring, primarily because of lack of game experience. When Gerke barked signals, someone often jumped offsides. When Seward called out its snap sequence, some Whaler was fooled and came across too soon. The penalties cut the heart out of any momentum Barrow could muster. And for a perfectionist football coach—as so many are—each whistle was like being nicked by a razor blade, not in and of itself a serious issue, but each drawing a little bit of blood. Enough whistles, enough bloodshed, and someone could die—or, nearly as painful, lose.

Things looked as bleak as the sky for Barrow in the third quarter when Seward put another touchdown up. Seahawk quarterback Dylan Beck completed a twenty-three-yard toss to Nick Spurr, and Beck kicked the extra point. It was 16–6 and while that was not an insurmountable lead, the Whalers had not exhibited the type of cohesiveness on offense needed to rally.

When Justin Sanders intercepted a pass at the beginning of the fourth quarter, the crowd stirred. That seemed like the type of big play that could be a catalyst. But when the Whalers could not capitalize the game seemed to be slipping away.

The attitude seemed to deflate in the stands and along the sidelines, where those in authority but without a seat like Trent Blankenship, paced back and forth and occasionally dropped to one knee to watch the action. There was a spreading feeling that the Whalers weren't going to win this one and that was too bad because it was such a great day otherwise.

Play was stagnant and there was a lull in emotion, almost as if the entire block of fans was suffering from low-grade Thanksgiving turkey overeating paralysis. And then came a wake-up call in the strangest possible way. The jangling alarm clock was from malfunction, not pre-meditated time setting.

All of a sudden, on the visitors' side of the field, appeared a naked young man sprinting across the end of the turf. A streaker! Wasn't that a Seventies thing? Wasn't that crazy sucker freezing his you-know-whats off?

A buzz energized the crowd. Parents tsk-tsked and were disgusted. Teenagers laughed. The burst of lightning, as they all are, was over quickly. Not everyone was sure what they had seen. Some had turned their heads at the right moment (or they wrong moment, depending on your point of view). Everyone agreed that for a streaker to strip down on such a chilly day, he must be highly motivated.

Then everyone agreed that the streaker must be dimmer than a forty-watt light bulb because he did not run off and disappear over the horizon. If there is a primer for streaking, the bottom-line rule would include the advice to keep on running once out of the park, and if at all possible jump into a waiting car—and to expose one's self in a place where there would be anonymity. Not only did the Barrow streaker not have a getaway car at the ready, he stopped running less than fifty yards outside the field to get dressed, and in a place as small as Barrow recognition was a certainty.

The inexplicable failure to leave the scene of the crime gave the authorities ample time to arrest the twenty-something man for indecent exposure and unnecessary buffoonery. Over the next couple of days the story leaked out that the man had done his dash on a dare and stood to collect something like $50 on a bet. However, the police threw the book at him. Not only was he held for hours he was fined many hundreds of dollars.

In the absence of touchdowns, the incident provided fodder for conversation in the stands and a little bit of spice to the event. By then it was late in the fourth quarter and the Whalers remained ten points behind, seemingly hopelessly so on a day when they needed a bulldozer to move the ball.

At long last, the Whalers got the offense out of four-wheel drive and into first, putting together a march sparked by Gerke–to–Luke George passes. With the Seward defense collapsing, Gerke put his own wheels into motion and darted around end nine yards for a touchdown with two minutes, forty-seven seconds left. Watching with a big smile on his face near the Barrow bench was Csonka, rooting for the team his talk inspired to do well. Barrow went for the two-point conversion, but it failed.

The Whalers trailed 16–12 and Csonka said, "Good for them. They made it look good."

The ball went back to Seward. By the time the Seahawks ran the clock down and punted, provided Barrow could even stop them on a three-and-out, it seemed unlikely the Whalers would have enough time left to make anything happen.

Anyone who knew anything about football knew that the only strategy was for Barrow to try an onside kick. But anyone who knew anything about football knew that Seward would be ready for the obvious attempt, and that onside kicks to set up last-gasp drives were recovered only slightly more often than a full moon came around.

Barrow put the play into motion. The ball floated, bounced, and in the scrum that followed, the Whalers came up with the ball. Barrow was alive! Csonka arched his eyebrows. Maybe.

The weight was on Gerke's slender shoulders. He was the quarterback, the leader, and he had to make things happen with his arm and legs. He took a snap, juked, faked, and burst downfield for a twenty-yard gain. Two-and-a-half minutes left.

Gerke rolled right, seemed trapped, and squirted to the 18-yard line. Less than two minutes to go. The handoff went to Edwards, who fought to the 11-yard line. Gerke started left, handed the ball to Edwards and he burst inside the 5-yard line. Barrow had first-and-goal at the 4-yard line with forty-five seconds to go. Fans were on their feet screaming. This was too good to be true. The Whalers might pull this one out.

Gonzales hiked the ball to Gerke. The quarterback rolled left chased by Seahawk defenders. On the run he fired a hard pass to Luke George that was a little off the mark. George reached one hand out, grabbed the ball, and looking like a professional tight end, gathered it in for the four-yard touchdown play.

Delirium. Barrow, 18, Seward 16. Hollywood would never buy it. It was too real to be believed.

The chant went up from the stands, the chant the Whalers shouted when they broke from a team huddle at the end of practice, the chant that had sustained them when no one thought Barrow would field a football team, and when everyone doubted this fabulous new field would be bought, installed, and ready for the opener.

"We believe!" the spectators yelled. "We believe!" Csonka yelled it, too. "We believe!" Blankenship paced the sideline bellowing, "We believe!"

When the clock ticked down its final seconds, fans issued one more group "Aarigaa!" and many rushed onto the field, to touch it, to admire it, and to touch and admire their boys, as well. First the team huddled at midfield and Parker led the Whalers in prayer. She wore her new parka and in the biting wind looked darned happy to have it.

David Gerke, Albert's father, was a proud poppa. The older Gerke, forty-two, operates heavy equipment for the local government. He likes to brag about what an arm his son possesses, but not even he was sure the sixteen-year-old had the poise yet to spearhead a rally like this one. Gerke hugged Albert and kissed him, right out on the field. Public display of affection between a man and his boy, something considered to be in short supply across America.

"That's my son," the older Gerke yelled.

It was a community's sons.

Gerke said the Whalers hadn't given up when they were behind by ten points with less than three minutes to go, but they weren't exactly overconfident, either.

"I think we were hoping we could come back," Gerke said.

Lineman Colton Blankenship said he always thought Barrow would make the comeback.

"Oh, yes sir," he said. "It fortifies my faith."

Voss stated the obvious, that the onsides kick was monumental and how badly Barrow needed to make a break to even have a chance to win. And he said that the Whaler defense kept the team in the game, and that eliminating mistakes at the end allowed the offense to show what it could do after the team grabbed the kick.

"It was pretty well scripted, wasn't it?" Voss said with a wink.

What was as far from scripted as could be was the way Robert Vigo utilized his speed from defensive end to terrorize the Seahawks' backfield in the fourth quarter. Vigo, a sophomore with considerable raw talent, was a backup running back still finding himself in formations. But he was the prime-time dude with a sack and fumble recovery when Barrow needed a game-breaker.

"That was amazing how we turned it around," Vigo said. "It's unbelievable."

Sandy-haired George, who besides catching the game-winning touchdown pass also intercepted two passes, has the wiry strength of a teenager who hasn't quite grown into his body. He was the hero of the moment, accepting congratulations of "Good game, good game," from fans.

On a day when the ball was slippery and hard to handle, George exhibited fingers that might well have been coated with glue. He made the catches others couldn't.

"I'll remember this day," George said.

Exuberant players thrust their helmets high in celebration, then they ran across the street, dropped their hats, in some cases pulled off shoes or pads, and ran into the freezing Arctic Ocean. How else do you celebrate little miracles in Barrow, Alaska?

One by one the players emerged, dripping wet, shaking their heads as if they were shaggy dogs drying their coats. They were lucky they were not all immediately struck down with pneumonia.

"I'm a little bit cold, but actually I'm too excited about the win," the younger Blankenship said. "Of course, I've been known to walk around in twenty-degree-below weather in shorts."

It is not every day that Blankenship can convince his Whaler teammates to court frostbite with him. But a day when Barrow wins a football game is one of them. He decided that every time Barrow won at home the players should dive into the Arctic Ocean. It's a tradition he felt was well worth starting.

Happy fans made their way to their cars—and their heaters. Cathy Parker Field emptied. The improbable victory capped what was probably the most magical day in Barrow sports history.

CHAPTER 9

# *Bad Old Days*

IN THE FALL OF 1966, fifteen-year-old Roy Nageak, who had been raised in Barrow, boarded the first of several planes that would take him from his home at the top of the world to Oregon to attend high school.

He left behind his parents, siblings, relatives, and friends so he could get an education beyond middle-school level. It was the only way. Barrow, like other rural Alaskan communities, had no high school to serve its Native inhabitants. If Nageak wanted to keep learning, he had to go elsewhere.

For decades, Alaska Natives with ambition—and their parents' consent and encouragement—moved from the Interior or the Arctic coast to Sitka in Southeast Alaska to enroll at Mount Edgecumbe for high school. Or they could go farther away, to Oregon, to Oklahoma, for high school programs catering to American Indians in the Lower 48, administered by the federal Bureau of Indian Affairs.

Nageak's leave-taking was not an easy one.

"It broke my heart," he said.

Alaska Natives of a certain age—Nageak was fifty-six when he relived his past in conversation—can identify with the emotions. As it had in so many of its dealings with its indigenous population, the United States government for decades treated the Eskimos, Athabascans, Aleuts, and other native groups of Alaska indifferently at best, and cruelly at worst.

As Barrow welcomed Cathy Parker to town and the 2007 football season was about to unfold, men and women like Nageak, who had been exported for high school, reflected on why the start-up of a football team was symbolically so powerful. What it meant to those individuals who had been separated from their families for the better part of four years, was that there was now no reason for a young man with football interest or talent to move somewhere else for the opportunity to play. One more activity, one more thing, had been added to Barrow to keep children close to their families.

In middle age, Nageak was vice-chairman of the Ukpeagvik Iñupiat Corporation (UIG). When the issue of providing land for the football field came up, he voted yes. A stocky man, with a ready smile and a generous demeanor, Nageak said he was scared when he left Barrow to attend the Chemawa Indian School near Salem, Oregon, but admitted to some excitement, as well.

He remembered taking a Pan American jet from Alaska to Seattle and then riding a bus from Seattle to Oregon.

"It was an adventure, but at the same time, we were without our parents," he said. "But when our parents signed that piece of paper to send us to Oregon, the commitment to education was there."

Other Alaska Natives and Native Americans from the Pacific Northwest were also enrolled at Chemawa. Nageak said one of the efforts made by the school was to assimilate Natives into American culture. That meant English language emphasis, above all, but it also meant, funny thing, that the school fielded a football team he could play on.

More than forty years ago, Nageak played quarterback on the Chemawa football team. He loved it. He thought the experience was great. When Barrow started talking about putting its own football team together in 2006, Nageak was stunned. He never expected something like that to happen in the community.

"No, not in my wildest dreams," he said.

Of course, there was a time when community elders would not have dreamed Barrow would even have its own high school. But then a combination of factors—from court rulings to oil wealth—made the construction of Barrow High School possible and even mandatory.

The United States of 2008 is a far different society than it was in the 1950s. Racism has not been rubbed out altogether, but things that are taken for granted now—intermarriage, adoption of foreign babies of a different skin color than the parents, political sensitivity (described as political correctness), and the out-of-the-home role of women—have transformed the social landscape.

The overt discrimination once practiced against African-Americans and Native Americans—banned from drinking from the same water fountains as whites, forced into separate seating in movie theater balconies, segregated schools, signs in the windows of establishments proclaiming that certain kinds of people would not be served—are unimaginable now.

While Native Americans in the Lower 48 were being massacred and relocated for their land and mineral wealth by United States government through force and decree, Alaskan Natives were basically ignored because they were so far out of the mainstream. Also because the Russians were busy doing the job, until Alaska was sold to the United States after the Civil War.

Ultimately, white America took notice of Alaska because of the turn-of-the-twentieth-century gold rushes, and eventually, oil wealth. Left to their own devices, a white-dominated government and oil-company partners would likely have left Native landowners and communities out of the twentieth century gold rush. The passage of the Alaska Native Claims Settlement Act, however, precluded that development and made Native corporations, their constituents, and some Native communities, rich.

For the first time, Alaska Natives had clout. They could buy what they wanted, whether that meant investing in infrastructure for a community, or spending corporation dividend checks on new snowmobiles, better homes, or more luxurious vacations.

Above all, the influx of oil money meant Alaska Natives could buy freedom. Freedom from old rules and old practices. To many, the absolute top priority was building new schools in the community, so that their children would benefit from the wave of oil wealth and not be wrenched from parents in order to receive a quality education.

Money alone did not provide the answer. Politics was involved, quite heavily, as well. Years before the Alaska Pipeline transported a drop of oil from the North Slope to Valdez a battle was waged in the courts, known as the "Molly Hootch Case."

Similar to what emerged by design in the American South, Alaska had developed something akin to the "separate but equal" doctrine. This meant that many areas had separate schools for white children and Native children. In the most rural areas there were no schools for Native children beyond a certain age.

In 1971, parents of children in the village of Kivalina asked the Alaska Legal Services Corporation, the state's version of a nationwide program to provide legal assistance to the poor in noncriminal cases, to sue the state so they could get a high school for the community. The state settled quickly. That was the forerunner of the class-action lawsuit filed by the organization in 1972, which was spearheaded by three villages near Bethel, a city in Southwest Alaska.

The first plaintiff on the list was a student named Molly Hootch of Emmonak. The state fought this lawsuit and it reached the Alaska Supreme Court. The court ruled that a trial should be conducted on the point that Alaska's failure to build high schools in Native villages represented a pattern of racial discrimination.

Then-Governor Jay Hammond was advised by his attorney general Avrum Gross to settle the lawsuit and immediately propose spending $20 million—money raised through a bond issue—to build a first wave of schools. That turned out to be the first step in a negotiation. It took a year of haggling, but the plaintiffs argued the amount up to $50 million. Expenses far eclipsed the initial estimates as time passed and prices rose.

Officially, when the case was settled by consent decree in 1976, it was known as *Tobeluk v. Lind.* Eighteen-year-old Anna Tobeluk lived in the Eskimo village of Nunapitchuk, about four hundred miles west of Anchorage. She wanted to attend high school, but her village did not have one, and she did not want to go hundreds or even thousands of miles away from home, to live at a boarding school the way Roy Nageak had.

The consent decree that grew out of the lawsuit required the creation of high school programs in 126 villages—unless the local community opted out—and Tobeluk and twenty-five others became students at Nunapitchuk High. Many of those secondary school programs began with temporary housing in small existing buildings, or converted one-room school houses—but eventually it evolved into a construction boom, with new buildings going up all around the state.

The first discussions of building a high school for Barrow began in 1977, and the cost was projected at $24 million. By the time the school opened in 1984, costs had escalated to $72 million. The state-of-the-art, weatherproof, gleaming school was declared the most expensive high school in U. S. history, and it drew national attention.

Under the court decision, in villages around the state, elders could sit in a room, hear a proposal that called for spending millions of dollars, and approve a plan to build a new school in their community so their children would not be forced to live away from home to obtain an education. It was a tremendous breakthrough in Native empowerment, as well as a commitment to the future.

In 1978, the Alaska Legislature, seeking the best way to pay for all of this new school construction, imposed a new corporate income tax on the oil industry. The first $100 million collected under the law was earmarked for school construction.

At the time of the consent decree, it was estimated that three thousand Alaskan teenagers were leaving home annually to attend high schools elsewhere. Gradually, even as rural populations grew, that number was reduced to a trickle, and those who chose to leave did so for personal reasons, not because they were forced out.

Trent Blankenship had been in town only a short while before he grasped the symbolism of the simple existence of the high school. Yes, it was an attractive building—with the words "HOME OF THE WHALERS" in raised, block letters on the outside. Of course it was important to parents to have their kids educated. But the well-kept high school that so much money had been poured into meant a lot because it also had a lot of hopes poured into it. The earlier generations that had shipped out to Mount Edgecumbe or the Lower 48 had an ownership stake. Blankenship studied the past and realized the colossal importance to villages and rural community psyches that having their own schools represented.

"It still is a symbol of self-determination," he said. "It's a big symbol of independence. It is a missing piece. It had to be done. It was sad to have kids going away for school. It was sad at home and the kids were sad."

There was no scrimping when it came to building Barrow High. It was the best money could buy at the time. If there were extras to be added, they were added. The community was immensely proud of the school. Similarly modern junior high and elementary schools were also built. Adding football became part of the symbolism for some. It was *here.*

But as the old saying goes, money can't buy love. For that reason there has been extra dismay and disillusionment that after being provided with all of these amenities—these modern schools staffed with highly paid teachers—the community's kids were still running into trouble. Call it a betrayal of ideas that contradicted the emphasis on closely knit families in the Eskimo community, but it was hard for elders to fathom how so many of their teenagers became dependent on drugs and alcohol and how so many of them dropped out of these fine schools.

The mayor of Borough, Nathaniel Olemaun, sixty-four, said the War on Drugs program is an outgrowth of adults realizing there was a serious problem that could not be remedied only by a school curriculum.

"We found that kids and young adults were starting on meth," Olemaun said. "We needed to educate the kids on the dangers."

Seeking solutions, alarmed borough officials, city officials, school officials, the police department, regional tribal leaders, the health department, and Native corporation officials banded together at a meeting for the first time two years earlier, he said.

Ads railing against the use of alcohol and drugs ran in the weekly newspaper, the *Arctic Sounder;* on the local radio station, KBRW; on cable TV; and counseling services were set up to help people with drug and alcohol problems. Olemaun said officials wanted to see the adoption of a community watchdog approach, "friends don't let friends drive drunk." They wanted residents to be their brothers' keepers. They wanted people to take better care of one another.

The officials hoped average citizens could be persuaded to help relatives stop drinking and taking drugs, rather than enabling them by ignoring their behavior or being in denial. In a live-and-let-live environment, that was no easy sell.

"It took a while," Olemaun said. "We have to stop being protective of our families. These are illegal activities."

For those who had grown up in a simpler age, when it was enough to take snowmobile rides into the countryside, to spend spare time fishing and absorbing nature, a community that had television, some after-school sports team participation, and VCRs that could play movies all day long, seemed to have plenty going on.

Then, when an assembly was called at the high school to get student input, the officials heard from their teenagers that they felt they had nothing to do.

"We thought we provided a lot of activities," Olemaun said.

As often has been the case over the last thirty years in Alaska, the community governments turned to the oil companies, still drilling at Prudhoe Bay after all these years, for small grants. North Slope Borough officials began sponsoring village and city picnics for all ages, a fireworks show, Native dance classes.

"Activities like that," Olemaun said, "where the community could look forward to being together."

Football fit into the big picture. A home team to root for not only gave at-risk teenagers something else to do, it gave little kids role models to appreciate, and it gave adults another common denominator representing their town. The attention that has followed beyond the city has been a surprise. From ESPN to a German film crew, those who stop by to film football carry the message of Barrow to the world, as well. Might even help tourism, Olemaun said.

"It has value," Olemaun said of football's addition.

Nageak said he became a Kansas City Chiefs fan when he played ball in Oregon, particularly rooting for the size-challenged halfback Warren McVea, whose nickname was "The Flea." He fondly remembered his own chance to play football, and was in favor of starting the game in Barrow because there was no reason a younger generation shouldn't have the opportunity close to home.

"There are shareholders in UIC," he said, "and a lot of them are children."

And he didn't see why a Barrow High football team shouldn't become successful. "We've always been together, working together when we are pulling up whales. It takes a community."

CHAPTER 10

# *It's a Girl*

THE WHISTLE BLEW ON the practice field and the slightly stocky, powerfully built defensive back retreated, shadowing the wide receiver. The play went the other way. Next play the defender back-pedaled alongside the receiver and this time the pass came their way. Incomplete.

There were no names on the backs of the nondescript, white practice jerseys, no numbers. From a distance, especially to a casual observer, the players were indistinguishable, their faces and heads hidden by helmets.

There were big, strong players; slender, wiry players; and players of all manner of height and weight combinations in-between. They were football players. It was only when that defensive back was sent to the sidelines for a breather and the player pulled off the helmet, that the world could see that he was a she.

Ganina Pili has long, black hair, and she tied it into a long braid, then tucked it into her shoulder pads behind her head when she played football. A high school junior—at an age when the separation between the sexes may be at its keenest, in the sense that the young people are looking for dates rather than friendly mates—she defied stereotypes to go out for the Barrow High football team.

The National Football League likes to trumpet the fact that women are an increasing element in its fan base. But there are no women playing in the NFL. A woman on a roster at a major football-playing college is virtually unheard of. A woman at a roster on a small-college team is a novelty. Girls at selected high schools around the nation, however, have convinced local authorities they should be eligible to play football for their hometown team. It happens. Not in great numbers. But in 2007, to see a girl dressed out in full pads is not the shock it would have been in, say, 1987.

The vast growth and expansion of girls high school sports in so many realms, with the looming, set-in-concrete Title IX law, transformed the sports landscape for girls in high school and college-age women. Team after team has been added. Sport after sport has been added.

We are not about to witness a Rose Bowl played on television featuring an all-girls University of Southern California football team, but the day is approaching when the kicker for the Trojans might be a Woman of Troy. Over the years, court challenges in many jurisdictions have established that high school girls cannot be banned from playing on a team in a sport where there is no comparable sport for them. Even more disconcerting for many than football, with its team nature and its thickly padded equipment, has been the proliferation of girls in an individual, close-contact, even intimate sport like wrestling. By comparison, football is impersonal.

Pili, sixteen, comes from a family of athletes. She is of Polynesian heritage, with light brown skin, very black hair, and dark eyes. She was an impact player in girls basketball and volleyball immediately at Barrow High, so she had a reservoir of respect built up.

When Pili informed Mark Voss that she wanted to go out for football, there was no major announcement, no big-time hand-wringing, no need for picketing and demands that a girl be allowed to play a boys sport. No need to get in a dither. Voss figured some challenges to making it all run smoothly would arise, but he basically shrugged and said, "OK." Unlike in decades past when society worked itself into a snit, it was not a big enough issue to faze him.

The most obvious challenge in a normal team situation would be sharing a locker room. But since the Whalers don't have a locker room, that wasn't much of a problem. At the end of the school day, the players who had not brought uniforms home to wash come to the football office and pick up their gear. One floor below was a girls bathroom and a boys bathroom. Pili dressed in there, and some of the boys dressed in the adjacent boys bathroom.

A key element in integrating an all-anything team—whether it be color, ethnic background, or sex—is the acceptance of the minority by the majority. In a reasonably small town where everyone knew everyone and everyone pretty much grew up together, familiarity was not an issue. Since Pili was admired as a top-grade athlete, she was given benefit of the doubt on the matter of appropriate athleticism. Pili was lucky. She had those advantages going for her.

As a competitor with the soul of an athlete, Pili was attracted by the challenge of playing football. Her toughest sell was convincing her parents that it was a good idea and quelling the doubts of her female friends, who pretty much thought she was crazy. But Pili knew what she wanted to do.

"It's another sport to keep in shape," Pili said when asked to explain her football motivation. "I would have gone out last year, but I didn't know it was going to happen. My friends were surprised. They think it's weird. But it's exciting."

Yes, she said, there was some talk among adults about whether it was good thing for her physically to come into contact with all of these boys, but her outlook was that football is all about blocking and tackling and hitting, and people's bodies are bouncing off one another's all the time.

"'Don't worry,' I told them," she said. "'That's the point of the sport.'"

Pili said her teammates are like a band of brothers, since she grew up with most of them. She has cousins at East High in Anchorage, boys, and they told her they couldn't believe she was playing football. For the most part, though, Pili looks at football through the prism of sport. She is an athlete who has strength in her arms and in her low center of gravity. She can run, maybe not as fast as the fastest guys on the team, but with endurance. She understands team dynamics. What Pili did not have going for her was much of an understanding of football rules and nuances.

"I kind of came into the sport not knowing a whole lot," she said.

Of course, in Barrow, that did not make Pili stand out. She was just one of the many beginners.

"There is so much information," she said.

Football players everywhere just starting out make the same comment all the time.

Pili was not a starter against Seward. She was not good enough, had not earned a position. But she was in the mix for playing time, as a backup, on special teams, and is as good as many of the other players on the team. To some extent she had already proven herself. Besides Pili's credentials in other sports, she made the Outside trip to Florida and the football camps with the other players in the spring. They got a taste of one another for a month, on the field and off, on airplanes and in other aspects of road trips. They learned to live with one another.

Trent Blankenship, who traveled with the team, said some interesting dynamics emerged. When Pili, the only girl playing in the camps, experienced some flirting by players from other states, the Whalers seemed to form a protective cocoon, he said. And, Blankenship noted, in a beach setting, away from Barrow, where players and coaches were thrust together day after day for long hours, the players who had always treated Pili more or less like a sister seemed to treat her more like a lady.

"Yes, she's a girl," Blankenship said of the players' apparent thinking, "but she's our girl. They seemed to look at her with new eyes."

There is no perfection in the world, however, and while no one made a fuss publicly, there were players raised in families who believed there was no place for a girl on a boys football team, that if it did not come perilously close to violating their religious beliefs, it threatened their view of what is right and wrong in the world.

Senior linebacker Tim Barr, a top wrestler for Barrow, was playing his first football because he spent part of his junior year abroad, studying in Mexico as an exchange student. An avid reader who likes the Harry Potter books, who started watching more professional games on TV when he started playing the game, Barr said he does not believe it is natural for Pili to play with boys. His family—his father is a pastor who has led prayers for the team—thinks it's inappropriate.

"Not to me," he said of Pili's seemingly natural fit. "Ganina is a really athletic girl, but I don't like coed contact sports. I'm conservative. Before wrestling I talked it over with my parents and we decided if I had a girl as an opponent I would forfeit the match."

Although Barr said he had absolute confidence in Pili as a teammate and as a player, he felt awkward during preseason drills if she ran his way with the ball.

"The first time I tackled her," Barr said, "I had to put my hands down low. I wouldn't put my hands on her chest."

If everyone in the Greatland Conference felt that way, Voss could simply hand the ball off to Pili every play for a big gain. But nothing like that was going to happen. Pili would not be afforded special treatment by other teams, who wouldn't think twice about decking her—and that's if they even realized there was a girl on the field.

To some extent that's what happened in a game against Monroe Catholic in midweek a few days after the Seward game. The Whalers were irked because the Ketchikan game fell apart and it was too late to schedule any more regular-season opponents. Instead, Barrow matched up with Monroe Catholic, a small private school in Fairbanks that was the next Alaska school planning to introduce football and was searching for exhibition games.

Monroe Catholic had a strong sports record in some sports, notably basketball and volleyball, but was in the struggling stage with football. Under state high school rules, schools cannot play more than one game a week, and since Monroe was a throw-in between two regularly scheduled games, it officially counted as a scrimmage. Barrow didn't mind. The Whalers were hungry for gamelike action, in need of all experience that fit the format.

The Whalers were still on a high a couple of days after pocketing the Seward win with the come-from-behind rally. Being 1–0 felt good for a team that was one-for-the-entire-season in 2006. The shouted phrase at the end of each practice—"We believe!"—was beginning to feel like more than just words. The Whalers, who for good reason did not have tremendous confidence the year before, were starting to believe. One of the coaches' goals was to instill belief, to make the players think they could win any game and every game.

The result was enough to make players think they knew what they were doing. Yet Barrow was still very green. There were freshmen out for the team who were rank beginners in the sport.

Linebacker Joe Burke, one of three ninth graders on the club, said the closest he had ever come to playing football before this season was horsing around playing hard-nosed rugby with his friends. He liked to think that was a credential.

"Football is just with gear," Burke said.

Although teenagers do not describe themselves in such terms, Burke, fifteen, felt he was probably one of those "at-risk kids" targeted by football proponents. He should have been a sophomore, but had goofed off in school in the past and lost a year.

"Football is making me do more in school," Burke said.

All of the visitors had departed, radio reporters and Anchorage newspapermen—and Cathy Parker, parka in tow and not knowing when she would be cold enough to wear it again, and her party, had gone back to Florida.

Barrow was back to being Barrow and the football team was back on the practice field, getting ready for the next chapter in the adventure. One thing was different. Practice was on Cathy Parker Field, not at rock-strewn, concrete-hard Bobby Fischer Field. The days of picking gravel out of elbows were over.

From now on, after school, Barrow players boarded a school bus and rode the few miles over to the new field for practice. Or, as Voss put it, practice would be "on the blue."

Before the ride, though, the Whalers crowded into an empty classroom, doused the lights, and watched game film. It is always so much more fun to watch highlights from a game that you know has a happy ending. Mistakes pointed out can be laughed off because they didn't make a difference in the final result. There is a softer touch to the critique than after a loss, where highlighted mistakes can feel like apportionment of blame and the tone of voice may evidence recrimination.

The players were in a good mood. The glow of victory stuck like glitter to them. Lineman Keifer Kanayurak, who at six-foot-one and 280 pounds had the build for it, dreamed of playing football his whole life. He had intended to lobby his family to send him to high school in Fairbanks so he could play. But here he was, soaking up the feeling of victory in the first game of his junior year in good old Barrow.

"I just wanted to be on a team," Kanayurak said. "The contact is the funnest part. Making the good hit and hearing the pads crash together."

And then winning in a spectacular manner.

"It just overwhelmed me," Kanayurak said. "It felt so good. It was so emotional."

For the film sessions, the players sat in chairs that could barely accommodate them in uniform. They sprawled on top of desks. They leaned against walls. There was good-natured teasing. Hey, they won, didn't they? Forgotten was the fact that much of the forty-eight minutes worth of play was sloppy, that they committed so many penalties they were just this side of the law, and that it pretty much took a miracle to win.

The coaches were cognizant of all this. They viewed the film session as a teaching moment. The game unfolded on film and every time poor execution affected the play, a coach stopped the film. Frequently, the film was stopped so a gap on defense could be explored.

"This is for you guys to learn something," assistant coach Jeremy Arnhart said. "It's not just to watch the game."

There were groans about poor punt coverage. The film focused on the way the cornerbacks lined up.

"If you bump, there's no way they can get that pass," Arnhart said.

Assistant coach Brad Igou chimed in about the video.

"It was an awesome job of backpedaling for thirty yards, but you need to turn and run," he said to defensive backs. "We need to get closer to the ball. We weren't urgent enough. We weren't getting our hands up when we were rushing the passer."

There was criticism revisiting the three or four dropped passes.

"Those passes were right in our hands," Arnhart said. "That's not acceptable. You correct those minor things and we're going to be a lot better."

On one play, Seward got easy separation on a punt return and Arnhart sarcastically let the coverage team have it.

"What were you doing?" he said. "Shaking hands with the streaker?"

Good line.

There was laughter, but determination to be better was written on faces as the team boarded the bus. Just the right mixture of levity and attitude to have a good practice.

Only the weather conspired against the Whalers at Cathy Parker Field. The wind whipped in off the Arctic Ocean, gusts practically lifting players off their feet at times and freezing exposed hands. Pili liked to wear gloves, but they weren't warm gloves so much as for grip. Any player who avoided packing a sweatshirt paid a price; on this day, the cheap, bulky gray sweatpants so common in gym class seemed to be government issue.

Only the occasional winter-hardened athlete peeled off the sweats to play in shorts. Pili was one of them. But standing nearby, Robert Vigo was shivering. "Hey," he yelled to Pili, "can I wear these?" She let him.

The plan was to drill on the kicking game, practicing extra points and punt runbacks. The problem was that once the ball was booted in the air with this wind, no one knew where it would land. Guys with frosty hands would have to catch it and make the runback, but the way the wind tossed the ball around it was like circling under a live eider duck coming in for a landing. Terrible conditions.

"We have to do it, though," Igou said.

Players not on the field jumped up and down in place on the sideline, hands stuffed into sweatshirt pockets. For warmth, Voss huddled them together like a herd of musk oxen circled against the elements. The players' problem was that they had less fur.

At one point, Vigo stood next to Pili. Perhaps feeling a little guilty that his legs were warming in her sweatpants, he asked, "You're not cold?" She said, "No, just my ears." The wind whistled through the earholes of the helmet.

After less than an hour on the field, Voss herded the players back on the bus so they could warm up.

"What a day," Arnhart said.

Thinking back to Barrow weather during the football season the year before, Voss added, "That was colder than any day we played last year."

A year earlier at this time, Dave Evikana was at hunting camp with his foster father, while his brother Joe was playing football. Evikana, a sixteen-year-old defensive back, was the boy Olemaun spoke about being torn between football and hunting.

Evikana, who said he became a Pittsburgh Steelers fan watching them win the 2006 Super Bowl, said he chose football for his junior year because his brother made it sound like so much fun, and he liked what he saw when he attended some games.

"It's really tough, though, because caribou hunting is my favorite," Evikana said. "I love to go hunting, too."

With no breaks in the terrain, Barrow is often windy. The gusts sweep off the Arctic Ocean and pummel those trying to walk in a straight line. For those trying to run precision pass routes, it is difficult to stay upright if the wind is in your face. While granting that it was difficult to run against the wind, Justin Sanders was a lot less concerned with the elements than if the Whalers had been practicing at the old rock garden.

There were no rocks, no slippery dirt. As far as Sanders was concerned the next sporting event to be held at Bobby Fischer Field—named for a prominent pilot—could be a chess match featuring the late grandmaster Bobby Fischer.

"It was great," Sanders said. "It's a lot easier to run on it. You don't slip and your timing's not off."

No, the shininess of the new toy had not come close to wearing off yet.

CHAPTER 11

# *Wild Life*

THERE ARE ALWAYS REMINDERS of Barrow's unique place in the United States. Sometimes it is in the wind calling from the Arctic Ocean. Sometimes it is in the guttural enunciation of the long words that are integral to the Iñupiaq language and that sound alien to the English-speaking ear.

And sometimes it is a whale surfacing next to shore, perhaps a hundred yards from a city street.

Brower's Cafe, overlooking the ocean, was just beginning to fill with a lunchtime crowd when shouts went up and a furor overtook patrons seated by the large glass windows.

Whales!

Even longtime residents became excited at the sight of two gray whales just about ten feet out in the water from the beach. Those eating in the center of the restaurant sprang up and crowded into empty booths to peer out the windows. Some diners hastily finished meals and ran outside for a better view.

Gray whales, which grow to forty-five feet or so and can weigh up to thirty-six tons with a lifespan of fifty years, are migratory. By October, when the sea ice is firm, they are gone for the winter. Earlier in the season, periodically the whales swim up to shore where their thick, rounded bodies can touch bottom. They are scraping barnacles off their massive chests. These gray whales, a species not hunted by the Natives, were on the move, swimming past, alternately ducking beneath the surface of mildly churning waves and then rising high enough to pierce gray water with their black fins. They took in air every five minutes or so. The sky, the color of the water, and the color of the whales' bodies were all about the same tone. Only the fins were darker.

The whales hugged the shore as they swam, occasionally ejecting sprays of water from their spouts. Sightings were not so unusual in Barrow in late August, but it was unusual for the whales to come so close to the sand. It was an illusion because of their size, but it seemed as if they were close enough to be touched: Come here, I'll rub that barnacle off for you. But really, the whales were always out of reach without some serious wading in an inhospitable tide on a cold and gray day.

The whales hung around and were readily viewable for perhaps twenty minutes before they turned out to sea.

"You don't see that every day in Chicago," said local radio personality Earl Finkler, who watched the whales swim away and snapped some pictures.

At the report of whale sightings at football practice, the players, who have all seen whales many times, still thought it was cool that they surfaced right outside the window of an eatery and put on a little bit of a show for observers. This was the type of event tourists pay good money to witness, or rather, to have the chance to witness, since whale sightings are never guaranteed in the price of an airplane ticket, hotel room, and tundra tour. At the same time the players take it for granted that whales are around. Like the absence of trees, and the arrival of wintry weather in August, it's just part of the environment.

The Iñupiat players tended to be born and raised in Barrow. The white players, the Asians, and the Polynesians, more likely had been born elsewhere and moved to Barrow with families that felt there were better economic opportunities in the far north. Sometimes it was possible to read backgrounds from the allegiances the players had to professional football teams. Receiver Austin Fishel, sixteen, said he was a Steelers fan.

"My mom was born in Pittsburgh," he said.

Junior Van Edwardson may be the product of a mixed marriage— or maybe even a schizophrenic one—since he is a fan both of the

Indianapolis Colts and the Seattle Seahawks. Upon further cross-examination, it seems he might be a little bit more partial to the 2007 Colts Super Bowl team, since he loves quarterback Peyton Manning and wide receiver Marvin Harrison.

Given that Foxboro, Massachusetts, is about five thousand miles from Barrow the way airlines fly, a surprising number of the Whalers were New England Patriots fans. Assistant coach Brian Houston nodded with approval every time he heard one of his charges praise the Pats. Houston's hometown is about thirty miles from where the Patriots play home games, and he has rooted for the team his whole life. He owns an appropriate mix of Patriots apparel, as well, so he regularly displayed his commitment with his wardrobe.

In mid-August, however, the football at hand was more important for the Whalers than the football to come from the pros. The sky-high emotion from overcoming Seward had to be channeled into a useful energy and there were only a few days of practice before Monroe Catholic brought its new squad to town.

Such highs for the Barrow program had been exceptionally rare, and the players wanted to savor the win. Fishel was reflective about how far the team had come in a year and what the event meant.

"I still can't believe the field is here," Fishel said. "A lot of people in the community didn't even want us to have a second season because of how bad we were. We have a lot more people who know what's going on now in fundamentals, in drills. This is a lot better than last year."

A cornerback and wide receiver, Fishel said he could sense a grassroots change in the community's embracing of the football team.

"Before, most people were playing basketball," he said. "Now you see kids throwing footballs around. It's pretty cool being a role model for kids. They ask, 'How does it feel to put on the helmet?'"

How *does* it feel?

"It feels pretty awesome," Fishel said.

Different sports have their special followings in different parts of the country. Basketball, football, or baseball may be prized more in one region than another sport is, but in an era where every community seems to have the same chain restaurants and chain warehouse stores, any cultural difference is appreciated.

Basketball remains the most popular sport in Bush Alaska. Football is spreading like breeding rabbits, but will never take over completely because many villages are too small to field teams. One athletic endeavor foreign to schools in the Lower 48, which is especially relevant in outlying, rural Alaska communities, is Native sports competition.

Traditional Native sports are taught in the city school systems, but they are more a fabric of life in the Bush. These games are all rooted in the subsistence lifestyle that has sustained Alaska Natives forever. The names of the events sound strange to outsiders, from the four-man carry to the two-foot high kick, from the ear weight to the blanket toss. There is a statewide competition each spring for youths in Anchorage, the Native Youth Olympics (NYO); in the summer for adults at the World Eskimo-Indian Olympics (WEIO) in Fairbanks; and every two years at the Arctic Winter Games, an Olympics-style event that rotates between Alaska and Canada and has also taken place in Greenland.

The events either reinforce skills that might be used on a subsistence hunting or fishing trip, or mimic the same kinds of movements and challenges. The Indian stick pull, an event Big Bob Aiken used to excel at when he was "a young pup," as he puts it, involves one seated contestant trying to pull a foot-long greased stick away from another. The greased stick represents a slippery fish trying to escape being caught by hand.

A crowd-pleasing event that has garnered much publicity Outside as a symbol of the North is the blanket toss. Perhaps a couple of dozen people ring a circular sealskin blanket as "pullers" and stretch the blanket taut. One person climbs up and in timing jumps when the blanket is pulled tight, sails into the sky. It is said that the origin of this game— in most cases best contested outdoors—relates to capturing whales. It was a method developed many years ago to send a signal to others over the flat land that a whale had been taken. Of course, these days it's more likely a cell phone would be employed to alert those tending the home fires.

Reggie Joule, a many-times champion in the blanket toss years ago, and now an Alaska state representative, once appeared on *The Tonight Show* with Johnny Carson to talk blanket toss. At the World Eskimo-Indian Olympics, where the event is held indoors, the goal of pullers and jumpers is to toss the individual high enough to touch the roof at Fairbanks' Big Dipper Arena. It happens once in a while. During the outdoor whaling festivals in Barrow, those in the blanket toss have no ceiling. They are reaching for the sun, the moon, and the stars.

As a younger man, Big Bob Aiken starred in the various strength events, winning gold medals galore. In recent years he has served as the master of ceremonies for hours daily during the four-day WEIO event, and has coached Barrow's young people for the NYO event in Anchorage. Football is not Aiken's favorite game, and though he has come around to it as a good thing for the community, if given the choice he would rather see the same enthusiasm for Native sports.

In the case of sophomore lineman Forrest Ahkiviana, who is five-foot-ten and weighs 215 pounds, both sports have appeal. Ahkiviana competed in the two-foot high kick—where competitors run up, leap, and try to simultaneously touch toes of both feet to a dangling seal ball—the preceding April in Anchorage. He was pretty good at it, too, with a high mark of eighty-four inches, a score that might indicate he could become a fair high jumper.

When the Whalers were just starting to put on their shoulder pads for a Monroe practice, Ahkiviana was in a corner outside the football office practicing a few high kicks. He also wore a Native Youth Olympics T-shirt under his football gear.

The victory over Seward paid feel-good dividends. For a couple of days, everywhere a football player went, friends, kids, parents, and unaffiliated adults said "Good game." It is not in the Iñupiat nature to be too outgoing, so every simple comment uttered probably carried ten times the emotion behind it.

Few heard such compliments as often as the blond-haired, blue-eyed George, who scored the winning touchdown and played brilliantly on defense. He marveled a bit at the swiftness of the football team's developments. Just a few weeks before he had actually gone swimming in the Arctic Ocean. It was 66°F that day, he recalled, and no big deal. It was a lot colder after the Seward game. That kind of mirrored how quickly things changed in Barrow.

"Before last year we never had football, so I never thought about it," he said. "Last year at this time we were still learning the basics and how not to be clumsy. And the field, that happened fast."

Houston walked past and without breaking stride said, "Don't believe what he says," about the angelic looking George.

Denver Enoch, nineteen, and his brother Dane, seventeen, are the type of outsized young men football coaches drool over. Denver is six-foot-seven and weighs 300 pounds. Dane is a little bit smaller. They are part of a family that has moved around a lot for professional reasons, living in Iowa, South Dakota, and other parts of Alaska. But Alaska is really his home, Denver said, with twelve nonconsecutive years living in the state, and above all he wanted to represent Barrow on the football field. If he was somewhere else he probably would have obtained his high school diploma already, but he wanted one season shared with his brother.

The main problem was that Denver Enoch's right knee was not cooperating with his goals. He hurt it over the summer, but thought it would be OK. He played against Seward, but he was back in street clothes for the first practice following the game. It happened to be a nasty day, with the wind ripping through town like a mini-hurricane. Instead of wearing football pads, Enoch was hunkered down in a heavy parka rated to –40°F, hood up, trying to stay warm on the sidelines.

Enoch said aloud what no one had said before the Seward game. Given that it was the season opener, given that the field was being dedicated, given that the Florida people who were so kind to them flew thousands of miles to see them play, there was a lot of pressure on the Whalers to perform.

"It was really, really stressful," Enoch said. "People said, 'Oh, no worries, you'll be fine.' The people who got us this field were there and we had just dedicated our season to Cathy Parker. There was so much on us."

The way it all turned out, with the last-minute win, and the celebrating fans, was like a movie ending. Lineman Keifer Kanayurak actually said to Enoch, "This was our Walt Disney victory."

"That was a good way to look at it," Enoch said.

It was a special memory to make and hold on to, but Enoch's next move was curing the bum knee. It was annoying. Almost as annoying as all of the people who come up to him and insist the Broncos must be his favorite NFL team.

"They're always going, 'Are you a fan of the Denver Broncos because of your name?'" he said.

He was not about to change his name to Indy, like Indiana Jones, but the fact is Enoch's favorite pro team is the Indianapolis Colts.

"That was the first team I ever saw," he said.

Jokes were starting to fly about the new field, too. The field was so close to the lake on the visitors' side that hulking defensive linemen wondered if they could hit a running back so hard he would bounce off of the hurricane fencing and roll into the water. Or better yet, fly through the air and land with a splash.

Um, not likely.

Junior Taylor Elbert sprained his right ankle during practice, and since there was no handy bucket of ice to soak it in, it was teasingly suggested that he hobble across the street from the field and soothe it in the Arctic Ocean.

Um, no, that wasn't going to happen, either.

What did happen that seemed wacky to the players and coaches was that in the middle of practice a Tundra Tours van pulled up, and out popped guide Ryan Oyagak with about ten tourists. Apparently, on the Home of the Stars Barrow map, Cathy Parker Field was the latest stop.

Lineman Colton Blankenship looked over at the visitors, none of whom seemed to be paying any attention to the Whalers, and said, "It's funny."

Mike Olson immediately figured out that this was not going to be a one-time phenomenon.

"Watch, they'll stop every day now," he said. "They all want to see the field."

It was suggested to Coach Voss that someone should sidle over to the tourists and tell them that the synthetic grass was really made of polar bear fur. See what happens, you know?

"Yeah," Voss said, "we'll tell them we had to kill eighty of them to make it."

Somehow that "factoid" got overlooked in Oyagak's presentation, and the gang piled back on the bus and motored away without turning the brief stop into a Save the Animals demonstration. The tourists got the Reader's Digest short version of how the money was raised and how the field was transported. To them it was probably not much different than hearing about the Wiley Post–Will Rogers memorial, or the Naval Arctic Research Laboratory building constructed near the end of World War II that now houses the offices of the North Slope Borough Department of Wildlife Management.

What was intriguing was how many Barrow residents stopped by during practice. Some pulled up as close as they could get to the fencing and just sat in their cars, staring at the field. Some climbed out of their vehicles, walked around the perimeter of the field, sat down on the bleachers for a few minutes, and admired the layout. Some did that and even watched a couple of minutes of football. It seemed as if people were still getting used to the idea that the bright blue and yellow field was actually there, that the field was actually theirs. It was so unreal that this fancy football field was presented as a gift, almost literally dropped from the sky, that they might have just been checking to see if it was still there, that since the Seward game ended it hadn't been rolled up and carted away. Few stayed very long. Yep, that's our field, they seemed to be saying, and that reassurance was good enough for them.

By the end of the workout, those departed tourists might have been needed for a Save the Players demonstration. The coaches were ready to kill their guys, whose thoughts seemed more preoccupied with the last victory than the next opponent. They performed with that type of space-cadet concentration all day. The three assistants took turns reaming out the players for "swelled-head syndrome."

"That," said Jeremy Arnhart, when the team huddled up, "was a sickening practice."

Just in case the players thought Arnhart's was a minority opinion, the other coaches had choice words designed to light a Coleman lantern under the guys' butts.

"If you think you can just lollygag around and be a team, forget it," said Coach Igou.

"You were lazy and not paying attention," added Houston. "Focus."

Some players, committing the ultimate faux pas, were not even present to absorb the verbal lashing. They skipped practice. Arnhart ordered the majority in attendance to pass the word.

"You can be a fan or a champion," he said. "The ones who missed practice are on the verge of becoming fans."

The threat was delivered with a flinty-eyed stare.

After the lecture, designed first and foremost to bring the players back to earth in time for the next day's Monroe Catholic game, the players grouped together on their midfield logo and once more shouted, "We believe!"

The mantra was still strong pouring out of their lungs, but what the coaches did was remind the players that faith had to be backed up by hard work. Houston verbalized that and gave it added meaning.

"It's not just for on the field," he said. "It's for all of life."

In Barrow, above all places with its harsh environment, the players needed to remember that nothing was given to them. Survival was often a team effort. The same was true on the football field. With group effort, working together, they could make special things happen.

CHAPTER 12

# *Monroe Catholic*

THERE WAS A LOT on the players' minds on the third Wednesday in August. The coaches were calling the Monroe encounter something less than an official game. It had to be a scrimmage, despite Monroe's addition to the schedule to replace the lost Ketchikan game, but the coaches stressed it was more than a practice.

It was also the first day of school. Lots to remember this day. The players had to bring whatever football gear with them that had been washed at home since the Seward game, and keep track of the new books they were getting, and be ready for a 4:00 P.M. contest after the final bell.

Inevitably, some players left cleats or a jersey at home. This was not as insurmountable an obstacle as it sounded, since everyone probably lived within two miles of the school and rushing home on a four-wheeler was possible.

Emerging defensive tackle Jason Ruckle, a seventeen-year-old senior who had never played the game before Barrow's introduction to the sport, laughed as he pulled on his equipment and reflected on the difference between 2007 and 2006.

"They don't have to teach us how to put the pads on this year," Ruckle said. "There's a lot of pads."

On the Monroe side, they probably *were* still teaching Football Gear 101. The Rams flew into town with a skeleton crew of sixteen players representing a student body of about 160. Voss found himself in the surprising position of leading an inexperienced football team with much to learn into a game with an even more inexperienced football team with even more to learn. Hmm. That old 89–0 Soldotna–Nikiski score went through his mind.

No, there was no need for humiliation. He was sensitive to that. The Whalers could well have been decimated a time or two by a bully team, but the blowouts suffered were within reason. It was decided before kickoff that the gamelike experience was enough for Monroe and Barrow alike. Nobody was going to officially keep score and timekeeping might be a little bit flexible, too. The plan was to play fifteen-minute running time quarters.

As Monroe approached the field in its team bus, the players studied the Arctic Ocean. And sure enough, they saw gray whales diving and surfacing. Heck, no matter what happened in the game now they at least had a story to tell to their friends back in Fairbanks. Cool! Whales.

In football parlance, it might be said that Big John Lambrecht (everyone calls him Big John, as if it was written on his birth certificate) was a whale. He is six-foot-six and admits to weighing 340 pounds. As might be guessed, the biggest player on Barrow's roster is not a kick returner, but an interior lineman. The nearsighted Lambrecht removed his glasses every day at the start of practice and parked them on the dashboard of Voss's station wagon. Most close encounters on the line of scrimmage don't require the big guys to see more than two feet away, anyway. The ball is snapped and they smash into the closest guy in a different color uniform.

"I can see the ball," Lambrecht said. "It's a brown spot. It's a little blurry."

Oh, the coaches would love it if Big John was as nasty as he was large, but while Big John is big-boned there is not a mean bone in his body. He can throw his weight around if riled, but away from the field he is more likely to be a candidate to babysit your first grader than to be an enforcer. Truth be told, Lambrecht seems a tad injury prone. There always seemed to be some small ding on his body in practice. The day before the Monroe game, Lambrecht finished practice groaning about a

# Thunder Scrapbook

⬆ Barrow High head football coach Mark Voss addresses his team during preseason two-a-day practice on the school's old dirt practice field, renowned for the number of rocks players had to cope with.

⬅ Assistant coach Brian Houston, who played NCAA Division II college football at the University of New Haven, nurtured the linemen, and could be counted on each week for uplifting pep talks.

⬅ North Slope Borough Superintendent of Schools Trent Blankenship is the man who spearheaded the creation of the Barrow High football team, as a way to lower the school's dropout rate among boys.

← Brad Igou, one of the Whalers' three assistant coaches, played college football at Arizona State.

↓ It does get cold in Barrow, especially when standing around on the sidelines. Assistant coach Jeremy Arnhart (right), who guided the offense and kept all the plays on a laptop, here instructs quarterback Albert Gerke.

➡ A view of Barrow High's new artificial turf football field, located across the street from the Arctic Ocean, which replaced the previous gravel. The yellow midfield logo honors the team; a freshwater lake is in the background.

➡ Cathy Parker of Jacksonville, Florida, wife of a high school football coach and mother of boys who play football, was inspired by a television documentary to raise $800,000 in cash and in-kind services to provide an artificial turf field for the Whalers. Parker, surrounded by players, was present in Barrow for the opening game when the new field was named Cathy Parker Field in her honor.

➡ Fan Price Brower, member of a prominent Barrow family, brought his own chair to the opening game against Seward and dressed warmly in his polar bear pants, periodically shouting for the Whalers through his blue "Go Whalers" megaphone.

⬇ Popular lineman Big John Lambrecht broke into tears on the field after the final game of his senior year, noting how much he would miss the game and his teammates.

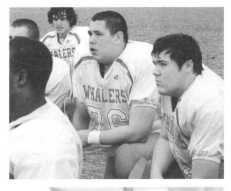

⬆ Whaler center Mike Gonzales was crowned Homecoming King at halftime of Barrow's victory over Nikiski, and shared the spotlight with his father, Chato.

⬅ Ganina Pili, a star Barrow athlete in volleyball and basketball, decided that girls could play football, too. She was readily accepted on the team from the beginning; here she holds a football during preseason practice.

❚ Fans on the Whaler side of the field showed their colors in the opener against Seward. The cars behind them were parked on the beach just in front of the Arctic Ocean.

❙ The Whalers brought out fans of all ages, like Robert Ahkiviana, four, who announced his primary rooting allegiance to his brother, defender Forrest, wearing number 69.

↑ Bill Rohan, father of Whaler Zac Rohan, at the controls of the Barrow football bus he designed from a four-wheeler. Note the full uniformed dummy at the wheel.

⬆ Big Bob Aiken, who is known as the World's Largest Eskimo, stands six-foot-four and once weighed 500 pounds, though he has slimmed down. Aiken, now in his fifties, stands in front of the huge bones on the beach that are symbolic of Barrow's connection to bowhead whales.

➡ The Barrow defense gang tackles a Sitka Wolves ballcarrier in the final game of the season.

⬇ Sophomore Anthony Edwards, a five-foot-eleven, 208-pound game breaker, was the team's biggest offensive weapon. Here Edwards is breaking into the clear at Cathy Parker Field.

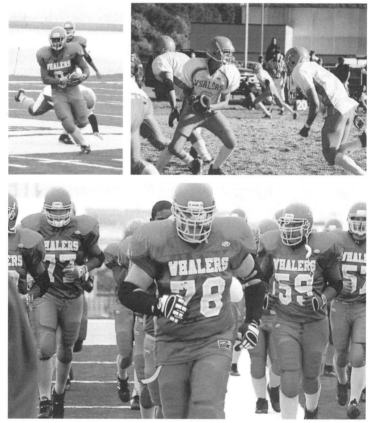

⬆➡ Strong-armed sophomore quarterback Albert Gerke made big plays on offense as the team's signal caller, and also by intercepting passes on defense.

⬆ Defensive tackle Colton Blankenship (78) leads the team onto the field at the start of a game.

↓→ It was not as hot during August two-a-days as it is in the Lower 48, but Barrow players Anthony Edwards, Justin Sanders, Dave Evikana, and Ganina Pili (left to right), were still plenty thirsty during a practice break.

↑Soft-spoken senior defensive tackle Jason Ruckle made his presence felt for the Whalers with hard hits all season.

→ Cheering on teammates during a game: Mike Olson (who stenciled his number 75 into the hair on the back of his head) and Jim Martin applaud the action.

↑Years ago, students in Barrow who wished to continue their education in high school were forced to attend boarding schools. Whaler Daniel Thomas (left), stayed home, while his sister Deidre chose to go to Mount Edgecumbe in Sitka.

↑→ Coaches all over the country, at all levels of play, make their linemen flex their muscles, as the Whalers are about to do here in preseason practice, by pushing a heavy blocking sled around the field.

After Barrow High started football, youngsters around town developed an interest in the team, and in playing with a ball themselves. Here four-year-old Simeon Ahkivgak entertains himself on the Whaler practice field.

↑ Yes, they really do have polar bear plunges into the Arctic Ocean in Barrow. This was the annual teachers day, when new school District hires dove in together. A late arriving Superintendent Trent Blankenship jumped in fully clothed.

← The death of humorist Will Rogers (pictured) and pilot Wiley Post in a 1935 plane crash focused national attention on Barrow for the first time. This memorial near the airport honors their memory.

back problem. He treated it overnight by rubbing on a heat ointment, though, and was ready to play.

"It doesn't hurt anymore," Big John said before kickoff.

There was a lot of banter in the team changing area, the pseudo–locker room area, at the school. Voss was thinking about a player and his relationship to the school now that classes had begun. He was talking out loud about the image of football players and the way they are perceived.

The thought seemed to be provoked by a joke that had a punch line about adding two and two.

"Some people think of football players that way," Voss said, "as big dummies. I teach computer skills. It's not like we're all idiots. We get stereotyped all of our lives. It's not as if they all turned down academic scholarships to play football, but a lot of them are above average guys."

Clearly, with only sixteen players in uniform, depth was going to be a concern for Monroe Catholic and with Barrow suiting up thirty-five, the Whalers were likely to remain a lot fresher. It is not as if Fairbanks is to be confused with the tropics (in fact, on singular winter days the temperature might well be lower in Fairbanks than Barrow), but it was Barrow weather, cool and windy. Fairbanks might well still hit 70°F in August, but in any case the city would be coming off something passing for a genuine summer, so the players were not seasonally adjusted.

Once the ball was kicked off, it quickly became apparent that Barrow was the superior team. Agile senior Cody Romine blocked a punt and the Whalers had good field position.

Coach Arnhart scripted the first fifteen plays for the offense and they worked. Justin Sanders, on his way to his NFL dream, plucked a pass out of the air thrown by Albert Gerke for Barrow's first touchdown. Soon enough he had another touchdown grab. Sanders is six-foot-one and doesn't have an ounce of fat on him. His belly looks as if he had been doing situps in the cradle. The Rams couldn't cover him and Gerke found Sanders roaming downfield.

There wasn't a huge crowd in the stands the way there had been for the Seward game, but then the game was being played on a weekday afternoon, on a work day, on the first day of school. The event had not been highly publicized, either. Steadily, though, once residents realized a game was in progress, they drifted over to Cathy Parker Field to watch. One minute, it seemed, there was hardly anybody there, the next there were hundreds.

The most energetic spectator was Trent Blankenship. If he sat still for more than a minute the entire season, the world missed it. When the Whalers were playing, he was pacing on the home team's sideline. This was his baby—in more ways than one, given that he had nurtured both the team and the defensive tackle known as Colton from infancy—and he nervously ached for success on all fronts.

Somewhere during the first half, Colton Blankenship made a rare play. He got a hand on the Monroe quarterback's pass, batted it in the air, grabbed the ball, and ran it back for a touchdown. That's a career combination for a defensive lineman. The older Blankenship recognized this and dashed off to Colton's side as the player exited the field huffing and puffing.

"I've got to congratulate my son on his interception," Trent Blankenship said. "I'll never have this chance again."

Daniel Thomas stole another interception, and then Robert Vigo turned in an electrifying run. During two-a-days Vigo was often the target of coaches' wrath because he didn't always line up correctly in formations, and talked a lot at inopportune times—which came across as bucking authority, even though it never seemed like he meant it. But he was probably the fastest guy on the team, and against Seward, on defense, he showed he had the propensity for making game-altering sacks and tackles.

Vigo hinted at the eye-catching, big play capability he possessed on offense when he took a handoff, slashed around left end, and scampered ninety yards untouched for a touchdown. It was a beauty of a play, an example of what can happen when all eleven guys on offense are clicking as a unit.

The feel-good play lasted about five seconds before being wiped out. Penalty flag. Barrow was charged with holding. The ball came all the way back to Whaler territory. Instead of standing as testimony to what good things can happen when everyone pulls together, the play became an example of what bad things can happen when one person makes a mistake.

The good plays far outweighed the bad for the Whalers this game. Luke George caught a touchdown pass. Austin Fishel collected an interception. Forrest Ahkiviana caught a fumble in mid-air. Anthony Edwards gathered in a flair pass and scooted eighty yards for a score. Then Vigo took another handoff, cut back, sliced through traffic, and rambled sixty-five yards for a TD. This time there were no flags. Until after the play, that is. Barrow was smacked with an excessive celebration penalty.

Monroe squeezed one touchdown out of all its opportunities, which were spread over the equivalent of six running-time quarters. Voss used all of his players extensively. He couldn't keep the starters in all of the way or he would have run up the score. The touchdowns came easily and while there was no scoreboard reading, Barrow led by six touchdowns to one.

"Our kids have never been in this situation," Voss said.

One player who benefited from the share-the-wealth playing time was Ganina Pili. In full pads, helmet on, hair hidden, and with no program listing names on the rosters, the casual observer would not know that a girl was playing for Barrow. However, the fans knew. When Pili caught a pass from Thomas while she was cutting across the middle, they roared.

"Nice catch," shouted Colton Blankenship.

When Pili trotted to the sidelines, Jim Martin gave her a high-five.

A few minutes later, with the Whalers back on offense, Pili made another catch. The sure hands that served her well in basketball and volleyball made her a good receiver. Pili also got some licks in, playing in the defensive backfield.

By most societal standards, Pili has a pretty face. She has large brown eyes and when she lets her long black hair free, there is no question she is a girl. The hair bugs her sometimes when she readies for practice. It's got to be twisted into a braid and it's got to be arranged in such a way that she can comfortably wear a helmet, and then the braid should fit into the uniform down by the shoulders.

"I keep forgetting about my hair," Pili said.

When the Monroe scrimmage ended, the players lined up on each side of the field, and single-file marched toward one another to shake hands. High school athletics demands that type of sportsmanship. Whatever the result, wherever the game, the handshake line is part of the deal. The line keeps moving. It's a quick process. Players don't linger and talk. Emotions are raw and their coaches are waiting to speak to them. When Pili moved through this handshake line she sensed something different. The Monroe players looked at her with surprise.

Was it possible they had just played an entire game against Barrow without even realizing one of the players was a girl?

"I don't think they noticed until the handshake line," Pili said.

As the Monroe players huddled for a quickie game analysis from their coaches, Barrow fans applauded and shouted, "Thank you for coming, Monroe." It was a nice touch, a genuine one, and it symbolized the realization that any trip to Barrow involves commitment from teams located in other cities.

The Monroe Catholic team spent the night rather than flying four hundred miles each way the same day, and the next day Pili ran into the coaches.

"One of the coaches came up to me and said, 'Are you the one who was beating up on our guys?'" she said. Her reaction? "I just laughed."

They would go back to Fairbanks marveling at the smooth-running unit that was the Barrow Whalers, and might incidentally mention that the Barrow team was so tough it had a girl who could steal your lunch.

That's how good the Whalers looked in the Monroe game. It was easy to forget that Monroe players were all beginners, and that a year before that was the Whalers.

"I'm enjoying football," Big John said. "It fits my stature. And I think we're better than last year."

Since the wind was whipping across the open field, it didn't take long for the fans to clear out. They're no fools. Barrow residents won't be intimidated into staying home if there is entertainment like a football game they want to watch, but they are not silly enough to linger a moment longer than necessary in bitter weather.

The Cathy Parker Field was emptied of players, spectators, and workers quite quickly. The blue and yellow still shone, though, under a rugged gray sky. It was only August, but weather was starting to deteriorate for the season. It was not the first time the issue had been addressed, but one had to wonder how the ProGrass field would hold up against the elements when they were as harsh as Barrow's and winter lasted so long.

"These fields are designed to sit out all winter," Trent Blankenship said. "They do in Minnesota and North Dakota. They made this thicker so it's designed to sit out under extra sunlight in the summer. They're not really worried about the weather. Once the snow covers it, they can just run a snowplow over it."

The field was a gift, delivered free of charge. The weather was very real and it would be a crime for the field to be threatened by the climate. How could Barrow and the North Slope Borough School District make the field last forever?

"Maybe we'll be seeking to put a dome over it," Blankenship said.

Parker probably called in all of her IOU's on the initial fundraising, and there is probably no one else out there like her willing to devote so much time to raising cash for a dome. On the other hand, pretty soon the cost of a barrel of oil was going to shoot over $100. No telling what oil taxes could build. Everyone had seen that miracle before.

CHAPTER 13

# *The Whalers*

MAC ROCK, A SEVENTEEN-YEAR-OLD Barrow High School football player who plays wide receiver and safety, was ten or eleven the first time he went whaling. It was fall whaling, the less optimum season, when the Arctic Ocean is rougher than it is in spring.

"That's the scariest time you can go out," Rock said.

Although he would not be an active participant because he was so young, Rock's grandparents wanted to introduce him to the cultural tradition. He was along for the ride, to "just watch and learn, just observe," as he put it. He remembers waking up early for the journey onto the ice and into the ocean, and helping to make tea and coffee.

But when the waves surged to eight feet and the skin boat was rocking and rolling, the only thing Rock wanted to observe was solid land. He was afraid he was going to drown.

"I started crying," he said.

Whaling is the soul of Barrow. The bowhead whale is the prey that, as much as winter, defines the culture of this northernmost place so remote from mainstream America, so reliant on the bounty of nature.

The bowhead is a symbol of life and culture. It is a payback to the people daring enough to live in the Far North on the shore of the Arctic Ocean. The whale sustains them physically and culturally.

If the place where the people hunt snowy owls has been transformed into a city with restaurants, a grocery store, a gas station, modern schools, and cable television, whaling and the bowhead link Barrow to the past and its lineage.

On a gray but dry day, a visitor walking through neighborhoods or driving up and down the unpaved residential streets might pass a handful of drying racks outside homes. The wooden contraptions, akin to clothes racks where people have no electric dryers, display salmon or whale meat.

Depending on the season, the freshness of the meat, and which way the wind is blowing, once in a while the aroma of drying fish in the air will attract a polar bear into town, always a dangerous prospect. Sometimes leftovers, scraps clinging to bones, will bring a prowler off the ocean.

"They go in the direction of the smell," said Big Bob Aiken, who has seen his share of polar bears in his life. He mentioned seeing a polar sniffing around on the beach only the week before. "It smelled all the rotten meat on the beach. It was chased off by the Wildlife people. They made sure it went back out on the ocean."

Spaced indiscriminately along the beach, thick, heavy, bleached whale jaw bones lay where they were abandoned at the end of a hunt. Given that they are not as collectible as sea shells, they rest on the sand, remembrances of the whales killed, symbols of a community sustained.

One tangible symbol of Barrow, a photo-op location, is readily visible on the beach next to Brower's Cafe, where two gigantic whale bones are planted to form an arch. Not a king-sized, man-made arch that soars above St. Louis, this arch still is large enough to swallow up a football-sized lineman as if he stood in a doorway. And maybe it was a doorway to the peoples' souls.

Whaling, for the most part, is private business in the Eskimo community of Barrow, not something tourists see when they visit, not something talked about routinely when the hunt is out of season. Whaling rituals are ingrained in the families who are fortunate enough to have a whaling captain or crew members in their midst, but whaling itself is not a conversation topic unless someone asks.

Whaling captains are esteemed members of Barrow society. Mayor Nathaniel Olemaun is a whaling captain. They are leaders, men with responsibilities not only to their families and friends, but to their community, for whale meat is shared with the masses. They make crucial, life-risking judgments on the hunt, and their crew follows.

The Arctic Ocean near Barrow is typically frozen for eighty percent of the year. Winter winds help form the ice and sometimes storms create jumbled blocks of snow and ice that masquerade as boulders. Whaling is primarily, but not exclusively, a springtime, April–May endeavor, when long hours of sunlight help hunters stay out longer and when the ice is breaking up a few miles from shore.

During the second half of the nineteenth century, and into the early years of the twentieth century (pretty much between 1848 and 1915), commercial whaling was one of the most adventurous professions a young man could sign on for. Wooden boats sailed from New England, and might be gone from port a year or more at a time. The times produced literature like *Moby Dick*, and the hub of the whaling industry was New Bedford, Massachusetts, coincidentally the home of Barrow High assistant football coach Brian Houston. Big Bob inherited his surname and his size from Irish whalers visiting Barrow perhaps four generations past.

Bowhead whales are among the largest mammals on earth. They grow to be sixty feet in length and can weigh up to 120,000 pounds. On the growth chart of a bowhead, a foot in length roughly equals 2,000 pounds, or a ton, in weight.

Whale by-products helped produce oil, hair ornaments, and corsets. There never was much of a Lower 48 market for muktuk, or whale meat. Changes in societal mores, which permitted women to run around in public without corsets, contributed to a sudden dropoff in demand, not to mention the diminishment of the bowhead whale population after an estimated nineteen thousand were harvested. As has been known to happen in various regions to various species, the enthusiasm of the hunters eventually overwhelmed the supply of the resource.

For quite some time, harpoons thrown by strong men with good aim represented the accepted method of killing a whale. Whales were so powerful many escaped with only flesh wounds, and sometimes they overturned vessels and dragged whale hunters to their deaths. The natives employed twenty-to-thirty-foot-long boats called *umiaqs,* made of seal skin, to pursue whales, and paddled their way out to sea. It took a skillful whaling captain to maneuver his boat close enough to the whale to make a strike, yet stay far enough out of its reach so the boat wouldn't be swamped or overturned. Survival time in the frigid water well before the age of waterproof suits could be measured in the time it took to light a match. Not long.

Whales have a longer life expectancy than humans; there have been whales captured and killed in the early years of this century that were discovered to have broken-off pieces of harpoons still embedded in their bodies. Scientists concluded that the harpoon remnants were in the whales for more than a century. Eventually, harpoons with small explosives were invented. This technology was more efficient, safer for the hunter, and resulted in a higher kill rate per strike.

Unlike the New Bedford whalers, the Barrow whalers were not wheeling and dealing in the commodities markets. When the Iñupiat Eskimos engaged in a hunt, it was both for personal use and because of cultural connection. This was the way the elders did it. This was the way the ancestors did it. To an Eskimo of the North Slope of Alaska, the whale was a life-giving animal, sacrificing itself for the common good, so that humans might survive. Iñupiat legend figures that whaling predates recorded time. Scientific reports estimate that whaling in the Barrow vicinity has been going on for at least two thousand years.

The Iñupiat people use every bit of the whale, except these days some of those jaw bones. Muktuk, the skin and blubber of the whale, is high in vitamin C, and the meat is high in calories and rich in nutrients. In the past, before the modernization of Barrow, whale bones were used in the construction of sod houses of the vintage used in the Disney movie filmed on the outskirts of town so long ago. Baleen from the whale was used to weave baskets. A single bowhead whale could feed a village.

Bill Hess, a respected Alaskan photographer, produced the seminal book *Gift of the Whale* in 1999, after many years of being an invited guest on whale hunts throughout the region. He refers to the bowhead hunt as "a sacred tradition."

Almost as a counterpoint to the traditional methods followed in the taking of a bowhead, Hess also included documentation of the hullabaloo surrounding the trapped gray whales. It was a time that Aiken refers to as "insane." This is an understandable position, given that most of the time the Eskimos of the area put all of their energy into harvesting whales, not rescuing them. Some of Hess's pictures are remarkable close-ups showing local men lying on the ice only a few feet away from a gray whale breathing through a hole in the ice. In one picture a man is reaching out to pet the whale.

But 90 percent of Hess's attention was focused on the annual ritual of the hunt, and it is a spectacular sight to see a photograph of women cutting the whale down to size with their traditional, sharp, wooden-handled *ulu* carving knives. The meat was cut into sections about six feet long and three feet wide. Stacked up, the sections resembled a pile of mattresses.

"The slabs were warm to the touch," Hess wrote, "slick with oil, and heavy—about 25 to 50 pounds each."

There was a certain irony in the eyes of the world being focused on Barrow when the attempt was made to save the gray whales trapped in the ice. That's because the eyes of the whaling world are almost continuously on Barrow and its environs to make sure that the Eskimos of the North Slope don't harvest too many whales.

What once was an abundant resource—before Outside whalers intruded—became an early environmental focus. Whereas men once so proud to harvest whales sliced the population, others now wanted to save them for future generations. The International Whaling Commission was founded in 1947 to regulate commercial taking of whales. Eskimos did not appreciate those efforts or this intrusion very much. Their relationship with bowhead whales was far more involved and intimate than someone who sailed several thousand miles into their territory, then took the whales and ran.

In 1990, the bowhead whale was declared an endangered species, further complicating Eskimo life and relations between the Iñupiat, the whaling commission, the United States government, and other countries who agreed to protect whales. For years, the Whaling Commission did not want to differentiate between Alaskan whalers and those representing countries like Japan and Norway where whales were supposedly taken for "scientific" purposes only.

Eventually, through long negotiating battles, Alaskan Natives were recognized as a specific entity worthy of being singled out for individual ruling. The freedom to live the way they had always lived was impinged upon, but Eskimos could still hunt whales. A quota system was devised to limit the numbers each year, but the numbers were high enough to live with.

The International Whaling Commission meets periodically to review the quotas and determine the numbers. Such a regular meeting took place in Barrow at the end of May 2007, and set quotas through 2012. Alaska's regular delegation to the international event consists of the Alaska Eskimo Whaling Commission, representatives from Barrow and nearby villages (such as Point Hope) where whale hunting is prominent, and the North Slope Borough Department of Wildlife Management.

It was agreed at the conference that 208 whales could be hunted over the following five-year period, by ten Iñupiat and Siberian Yupik communities, because the estimated bowhead population was about ten thousand. The meeting's result was welcomed by Alaskans who found the number—the same as had been approved for the previous five-year period—satisfactory for sustaining subsistence levels. There had been times over the years when discussions between Natives and the commission had been contentious, but this time the quota was set by a no-sweat consensus.

In the past, this small group of indigenous people had been threatened by international politics. While the Eskimos were lobbying for a way of life, delegates from Japan had initiated hard-nosed debate, in essence saying, "Why should they get to take whales when we can't?" There was a period of time when there was a failure to differentiate between whales taken for subsistence, in a tradition dating back thousands of years, and whales taken for what many assumed was a smoke screen of science, but really was for commercial reasons. This was a battle fought by the Iñupiats, with the aid of U.S. Senator Ted Stevens, for years. A truce finally prevailed and after the May meeting Alaskans could exhale for five more years.

Borough mayor Ed Itta expressed pleasure at the decision in an interview with the *Arctic Sounder* weekly newspaper. "The science was on our side," he said. The estimated size of the bowhead population helped the cause.

When a whale is spotted not too many miles offshore—often through the old-fashioned way of a scout standing atop crumbled ice at Point Barrow—word is passed and whaling crews mobilize.

It is the whaling captain's responsibility to provide the boat that can carry a dozen men and all of the equipment. A captain might inherit his family's title and gear as a youngish man in his thirties and retain the job for decades. He may have a right-hand man whose advice, based on years of experience, is valued; and there might be a teenager along to get a firsthand look at what whaling is all about, so that he will eventually slide into one of the seats in the boat.

Boats and equipment that used to be taken by dog team or carried by human power are now hauled across the ice to the open water by snowmachines. Boats slide into the cold, gray water and the captain starts the outboard engine, another concession to the modern age, replacing the use of oars.

It is not always easy to get close enough to a bowhead to make a strike, but if a harpoon with an explosive hits just right, the tip will pierce the thick skin of the whale and the explosive will go off, wrecking its innards and killing it quickly.

Then it becomes the job of the crew to swiftly secure the whale so it doesn't sink, and drag the huge beast back to the ice. Word is transmitted quickly that a whale has been taken, and the entire town mobilizes.

Once the many-ton whale is tugged across the water to the shore ice, teams of dozens of residents work together, rigging a block-and-tackle and pulley system to lift the catch onto the ice, where it can be butchered. Barrow whale hunters harvested a fifty-ton-plus bowhead in the spring of 2007, and the slicing and dicing work—the women's assignment—took hours.

"Up here," said Clancy Itta, the fire chief, "whaling is something we live for. We prepare year-round."

After the bowheads finish migrating past Barrow for the spring, the strikes are complete, the hunt is shut down, and the booty is divided. Whaling is an all-for-one and one-for-all community activity. The captain guides the crews. The people act as pullers. The women cut up the whale. According to custom, the whaling captain keeps a certain percentage of the whale for his family, divides up a certain amount among the crew, but also disperses some to those who helped in other tasks. Also, so they are not left out, whaling captains give muktuk to elders too infirm to hunt anymore.

Each June, once the equipment is put up for the season, the community gathers for a festival called Nalukataq to celebrate a successful whaling campaign. The festival includes a blanket toss, Eskimo dances, and sharing of the muktuk. People sit in a circle or square as the whaling captain walks around serving muktuk, scooping it out of his container and placing it in white plastic buckets with handles. While people are partying, caribou meat, duck, goose, and fish are eaten, as well. The festival can go on for several days.

Nalukataq is an occasion where time is shared between people of all ages, and thanks is given to the whaling captain, the crew, and to a higher being for, as Hess put it, the gift of the whale.

Barrow Whaler defensive lineman Forrest Ahkiviana, fifteen, lived in Anchorage for a couple of years and was sometimes quizzed about his Eskimo heritage.

"I was asked, 'Do you eat muktuk?'" he said. "I said, 'From time to time.'"

Like other natives from Barrow, he was raised on the chewy, salty whale meat.

Big Bob Aiken said that when he was nine years old he saw an elder dance for joy at the report of a whale taken, and it made an impression on him. He learned quickly how important it was to land a whale.

"Everything we need to survive in the cold winter months is contained in the whale," Aiken said.

On May 16, 2007, Barrow cutters dissecting a fifty-ton whale came across a stunning archaeological find. A 3.5-inch-long, arrow-shaped weapon fragment was discovered embedded in the neck of the bowhead. Because of distinguishing markings, scientists were able to identify and date the tool. This particular whale had escaped capture and death at the hands of whalers—either from New England, or locals using Massachusetts-made equipment. Scientists guessed that the whale was between 115 and 130 years old! That would make the bowhead one of the granddaddies of all time in the Barrow area.

Craig George, a local wildlife biologist who was called to the scene, said the age estimate was shocking and confirmed what Natives had said for a long time—that bowheads live the equivalent of two human lives.

Ahkiviana was so excited to be invited by his uncle to participate in his first whale hunt in April that he didn't sleep for about twenty-four hours before going out. Ahkiviana imagined himself sighting the whale and with harpoon in hand, being part of the kill. It didn't quite work out that way.

"When I got out there," Ahkiviana said, "I was told, 'You're making coffee.' You have to start at the bottom. We saw a whole bunch of whales, but we really couldn't get to them."

But another crew had a strike and Ahkiviana was among the fifty people who pulled the fifty-foot whale to shore, straining their muscles for four straight hours. That exercise was definitely tougher than two-a-day practices.

"It was a lot of work," Ahkiviana said. "You could feel it all up in your forearms."

Exhausting work. Ahkiviana fell asleep out on the ice. His father put him on the back of a snowmachine and drove him home. Later, he compared the experience of being involved in a bowhead whale harvest and playing football.

"Pulling up the whale was harder, but being a lineman is funner," he said.

CHAPTER 14

# *Seasons*

A SCHOOL ACTIVITY WAS PLANNED for the beach on a Friday night before Barrow was scheduled to play Eielson. A bonfire. Just like a real football program.

Only the coaches were not so excited about this event. They could see their guys getting caught up in the excitement, staying out late, and not getting enough rest. In a team huddle on Cathy Parker Field after practice, Mark Voss delivered the message: Do not stay out late. Do not overdo it. Do not jump in the water. There were a fair number of common sense do-nots.

Jokester Daniel Thomas could not resist a remark.

"I think I'll go undercover," he said.

"We've got James Bond here," Voss said, keeping it light.

A pregame bonfire. Barrow was catching on to football traditions. And don't think the players didn't notice or appreciate it. In a city where demonstrative displays of group affection might be limited to the whaling festival, the football team gave people something else to rally around, provided reasons to get together in public, to share a common rooting interest.

Sophomore Mikey Stotts, sixteen, a cornerback, thought back to life without football and said he wasn't sure what he would be doing for amusement if he wasn't on the team.

"Nothing really," Stotts said. "I'd be at home watching TV. Or I'd play games, car racing games, Xbox."

Austin Fishel said he would probably just be hanging out with friends. "Actually," he said, "doing homework."

Mike Gonzales, seventeen, the senior starting center, said he originally went out for football to keep in shape for his primary sport, wrestling, but fell in love with the game, with the hitting, particularly.

"I like contact sports," he said. "You get pads and you can't go wrong. When I was a sophomore we used to joke around, 'What if we had football?'"

Much to his amazement, football became reality a year later. He felt fortunate. If there was no football, Gonzales said, he would definitely be involved in something else after school, whether it was running cross-country or lifting weights.

"My dad would make me do something," he said.

Besides the fact that Eielson was a respected opponent with a long history of success and discipline, there was a curiosity factor involved in the game for Gonzales. The Ravens represented the school on Eielson Air Force Base located about an hour south of Fairbanks. This meant something to Gonzales. His brother was about to graduate from an Air Force training program in Texas, and within the year, after his own high school graduation, Gonzales planned to join the Air Force. That was the future he had mapped out for himself. He wanted to fly jets.

The coaches pour themselves into game planning. They kick around fresh ideas. But they worry about their players. If a player misses school, they want to know where he is. If a player is sick, that is one thing; if a player is a no-show, they get angry. In a place where the dropout rate is high, where kids get entangled with drugs and alcohol with regularity, the coaches try to keep close tabs. They are trying to establish something special as a team, but they recognize that many things pull at their players away from the field. It may be girlfriend troubles, classroom challenges, or difficulties at home. One player who was going to come out for the team, and who was listed on the preseason roster, decided not to play football this season because his mother died. No one could blame him for being depressed. But they wish he had come out, had accepted the schedule routine, and the camaraderie.

No one was more finely attuned to kids at risk than Brian Houston. He was not a teacher at the high school, but spent his days working with teens in a special program at an alternative high school called "Kiita." The word means "Let's go," in Iñupiaq, a rallying cry for those who had been identified as needing help in one way or another. It might be their slowness in the classroom, it might be because of physical problems, or psychological problems.

The year before, a special education student had been a member of the football team. This year, with some forty students at the center, Houston was pretty sure none of them were playing on school teams in any sport.

"It's an alternative for kids who are not successful in a regular classroom setting," Houston said. "They need more structure. Some of them have all they can handle going to school."

There was definitely a bit of the preacher in Houston. At the end-of-practice huddles, perhaps thinking about those kids who were having it a little bit tougher at the center, he frequently reminded the Whalers that it was a privilege to play football for their school, that they were lucky to have this chance and they should be sure to make the most of it.

Houston seemed to understand that you had to say these things to players over and over again to compete with the noise rattling around in their heads from constant exposure to television, a distant Lower-48 world making itself known through commercials and contemporary music. He didn't say those were bad things, but it was apparent that he considered football a more wholesome world.

For three months, the coaches wanted football to be the most important thing in the players' world, rated in importance slightly above girlfriends, socializing, and even going to hunting camp. The last thing in the world the coaches wanted to do was get in a spitting contest with elders. They had no intention whatsoever of doing that. But they did demand commitment, and a kid who skipped practice for days was letting down his teammates by his absence. The whole system collapsed if players blew off practice. They fell behind in school. They disrupted drills. They couldn't keep up with execution.

No, the coaches were not going to tell a young man he had no business following a path laid out by his ancestors generations earlier, but they had made it clear when a player signed up for two-a-days in July that they were part of a team and they were needed. In a sense it was joining a brotherhood, at least for a little while, where the common good had to take precedence over individual wants or there would be chaos.

Again, players whose families retreated to hunting and fishing camp for days or weeks had to surrender something precious in their lifestyle—or make that *trade* something—for the time being. There was still a lingering desire to be in both places for some. Though no one left the team to go hunting or fishing, there was plenty of thought given to how families, friends, and neighbors were spending their time.

Robin Kaleak, fifteen, a soft-spoken, muscular, sophomore lineman with considerable potential, went to camp to fish for whitefish as usual as a freshman. He was gone two weeks and when he returned he discovered Barrow had a football team. It was too late to play. This year, he stepped back from a family subsistence activity he had been part of since age seven to go out for the team.

"It was hard to miss it," Kaleak said.

Kaleak wanted to go to camp sixty miles down the coast, but somewhat surprisingly a grandfather said he should try football instead.

"He made me change my mind," Kaleak said. "It's good for me. Last year I was failing in school. Football helps me get my grades up."

It is not as if wild game is bountiful around the calendar in Barrow. Spring bowhead whaling is the prime time for that hunt. Additional whaling can occur in the fall, but spring is busier. The migration of the Western Arctic caribou herd takes place in March or April and August. Commuting ducks and geese are in the air in August and September.

The grocery store's doors are open year-round, but the windows to hunt and stockpile food for the cellar are open for much shorter periods of time. A person with money will not starve in Barrow if he does not go hunting or fishing, but he might be deprived of important, favorite elements in his diet. And not every person can afford the high grocery store prices all of the time.

The anticipated arrival of pack ice for the winter and later or earlier comings and goings of animals lead the Eskimos of the North to believe global warming is far from a myth. Trends of centuries have been altered, and some surprises occur. It was August 24 when Big Bob Aiken discussed hunting patterns.

"Broken up ice should have been here by now," he said as he gazed out at a wide-open, wet Arctic Ocean. "My uncle went out twenty-five miles and he didn't see one iceberg."

The day before, Aiken had strapped his .223 rifle and 30-30 magnum on the back of his four-wheeler and cruised out toward Point Barrow to see what type of game might be available. He did not have to go far out of town before he saw a flock of eider ducks. He shot three and brought them home for the freezer. The oddest part of the entire excursion, though, was that it was sunny and the temperature climbed to sixty degrees.

"Something is not right," Aiken said.

Global warming was in the news all summer. Not only was former vice president Al Gore raking in honors—from an Oscar to the Nobel Prize—for his lobbying efforts to raise awareness of the environmental problem, Alaska Natives were often held up as examples of people whose lives were already being affected.

In June, Barrow hosted a United Nations Environment Program as part of North American World Environment Day. The theme of the gathering: "Melting Ice, A Hot Topic."

While many around the country might think Barrow would be happy to have fewer –30°F days, and a little longer time with open ocean instead of Arctic pack ice, the lives of Iñupiats in the North are dependent on the rhythm of the seasons. In a memorable comment at the forum pertaining to additional days of warmer temperatures, Wesley Aiken, another Big Bob relative, said, "We don't grow vegetables."

It was apparent at the meeting that those who had followed the footsteps of their elders for years were worried that the hunting culture they had long relied on would disappear. When a UN program official said the future was about adapting to climate change, he was uttering words Natives did not want to hear.

"In Barrow," Mayor Nathaniel Olemaun replied, "We know about adaptation. Iñupiat hunters at every single outing on the land or sea ice base their behavior on the conditions of the day." That was true, but they also based their behavior on experience and what they sometimes encountered were new conditions they had never seen before.

Supporting Big Bob's comment about the ice being far offshore so late, hunters from Wainwright, another Eskimo community of six hundred residents west of Barrow, reported only a week earlier that the sea ice they expected to see within thirty miles of shore was still three hundred miles north. In Wainwright, those changed conditions wrecked the traditional walrus hunt, reducing the harvest by 90 percent by late August.

Mac Rock is one Barrow player who ordinarily would be at fall camp if he were not a member of the football team. Even before he took that scary little autumn whaling trip, Rock had been out hunting caribou with his family. At age eight, Rock hunted with his brother and uncle. They helped him line up a shot at thirty feet using a .223.

"I closed my eyes before I shot," Rock said.

But he knocked down the caribou. Of course, then the other older males had to take care of the butchering, because Rock had no idea how to do it. As hunting season swirled around them, with men riding out to the Point to shoot waterfowl, with nets being placed in the lake to catch fish, and with families evacuating to camp for caribou hunting, the players were coaxed to focus solely on Eielson.

Eielson was a preseason Greatland Conference favorite, a team that had the capability of butchering the Whalers, if they were not careful. Eielson did not traffic in fancy plays. You knew what you were getting when you faced the Ravens. They were going to run the ball. It might be around end, but more often it would be between the tackles. The Ravens were less likely to come out throwing than Alaska was to become a spring break destination.

"Eielson is going to run the ball 93 percent of the time," announced assistant coach Brad Igou at a skull session. Not 90 percent, 93 percent. Even if accurate, the assessment was probably more from perception than calculation. Oh, the Barrow coaches were definitely familiar with Eielson. And pretty impressed, too.

"They come across and lay a lick," said Jeremy Arnhart. "You've got to play with some attitude. We should lay it to them."

Houston chimed in.

"We can't be catchers," he said. "We've got to deliver."

Cutting through the verbiage of this exhortation was a message of some substance. What the coaches were saying was that Eielson was a good team and very tough and for Barrow to win this one it would have to play harder, hit harder, and make fewer mistakes.

This didn't mean there was no room for levity when the Whalers watched some game film from their official triumph over Seward and their unofficial triumph over Monroe Catholic. When the images showed Robert Vigo leveling a quarterback he proclaimed, "He got a good chunk of muktuk."

Nobody was even 93 percent sure what Vigo's comment meant, but it sounded funny and brought a group laugh. Maybe Vigo was suggesting the opposing player got run over by a whale. Now that would be something to picture. A bowhead whale on the defensive line rushing the quarterback. Steamrolled again.

A common practice at sports festivals like the Arctic Winter Games is apparel trading. An Alaska team jacket might look very cool to an athlete from the Northwest Territories and vice versa. Before the closing ceremonies bartering takes place. It was a bit surprising, but not astonishing, when Daniel Thomas and Tim Barr showed up to practice wearing Eielson T-shirts. It was initially presumed by some to be a fashion statement, the logical progression following one of those trades that must have taken place the season before. Is that what Barr did?

"Heck, no," he said.

Trading was not the origin of the shirts at all, it turned out. On the weekend Barrow did not play Ketchikan, Voss deployed assistant coaches to other cities to scout several games. Houston went to Eielson and brought back a couple of T-shirts in preparation for this occasion.

"Coach made me wear it as a motivational tool," Barr said.

Houston admitted to the purchase.

"We're gonna tear these up," he said.

You know, sort of like feasting on the Ravens. For all of the talk of ferocity, it was a light, no-pads, just-helmets practice the day before a game. The sun was bright and the newness of the field still seemed to glow.

"This field really does look pretty in the sun," said Jarid Hope, still hobbled by a cast on his broken leg.

Voss wanted to practice long snapping and holding for field goals and extra points, not a terribly strenuous exercise. Instructions were to go stand on the 40-yard line to retrieve kicks, but Cody Gleason kept retreating.

"The 40-yard line, Cody," Voss said. "The one with the four and the zero."

➡ ⬅

There was one distraction during the workout, however. A twin engine prop plane kept flying over the field. It passed directly overhead, flew away, turned around, and came back a few minutes later. Maybe practicing touchdowns on the runway? No one knew for sure. Voss said he was told by several people that the field looks spectacular from the air with its vivid colors. Or, there could have been another explanation for the repetitive flyovers.

"Spies," Voss said. "Those Eielson guys."

That's right, they were the Air Force, and the Ravens were stealing the game plan from one thousand feet. That was about as likely as the fleet of vehicles that kept coming and going outside the fence, watching a few plays at a time, then driving away, being affiliated with the CIA. (There are a lot of beat-up vehicles in Barrow. Because of the phenomenal price of shipping cars in, a service that adds thousands of dollars to costs, drivers hang on to their wheels through cracked windshields and rusted bottoms longer than drivers do in the Lower 48. These cars were good till the last drop of oil.)

On the sideline, Barr bent down, picked up a pebble and heaved it away.

"I thought I was done throwing rocks off the stupid field," he joked.

Pili was on the sideline, too. Big tackle Mike Olson ambled up behind her and after a bit twirled the braid hanging down her back. She didn't even turn around.

In the postpractice huddle, Voss's voice was firm. All eyes were on him and all ears were open. He spelled out the next morning's pregame plan leading up to the noon start.

"Anyone who is not there by 9:30 is running a risk of not playing," he said. "Be dressed and taped by 10:00. The bus is not waiting for any of you."

Igou, veteran of a career as a lineman, knew what to expect from a team like Eielson that lived and thrived on the running game.

"This is possibly the best team in our league," he said. "They're going to come in and smash you in the mouth."

Arnhart announced, "We've got to execute to win."

Nobody knew that better than players who had lived through multiple-penalty, multiple-fumble games, and felt they could execute better.

"I wanted to be better last year," said Cody Romine. "But it's a lot better this year. There are a lot more people. We're pretty good."

Arnhart, also the Barrow basketball coach, a sport the kids did know, still wasn't sure how good the football players were so soon after having a team invented out of thin air. But he was optimistic about this bunch and he was optimistic about the future of football in Barrow regardless.

"I knew we had a ton of athletic students who didn't play anything," he said. "Well, we've definitely got some football players. We have been busy, busy, busy this last year. Our kids would not be where they are now without going to those camps in the spring. They did a lot of learning."

Yet the Whalers were still light-years behind some schools in executing the plays the coaches taught, in reacting the quick way they had to when the ball was hiked. While more experienced teams reacted with instinct, Barrow players were still pausing to think, then react. Often, those few seconds were costly. The play had already passed them by, or they committed a penalty trying to catch up.

"Some of these kids are starting to get the big picture," Arnhart said. "But it's not in their brains yet."

Arnhart thought of his players as pioneers, as the first class paving the way for others. Never before in his seven years in Barrow had he driven down streets and seen youngsters flipping a football to one another, or acting out games in their yards.

"Now it's all of the time," he said. "It's all over. In the Bush, everybody loves sports. Football will get so many more involved. There will be forty-five or fifty out soon. And hopefully our kids will continue on to something else during the school year, like basketball or wrestling. Once a kid is successful at a sport, they say, 'I can do this,' about something else, too."

At that moment, what Arnhart really wanted to see was a Barrow Whaler football team be successful against Eielson.

### CHAPTER 15

# *Getting Ready*

THE PLAYERS BEAT THE CLOCK on Saturday morning, their on-time arrival rate better than that of most major airlines. By 9:35 A.M., they were pulling shoulder pads over their heads and tightening belt buckles.

When David Gerke dropped his son off behind the school building where the back door entrance was propped open with a block of wood, he encountered Coach Voss.

"Are you guys gonna stop the run today?" the older Gerke asked rhetorically. "You better."

Absentmindedly, his thoughts on the game, but politeness ruling, Voss said simply, "They've got lots of run offense."

Not that Albert Gerke was ready to be a Brett Favre type of leader, like the family's Green Bay Packer favorite, counting on a slingshot arm to take care of all worries, but it wasn't passing weather, anyway. The temperature was only a handful of degrees above freezing that morning, and it was not expected to exceed 44°F during the early afternoon game. Then there was the wind, an ornery creature that day.

There was joking, some chatter, but it was pretty quiet among the players as they dressed and marched down the hall to an empty classroom in stocking feet—cleats to be put on by the back door before boarding the bus.

Coach Houston was at the front of the classroom, already diagramming formations with the enthusiasm of Albert Einstein, who for most of the players only a few months earlier would have been more understandable.

As Houston and Arnhart split the chalk talk, Igou taped ankles. That was one of his jobs. He was an artist with adhesive tape, the man who could make vanilla stick-em become part of an ankle with expert wrapping.

It was early in the season, but Eielson was 2–0 and ranked number five among Alaska small schools. The Ravens were a preseason pick to either win or be in the top two in the Greatland Conference. Under the small-schools playoff system, the first two finishers in the league advanced to the playoffs.

Eielson had more experience than Barrow, an historically powerful running game, and a tradition begun by the late Buck Nystrom a couple of decades earlier. Barrow's advantage, besides their glorious home field, was size.

The Whalers were a team of many components. There were Caucasians, African-Americans, and Polynesians on the team, as well as Alaska Natives, and there were players the product of mixed marriages. Quite the mix ethnically, but also quite the mix when it came to football player size. Barrow actually had the largest group of linemen in Alaska in the small-schools division.

The Ravens could fly like their team namesake, but they did not have the same kind of bulk Barrow did. A primary piece of advice offered by Houston in his pregame briefing was aimed at the Barrow linemen: Fire off the ball. He said it several times. The idea being that the Whalers could use their size advantage by quickly erupting forward after the snap and making immediate contact.

"We need to make some big holes," Houston said.

Arnhart was very much in tune with the theme.

"They've got 160-pounders," he said. "You should just kill 'em."

Houston looked at John Lambrecht, all of his 340 pounds, and at Keifer Kanayurak and Colton Blankenship, two more big bruisers who looked as ready as anyone to lay waste to an all-you-can-eat buffet.

"I need to have a big day from you today," said Houston, who—given his own Mack truck size—understood lineman mentality completely.

The Whalers were a rapt audience. They listened acutely to every word coming out of the coaches' mouths. This was the assistant coaches' time to shine, to be the mentors who soothed nerves, who reminded the players how hard they had worked, and spelled out on a blackboard what it was they had learned.

Houston, Arnhart, and Igou took turns reviewing different facets of the game plan and interspersing comments about what their young men needed to do, and were capable of doing, to win.

"Defense is going to win the game," Igou told the players. "If you guys have your heads up your butts, it's gonna be a long day. The scouting report is that they run 93 percent of the time. Maybe more than that. You can't let down with their team. You can't take a break."

Arnhart passed out photocopies of the fifteen start-the-game-right offensive plays he had scripted. Luke George folded his copy into a wrist sleeve.

In a way that differs from baseball, basketball, and hockey, football preparation and halftime reevaluation have long been linked to the pep talk. It dates back at least to Knute Rockne at Notre Dame in the 1920s, a man who was famed for his oratory. Those talks are rooted in a recipe of homilies, clichés, and ego boosts. Football game speeches have been parodied and pilloried. But they continue, and maybe it is because they work. Or maybe because they sound as if they should work and they are calming to the jumpy game-action mind.

Whether they saw it in the movies, heard it all from their coaches as they grew up, or it just came naturally to them, no team had an advantage over Barrow based upon a shortage of exhortations. Houston was the king of homilies, not only because he knew them all, but because he was sincere. Sure, some of the stuff that came out of his mouth sounded hokey. But he was talking to sixteen-year-olds nervous about what would come next, not sophisticated voters at the Democratic National Convention.

"Nobody beats us on the blue and gold," he announced.

It was a nice thought, but every team believes it should be undefeated on its home field and few are. Still, the concept of defending one's home as a castle from the marauding hordes appealed to warrior-football players. It broadened the mission. Win the game, protect your families. Repel the invaders and earn the fight for respect.

"We're gonna start something new here," Houston added. "It's gonna take will, determination, and a big heart. If each man on the field wins his one-on-one battle, we have nothing to worry about."

There was a determined rah-rah tone in Houston's delivery. It was talk that would make the players feel good about themselves without leaving them frothing at the mouth and smashing the desks in the classroom.

Voss took a turn, offering a gentle reminder that needed to be said. Only a week before the Whalers had broken in Cathy Parker Field with a come-from-behind victory. Then they trounced Monroe Catholic in a scrimmage. They were feeling pretty good about themselves. It was Voss's job to bring them back to earth without crashing the space shuttle.

"Gentlemen," he said. "Ladies," he added in a nod to Ganina Pili. "That's all past. Everything now is in the future."

Like the kickoff, in about an hour and a half.

"You have the opportunity today to take the lead in your conference," Voss continued. "This is your toughest game of the year. We're gonna take it to them."

Reverend Scott Barr, linebacker Tim Barr's father, gathered the flock in the room and told the story of an 1811 battle in the Peninsula War, during which a seriously wounded English colonel urged his troops to "die hard, men, die hard."

Always good advice to follow in combat, but the comment seemed a tad too grim leading up to the Eielson game, where the goal was to not die at all, but to walk away triumphant.

Pastor Barr also appealed directly to God to protect the Whalers from injury, to allow them to play well, and to give them encouragement if their will faltered. He asked that the Lord help the Whalers do the right thing and "just give them a good game." Barr also slipped in a teeny request for a victory.

Once again smoothly picking up on the theme, Arnhart yelled, "Let's go to battle!"

As the players streamed out the back door of the school and onto the bus, Robert Vigo shouted, "Game time!"

It was 10:45 A.M., one and a quarter hours after check-in time and one and a quarter hours shy of kickoff, when Pili asked out loud, "Where's Dave today?" Others echoed her question.

Dave, as in Dave Evikana, was missing in action. Or rather, missing before action. No one seemed to know where he was, but it was obvious he was not present and that he was not going to play against Eielson. It turned out he overslept.

As the bus pulled away from the school, Houston, the sole coach riding with the players (the others having piled into Voss's beat-up car), stood up at the front seat and said, "Let's keep it quiet, guys. Get focused."

A funereal silence descended on the players during the ten-minute ride to the field. Many looked out the window, but there was not much to see on a breezy, gray-sky day that they had not seen a million times before. It was their hometown and they knew every inch of the handful of roads, the shape of every business or house. There was no reaction when the bus drove past the hard-earth-and-gravel remnants of the field used briefly the season before.

The old field had been returned to its primary pre-football usage— a flat, open area employed as a training ground for the North Slope Borough's new heavy equipment operators. There was more than enough room to turn those Big Cats around without smacking into a fence or building.

As the bus pulled up alongside the field, early arriving fans were driving up as well, eyes scouting for the best parking space. It was going to be too crowded to find a vantage point that would afford a clear view of the game from the car. But it was good strategy to find a place near the field or near the concessions booth. That way if it got too cold (and given that the prediction was for 15–20 mph winds, it was shaping up that it would be) it would be easy to retreat to the vehicle at halftime, run the heat and sip a hot drink, while still being well-positioned to race back to the bleachers for second-half action.

Before the driver opened the door and the players jumped off the bus, Houston addressed them one more time.

"We believe!" he yelled. "Those are the only words we need to say."

One by one, as they exited the bus, the players slapped bare hands against a large, heavy, chunk of rock. It was a good-luck talisman, and no player skipped the touch before disembarking.

It took a big, strong lineman to deposit the rock on the bus, and Robin Kaleak did the heavy lifting. But it was not his rock. He was only helping out. This was something new for the Whalers, a new tradition taking shape, this connection between the players and the land they represented.

However, the rock was not a rock at all. It was a whale bone. Coach Houston had been taking a spiritual walk on the beach at Point Barrow one day the previous spring, absorbing the sight of the roiling waves of the Arctic Ocean, peacefully inhaling the scenery, when he came upon the bone.

"It was just there," Houston said. "I said I'm going to give it to the team as a pride thing."

Maybe he was in a particularly thoughtful mood. Maybe his mind was relaxed and open to new suggestions. But the whale bone moved him in a certain way. He couldn't help but think about the importance of the bowhead whale to the Iñupiat people. He thought about the bounty that came from one of these humongous whales. He thought a little bit about God and life and death.

And then he decided this whale bone had to come home with him instead of rotting on the beach. The sucker felt like it weighed a ton if you wanted to move it any distance, but in reality it weighed no more than an overloaded backpack, if you think of forty or forty-five pounds as just a tad heavy. It was work enough for Houston to get it into the car and take it home.

Houston held on to the whale bone for a while (talk about your oversized doorstops) and then at the preseason dinner when the Florida people visited, he unveiled it. His show-and-tell speech revolved around the fact that it had taken hundreds of people to hunt, capture, skin, and carve up the whale.

"It took many people to get this whale," he said. "Teamwork."

It was one thing to get the whale bone home, but it was a whole 'nother effort to bring it along in the bus to home games. (The bone was definitely not going to be making road trips in carry-on luggage.) Here in Barrow it felt right for the players to have a touchstone that connected them to the harsh place where they lived, and that tied them even tighter to the nickname of their team, the Whalers. It would kill Houston's back if he had to tote the whale bone around himself, but that's what growing, 250-pound teenage boys were good for—free labor for adults. As long as the Whalers bought into the idea of the whale bone as a special item, they would want to bring it with them to games. They did, and they did.

"We just started it," said end Justin Sanders of the whale bone's inaugural journey to the Seward game.

It was all part of the unity being taught and established. There were different ways to build that attitude. Some of them might seem hokey or artificial to outsiders, but when it came to teams you never knew what would take hold.

The Pittsburgh Pirates won a World Series in 1979 unified by the theme, "We Are Family," because of the popular Sister Sledge song. The 2005 Chicago White Sox were inspired by the song "Don't Stop Believin'" by the rock band Journey as the Sox battled their way to a World Series title. Presidential campaigns have been identified with slogans or songs to build unity and rally supporters. President Franklin

Delano Roosevelt's 1932 campaign featured the song "Happy Days Are Here Again." President Dwight Eisenhower's 1952 and 1956 campaigns featured the theme, "I Like Ike."

The oddest of traditions or slogans have been linked to a championship and never forgotten, part of a single magical ride, or sometimes enduring through many seasons. The Barrow Whalers were too young to have old traditions. They had to start somewhere.

"We believe!" the players chanted as they dashed off the bus, making sure to give that solid, unyielding whale bone a good slap. "We believe!"

CHAPTER 16

# The Ravens Are Ravenous

THE WEATHER WAS UNCOMFORTABLE for those bundled up on the bleachers who were exposed to the wind, but it didn't take very long for Eielson's hurricane force offensive attack to make the Barrow fans and coaches do some additional squirming.

Although it would be hard for most people to believe, Eielson is located in a spot in the Alaskan Interior an hour from Fairbanks where it might get colder in the winter than in Barrow. So it was wishful thinking to believe the Ravens were going to be intimidated by unseasonably coolish temperatures.

Igou was right in his scouting. The Ravens loved running the ball. Many years ago when the University of Southern California seemed to manufacture tailbacks more readily than teachers or engineers, it was said that the Trojan offense was as simple as calling, "Student body right," for a running play to that side, or "Student body left," for a running play to that side. There wasn't much trickery in Eielson's play calling. It wasn't needed. The Ravens ran right. The Ravens ran left. In both geographical choices, the Ravens found daylight. There were holes large enough to drive a four-wheeler through in some cases.

Barrow defenders just couldn't tackle the Ravens' feature runners. The Whalers always seemed to react a second late. And by that time the runner was past the line of scrimmage and the defense was playing catch-up. It was a demoralizing sight if you were a Whaler.

Eielson did not make many mistakes, either. The Ravens were well-drilled and from the first quarter on they drilled the Whalers. Less than three minutes into the game, Eielson led 6–0 when running back Chance Renfro dashed twenty-nine yards for a touchdown. Four minutes later, quarterback Austin Samulowitz tucked the ball under his arm on a keeper and ran sixty-five yards for another touchdown. Eielson added a two-point conversion and the Whalers trailed, 14–0.

The nippy wind delivered gray clouds and drizzle. Perfect hypothermia weather for those sitting still. Somehow being in the stands at a sporting event is an endurable experience in bad weather if the team you are rooting for is winning. But if the team you are cheering for is getting its clock cleaned, mist, fog, and light rain definitely contribute to making for a discouraging afternoon.

The second period was not any friendlier for Barrow residents, either on the field or in the bleachers. Once upon a time in the National Football League, there were a couple of fine players whose last name was Renfro. In the 1950s and early 1960s, there was Ray Renfro, a sturdy runner and punt returner for the Cleveland Browns. In the 1970s, there was star defensive back Mel Renfro for the Dallas Cowboys. At least six other Renfros have played at the top level of the sport. For one day, at least, Eielson's Chance Renfro proved as challenging to contain. He scored his second touchdown on a forty-six-yard burst in the second quarter after Samulowitz scored his second touchdown on a two-yard run.

It was 26–0 Eielson before the spectators made a halftime sprint to the concessions area for coffee and hot chocolate. The crowd included a couple of football fans from Long Island, New York, who had heard about the creation of a football team at the Top of the World and wanted to see a game above the Arctic Circle. So, crazy as it sounded, they flew in for the occasion. Let's take a weekend in Barrow, Alaska! The Whalers were developing a cult following around the United States.

For one brief shining moment in the second quarter, it appeared that Barrow was putting together a stick-moving drive down the field, piling up those first downs. Suddenly, the players executed with fresh crispness. Those plays drawn up on the blackboard worked. And then, at a crucial point, the Whalers were whistled for a five-yard illegal procedure penalty. On the sidelines, it seemed as if Arnhart might snap his clipboard in half out of frustration.

A stupid little lack-of-concentration penalty like that ruined it all. The infraction was a momentum killer, a drive stopper. The nasty weather felt even worse after that play, especially for guys on the sidelines not seeing much action.

Big defensive tackle Trevor Litera summed up those feelings.

"I'm freezing," he said.

Taylor Elbert, sidelined with a sprained ankle and under doctor's orders not to do anything too active on it, was so cold he couldn't sit still. For warmth he actually jumped up and down on the wounded ankle. Somewhere a member of the American Medical Association slapped his forehead in disbelief.

Then things got worse.

An Eielson player intercepted a pass and ran down the sidelines past his own team's bench on the visitor's side. Barrow lineman John Wilson, a hardworking tackle with an upbeat attitude, tried to head off the runner, but at the end of the play was lying on the ground far from the clear view of his own bench and home fans.

An injury. Wilson remained down at first. He tried to stand and fans applauded. But he fell down, rolled onto his back near the orange fencing, and stayed there. From a distance, it was difficult to see what was wrong, but clearly Wilson was in pain. Tim Barr, one of the first teammates on the scene, trotted back across the field.

"He messed up his leg," Barr said.

Wilson writhed on the ground in obvious agony. Officials clustered around. Superintendent Trent Blankenship and Coach Voss investigated the situation. Wilson sat up, peeled off his shoulder pads, and slammed them to the ground. He rubbed his own head, in pain and anger.

An ambulance was called and the siren grew louder as it approached the field, covering the few miles from downtown. There was not much chatter in the stands. At first the fans didn't know which player was hurt. Then they didn't say much because nobody knew what was wrong.

Paramedics arrived and stabilized Wilson. Then he was placed on a stretcher bed and transported to the ambulance. Austin Fishel carried Wilson's helmet off the field. Blankenship carried Wilson's pads.

"Torn ACL," Blankenship said.

Anterior cruciate ligament. They would find out for sure soon at Samuel Simmons Memorial Hospital. If so, bad news for the Whalers and Wilson, whose season would be over. As he left the field, Wilson was crying from the pain, and probably the frustration of an early season injury. As Wilson was wheeled off, Cody Romine yelled words of encouragement. Barrow and Eielson players both ran over to the stretcher and wished Wilson well.

After a delay of about half an hour, the game resumed. Eielson promptly scored another touchdown. 32–0. The Ravens' sympathy did not extend to the scoreboard.

Barrow finally introduced itself to the scoring column in the third quarter. Anthony Edwards took a handoff and darted around left end. His powerful legs pumping, he scored from seven yards out. Although he had been bottled up much of the day and the Whalers had sabotaged their own offense with too many chintzy penalties, when it was on display, Edwards's raw athleticism always made people smile. His shoulders are broad and his thighs immense, excellent physical equipment for a running back. Edwards had speed as well as power, and those who were most dreamy-eyed about his potential seemed to repeat the same phrase independently—"And he's only a sophomore."

Edwards's touchdown turned out to be an isolated occurrence instead of a momentum changer. Shortly thereafter the Ravens scored on a safety for a 34–6 lead. Then, as the quarter's end approached, Eielson pushed its lead to 41–6. And there was still a twelve-minute period to go. Even if Eielson was of the mind to take it easy on the Whalers, given that the Ravens only traveled north with seventeen players, coach David DeVaughn didn't have many options to hold down the score.

Still, Eielson only managed to score once, on an interception, in the fourth period, mopping up for a 47–6 victory. Barrow was never really in the game, looking very much its baby-stepping age. If Eielson was the class of the Greatland Conference, the Whalers understood a little bit better where they fit in. It was a lot to ask, to even think, that a team formed so rapidly and recently had the savvy to contend with the best of the bunch.

The coaches were realistic, not downbeat. If they had suspected they were in for a licking that Saturday, they never hinted in advance. Now that they saw firsthand how an experienced, smoothly running team operated, the Whalers had something to compare themselves to, even aspire to.

"That was a very good football team," Coach Igou said to his wet and chilled team gathered at midfield. "I still don't think you understand the intensity you need to bring on every play. But I don't want anybody hanging their heads, either."

Arnhart, too, brought perspective.

"Use this as a learning experience," he said. "But don't be satisfied with losing. You should be mad. This should hurt."

If losing by forty-one points didn't hurt at least a little bit, then the players didn't own a competitive streak. Anyone who has played on a sports team crushed in a game by an opponent passes through several stages. When it is happening, when the deficit mounts, it seems almost unreal. There is a sense of denial that it is happening to you. The differential also seems to grow very quickly, almost too fast to fathom. Then depression sets in. The key is overcoming the depression, not letting it linger, trying to take something useful from the loss. It is important to remember, but move on.

"That's what we want to strive for," Voss said of Eielson's efficient performance. "A better ballclub is what it was."

After shaking hands with the Barrow players, the Ravens ran across the street, shedding uniform parts, and jumped into the Arctic Ocean. They must have heard about the Whalers doing so after beating Seward. The maneuver surprised Barrow players.

"They jumped in the ocean!" Jim Martin exclaimed.

"They won the game," Voss said. "They can jump in our ocean."

More softly, Martin said, "But it's our tradition."

Never did a crowded school bus, featuring seats with perhaps an inch of padding, feel so terrific to Barrow players. The heat was on and boxes containing hot dogs and hamburgers were on the front seats. Damp and cool, it was definitely a calorie burning day—and fuel of any sort that fit under the definition of food was very welcome.

There was more talk about the burgers being naked than the team getting demolished. "No tomato, no lettuce, no ketchup, no cheese," said Robert Vigo.

Condiments were unnecessary amenities at the moment, however. They were tempted to eat the wrappers, too. With the players spread out among the seats, most out of reach of the food, cocaptain Justin Sanders stepped up and tossed seconds in hamburgers and dogs to players. You could almost hear the coaches say that was demonstrating leadership.

The instant nutritional intake, regardless of how minimal, seemed to reinvigorate the team. The burgers and hot dogs seemed to possess a mind-cleansing potion. Suddenly, rather than mooning about the loss, the players started to joke and laugh. Which was more than Coach Houston could take. Too much frivolity, too soon.

He stood up, faced the seats, and in a short bark yelled, "Hey." It got quiet in a hurry. "You guys just lost a game. Reflect about it right here."

The rest of the ride back to the school was very quiet. Whether the Whalers were contemplating getting waxed by Eielson, were planning their Saturday evenings with girlfriends, or were thinking about just how good those burgers and dogs tasted, would remain unexplored territory.

A surprise awaited back at the school: John Wilson was there. He used crutches to stand up, but he was already out of the hospital. Players smiled at Wilson, asked how he felt, said they were glad to see him.

Wilson said that he got hurt when he was trying to fight off a block that knocked him out of bounds. The knee was swollen like a balloon and the doctors at the hospital weren't sure of the extent of the damage yet. There was some, he said, but he might not have a tear. At the least the tendons were stretched on both sides of the knee. He had never suffered any kind of major injury before, Wilson said, and was stunned by how much this hurt.

"Worse than anything," he said.

Wilson told everybody he was fine, but he wasn't really. It was the macho thing to say, the right thing to say as a football player. An opponent could break every bone in your body on a hit, but you weren't supposed to show pain. It wasn't manly.

In Wilson's case, after the swelling went down and he had the knee reexamined, the doctors thought that the injury wasn't as bad as had been feared. It was possible Wilson would be able to practice again and play in a couple of games before the end of the season.

For the moment, though, it was as sad a Saturday as a football team could have. Pummeled by forty-one points on your own field, with a team flaunting your own celebration tradition in front of you, and losing a starter to injury—that was a trifecta of bad news.

Taking the rest of the weekend off seemed like a grand idea. Maybe the Jaguars would be one of the NFL games on TV and the Whalers could see their buds whipsaw a conference foe. In front of the TV set, the Whalers could dream of warm-weather Florida and what they would do to their next opponent.

CHAPTER 17

# *Road Trip*

THE SHOPPING INVASION OF the Sports Authority store was a bonanza for Whaler football players and business owners alike.

Fresh from the airplane that delivered them from Barrow to Anchorage on the Thursday afternoon before their Saturday game, the coaches led the expedition to the spacious store on the south side of the city before they even left the general vicinity of the airport.

This was a treat. Anchorage, with its 260,000 people, located about eight hundred miles south of Barrow, was a different world. It is a far more sophisticated city than Barrow, but not everyone likes that. There is a saying uttered by those who dislike cities that the best thing about Anchorage is that it is only twenty minutes from Alaska. By that the critics mean that the wilderness, the true Alaska, can be found outside the city limits.

That is an exaggeration. There is plenty of wilderness inside the city limits, with the Chugach State Park, Turnagain Arm, and the wild animals that roam the subdivisions. Often enough, besides the moose chowing down on trees alongside heavily traveled streets, the appearance of a brown bear in town serves as a reminder that this is not Seattle. Yet Anchorage might as well be New York City compared to Barrow. It has a wide variety of restaurants and a multitude of big box stores.

Barrow was scheduled for its first road game of the season on the last day of August, but Anchorage was just a way station. The eight football-playing high schools in Anchorage are in the large schools division. Barrow's Greatland Conference opponent was Houston, in the town of the same name located about sixty-five miles north on the main highway between Anchorage and Fairbanks.

Coach Mark Voss knew his guys, though. He did not immediately drive them in their trio of vehicles to the Anchorage Museum of History and Art. The Whalers were quite content gazing at the artifacts on display at the Sports Authority. Appropriately enough, Austin Fishel made a beeline for the football display section. On a layer of shelves, footballs for kids, for serious players, and at all prices, were for sale.

"I collect them," said Fishel, who said he owns eight footballs.

Quarterback Albert Gerke looked over the choices, too.

"I like that one," Gerke said.

The ball cost $39.95 and was advertised as an "NFL Pro Replica."

Robin Kaleak eyed the $29.95 NCAA college football model. He said he likes to have a football in reach at his house. He either looks for somebody to throw with or handles it himself, "Whenever I'm bored at home."

There are no supermarkets of sports merchandise in Barrow. If the guys wanted to find any of the vast array of gear filling the aisles of the Sports Authority, ordinarily they would have to search the Internet and buy long distance.

Colton Blankenship said he was in the market for a cushioned neck roll to wear above his shoulder pads behind his head. The item cost $54.99 and he thought that was a little bit steep. He might be able to find it cheaper shopping online, but it might not be delivered until the season was almost over.

"It would take three weeks," he said.

Stair climbers have grown in popularity for indoor exercise in recent years, and the players stumbled onto a cross section of mini-steppers—$49.99 apiece—smaller versions that were much more portable.

Justin Sanders tried one out and so did lineman Alastair Dunbar. Voss wandered up. Dunbar looked up and said, "Will you buy me this?"

Voss laughed and replied, "No, but I love you dearly."

Those guys were bargain shoppers compared to Mike Gonzales and Blankenship who discovered a store corner with the major Bowflex lifting apparatus. Those babies cost $1,899.99 each. This was not an impulse buy, and the postage alone would dent the pocketbook severely trying to get it back to Barrow. Gonzales preferred free weights anyway.

"I just like to lift," Gonzales said.

The twenty-one players who made the road trip were scattered all over the store when Voss sent out the word, "Whalers up front." Shopping trip over after half an hour.

The full team did not make the journey. Not possible. The budget would be a million dollars a year if Voss took all thirty-five players on every road trip during the season. The coaches in consultation had to decide who didn't make the cut. It was a tough role to play. You wanted to treat all players equally, and you tried to do that during practice all season. But this was a major reward and the dividing line was very distinct. Much went into the choices. Obviously, the starters, the regulars, the best players, were going to Houston. But where there were close calls, things such as practice attendance, tardiness, attitude, and other intangibles came into play. It was not particularly fun to play God, but it was a responsibility that came with the territory and Voss had to be firm without harming players' feelings. He didn't want those who stayed in Barrow to quit the team. He wanted them out for practice again on Monday morning ready to go.

Some of the selections were easier to make than others. John Wilson was injured. Taylor Elbert was injured. No inexperienced freshman had played his way onto the trip. Ganina Pili wasn't in the top group of players. Most of the players knew who belonged. Some of them brought the best possible attitude to the process. They made it their goal to improve enough during the season to be chosen for the next road trip. That was the kind of spirit the coaches wanted to nurture. But geez, it really didn't make you feel great to leave forty percent of the team at home. The Whalers wouldn't have to do this if they lived along the road system and everyone could just pile into one bus for a game fifty or a hundred miles away. But the Whalers didn't live along the road system. They lived in Barrow, and this was one aspect of the remoteness.

"It's real hard," Voss said of his role. "It's one of the worst things about doing this."

Until a few days before departure, in fact, Voss thought he was going to be able to take twenty-five players to Houston. Then he was told no, there wasn't enough money available to cover that.

"It's one of the facts of life in Barrow," he said. "It's tough. Everybody will be evaluated. Week to week it could change."

One of the other facts of life in Barrow—and not just in Barrow, but all over Alaska—is that players in all sports get used to sleeping on the floors of gymnasiums. As teams shuffle between remote villages and even somewhat larger cities, transporting anywhere from a dozen to a couple dozen players at a time (depending on the sport) great distances requires overnight stays. In Southeast Alaska, where roads are at just as much of a premium as they are in the Alaskan Interior, teams commonly travel by ferry on the Alaska Marine Highway system.

Teams do not stay overnight at the Marriott, the Radisson, or even the Motel 6. Once in a great while logistics demand that teams bunk in hotels for a night, but it's not as if anyone is going to have a single or be staying in a place that offers primo room service. The budget is always monitored.

On this trip, arriving Thursday, playing Saturday afternoon, the Whalers couldn't get home until late Sunday afternoon, the Alaska Airlines jet scheduled to land in Barrow just after 5:30 P.M. On the third night, the team would stay in a hotel, but the first two nights their home away from home was to be the Hotel Houston. Actually, the Hotel Houston doesn't exist. The players were scheduled to reside in a room behind the gym at the school. When you play high school sports in Alaska, there is a very good chance that you will become an expert at evaluating camping equipment such as sleeping bags and mattresses.

Outside the Sports Authority, Robert Vigo showed off some snazzy new yellow arm bands he could wear wrapped around his biceps. They seemed to be more fashion accessory than football necessity, however.

"I like looking good," Vigo said. "It's for the cameras."

Cody Romine sighed as the players streamed out of the store.

"I could spend all day here," he said.

Several fast-food restaurants were nearby and players, deprived of such fare in Barrow, enthusiastically split up between McDonald's and Taco Bell. Compared to Barrow, with its automatically inflated food prices, these places were bargain central.

Coach Brian Houston spent $6.60 for two double cheeseburgers and a large drink and couldn't get over how inexpensive it seemed. The biggest eater on the team was probably Big John Lambrecht. He downed a couple of Big Macs and some fries.

"But they're small," he said.

Most things are small compared to Big John.

For a bit, the lunch break was just like any kind of field trip with a bunch of high school boys. There was chatter about girls. There were jokes about intimate matters best left unrepeated. Houston looked around at the group of teenagers, most of them seventeen years old or younger, making up this roster of football players.

"Sometimes we forget we're teaching brand-new kids," Houston said. "Even the terminology, they don't know. I grew up with it. We've got to explain it to them. We've got to slow it down a little bit."

It was not prime lunchtime, so the wait for food was only about as long as it took to take care of the Whalers themselves. There were a few other patrons who looked over the players, all of whom wore their numbered blue jerseys.

"What school are you from?" someone asked Gerke.

"We're the Barrow Whalers," he said.

"Oh, Barrow," the person said.

At the Taco Bell, someone asked the players, "How do you guys like your field?" He knew all about the gift of Cathy Parker Field.

Next stop Wal-Mart. For anyone who considers the United States to be a homogenized country, with too many chain stores and fast-food restaurants selling too much of the same thing, it might prove educational to spend a day with people who don't live within easy access of the American spending dream. It's not as if the Whalers don't appreciate their home as a unique place, but they want everything else other American teenagers want, too.

Football is emblematic of that. But so is music. So are electronic games. So are movies on DVD. The Wal-Mart in South Anchorage is large enough to lose an entire football team in—and Voss did. The players split into small groups, fanning out down the aisles as good consumers searching for excellent deals on items hard to come by in Barrow.

Jim Martin was pleased to see a PlayStation game featuring golf.

"Hey, I'm going to get Tiger Woods," he said.

Informed that would put him ahead of the curve when Barrow started a golf team (hey, no one expected football), Martin laughed and said, "I'm not gonna do that."

There was a music player selling for $19.87 and the Whalers couldn't get over the low price.

"Holy cow!" said Martin.

Colton Blankenship checked it out, looked at Martin, and said, "If you don't buy it, I'll kill you."

The players focused most of their time on electronic opportunities, urging teammates to buy a movie that they had especially liked and talking up favorite singing artists. Given that they lived at the Top of the World, the players did not seem particularly out of touch with mainstream popular culture. A lot had changed due to the installation of more elaborate communications over the years. Show business developments that at best might have been rumors in Big Bob's high school days were well-known to today's high schoolers. That could be viewed as an advancement or not, depending on how much gossip about Britney Spears one thought was useful.

Voss was on a completely different mission. He wheeled a shopping cart through the Wal-Mart grocery section, looking to pile in large boxes of snacks for late-night munching. Once the team was ensconced at the Houston Hilton, it was not going out again.

Cheez-Its. Pringles. Representatives of all the essential food groups appeared in Voss's cart. If you had an aversion to salt you had best buy your own Gummi Bears or something. Well, there were Pop Tarts.

Coach Jeremy Arnhart stood around at the front of the store. With a less urgent need to scope out movies and music, he paused for a moment or two of downtime. Arnhart wore his dark blue, short-sleeved team jersey with a yellow football and a football helmet on the front, and with "Barrow Whalers" on the sleeves. He couldn't have been more of a human advertisement for his team if he'd held up a banner.

Yet two different women approached Arnhart and asked directions to store departments, erroneously taking him for a Wal-Mart worker. Excuse me, could you tell me how to find furnishings? Voss, the other coaches, and the players, about died laughing when they heard about these cases of mistaken identity. If they had been sipping soda pop it would have come out their noses.

As for Mr. Clean Cut, average-sized, short-haired Arnhart, whose build did not scream football, it was comforting to know that he had other employment options if teaching and coaching didn't work out.

CHAPTER 18

# *Everyone Knows the Whalers*

As THE BARROW WHALERS broke up into small groups for their first Alaska State Fair visit in Palmer, a town just down the highway from Houston, a stranger yelled, "Way to go Whalers, winning your first one!"

The man had obviously clued into the comeback against Seward, but missed out on the news about Eielson. That was OK with the players. If they could have kept the score from the Eielson game secret they wouldn't have minded.

"That's pretty cool," said tackle Mike Olson of the commentary.

The man not only recognized the Barrow guys as the football team, he knew something about them, too.

The Alaska State Fair was no more than a carnival concept to most Barrow football players. They had never visited the end-of-summer, two-week-long spectacular that features everything from demolition derby and concerts to rides and all of the junk food you can imagine, spread out over acres of land just off the Glenn Highway less than an hour north of Anchorage.

One of the unique staples of Alaska State Fair viewing was the collection of giant vegetables. It sounded silly, but intense competition had evolved over the decades to see who could produce the world's largest vegetables. This might sound more like a contest for the Iowa State Fair in the nation's heartland, where corn might grow as high as an elephant's eye, as it were. But Palmer, in the heart of the Matanuska-Susitna Valley, was settled in 1935 by pioneer farmers relocating from the Midwest.

The soil was good, the summer sunshine magnificent enough to accelerate the growing season, and while the transplants never quite developed the area into an agricultural nirvana, the community remained and the spirited vegetable growing battles endured. None more so than the cabbage field. Growing the largest cabbage in the world captured Alaskans' fancy, and each year at the end of August at the Fair, the fruits of the harvest were unveiled.

"I like the vegetables," Mark Voss—who unlike his players, had been to the Fair before—had said a day earlier.

Voss put his team through a light workout before loading them into vehicles for the short ride to the Fairgrounds, but he was distracted. He had received a disturbing phone call: his ninety-nine-year-old grandmother had died of a stroke in Arkansas. At times Voss sat on a bench away from the players, talking on his cell phone to family members spread out around Alaska and the Lower 48.

Periodically, Voss grew misty-eyed. He tried to figure out how to fly to Arkansas for the funeral, but it was a formidable challenge as is common in emergencies among Alaskans because of distance and logistics, and he probably would not be able to go.

"I spent time with her over the summer," Voss said of the block of time between the end of the last school year and when he had returned to Barrow for football practice.

The players dispersed across the Fairgrounds. Big John Lambrecht wanted to see the famous cabbages, perhaps to see if any were bigger than he was. Not so. The 2007 contest winner weighed in at 87-plus pounds, shy of the 105.6-pound record. That's a lot of cole slaw, but the cabbages did not approach Lambrecht territory.

"Where are the girls?" asked Cody Romine.

On a sunny Friday afternoon, with temperatures climbing into the 60s, and with school not yet underway, there would be plenty of flirting opportunities for a high school guy wearing a team jersey in a playland like this.

Some Whalers came upon a pony ride. Romine, who had a gleam in his eye, did not really resemble John Wayne and it was hard to guess how a Barrow teen would perform on horseback, regardless of the size of the horse.

"Are we too big?" he asked.

Romine is about five-foot-ten and while even his feet might have dangled on the dirt as the ponies marched in circles, other players were definitely too big.

Justin Sanders had been to a fair, the Tanana Valley State Fair in Fairbanks, but in comparative size to *the* Alaska State Fair, that was a lake next to an ocean.

This Fair had a multitude of big-time rides, the kind that would scare the bejeezus even out of a football player, the kind that might even make one puke. Some Whalers were more daring, or reckless, than others. Mike Olson was trying to round up candidates for a bungee cord drop that looked like it might cause whiplash. There were no takers and Olson, thinking back to the spring football trip to Florida, lamented, "You made me go on the roller coaster in Orlando."

The appeal to conscience did not help his cause. "Are you scared?" he asked aloud to teammates.

Quarterback Al Gerke had an arm that could produce the same kind of whiplash, but he wanted no part of this bungee jump. "Yeah," he said. "This is different."

State fairs are junk food havens. All rules affecting diets and culinary common sense must be suspended upon entering the grounds. Hot dogs, hamburgers, popcorn, chocolate candy, corn on the cob, ice cream, turkey legs, pizza, soft drinks, hot drinks, cotton candy, nachos, cream puffs, and items such as fry bread never otherwise seen outside the gates of these fantasylands create seductive sights and smells.

Colton Blankenship was paralyzed in his tracks when he spotted a booth with fry bread, basically licking his lips. Fry bread is a Native American food made out of flattened dough deep fried in oil, shortening, or lard. Blankenship was introduced to fry bread in Wyoming.

Historically, it was used as a wrap for ingredients that are also often found in tacos, such as ground beef, beans, and shredded cheese. However, fry bread has also evolved into a dessert, with powdered sugar sprinkled on top. Alaska State Fair fry bread is the dessert variety, a calorie killer.

"I can make fry bread," Forrest Akiviana said.

You half expected Blankenship to demand the recipe on the spot.

Sanders and Romine strapped themselves into seats in the front row of a ride that rocked back and forth.

"I'm dizzy already," commented Sanders, who had not yet left the ground.

Then the ride really got going, lifting the riders into the air, pausing at the apex of the seats' extension for a moment, ("It's pretty cool, you can see everything," Romine said later) and then plummeting in controlled free fall.

"My stomach hurts," Sanders said as he staggered away after the ride he had paid $4 for the privilege of taking.

Gerke, Olson, and Austin Fishel committed to a spin on the Super Roundup. No sitting on this one. The trio was belted into adjacent compartments standing up, and once started the ride spun faster and faster, with the players looking as if they would possibly disappear into time travel. Each time they rotated past earthbound spectators looking upward at them, they wore goofy smiles plastered on their faces. At one point Olson and Gerke reached across their capsules and gave one another a high five.

When the ride stopped and the Whalers disembarked, Olson admitted to being dizzy.

"When I stepped off," he said, "I was, 'Oh, which way is the ground going?'"

"That," chimed in Gerke, "was awesome."

Sanders raved about a more frightening ride. The feeling grew that the guys who took the greatest dares on the rides would be most likely to host a *Night of the Living Dead* movie festival. Apparently, Sanders had anted up $25 for the bungee jump.

"It was scary," Sanders said. "I screamed all the way down."

As they wandered the Fair, surprisingly often a player would hear a comment from a passerby up-to-date on Barrow football. A man wearing a Maine T-shirt yelled, "How do you like the new field?"

"Love it!" yelled back a few of the players.

This happened throughout the afternoon. The novelty of Barrow football, played above the Arctic Circle, certainly seemed to be well-known among Alaskans, or anyone who had been spending any time in Alaska recently.

"We're like celebrities," said Luke George, with a bit of disbelief in his voice.

Players kept checking their watches. They had a 4:00 P.M. rendezvous at the back gate to meet the coaches, since the Fair was not the only event on the day's agenda.

"If we had more time we could have more fun," grumbled Olson.

Mike Gonzales, Robert Vigo, and Anthony Edwards decided to bring some of the fun home with them. They each invested $5 to buy Chinese-style straw hats. They were great for keeping the sun off their faces at the Fair, but they seemed flimsy enough to be shredded by the first substantial gust of wind off the Arctic Ocean back home.

Coach Houston took one look at the approaching trio and couldn't decide whether to laugh, worry that the players were a walking affront to Chinese people, or just shake his head.

"You should be bending over picking rice," he said.

Their teammates laughed, but the tone in which Houston made the comment indicated perhaps they should be thinking about how hard people who wore those hats in daily life worked in the fields.

Robin Kaleak relayed a story about running into people who had seen a TV news item about Barrow and Cathy Parker Field. "We saw your field," they said. "It looks pretty nice." Kaleak assured them it was very nice indeed.

With certain exceptions, the coaches did not tell the players exactly what was planned each day on the road, or for what time. They had to stay fluid because of the availability of practice times and sites, and it was always a mini-military operation getting everyone loaded into vans to go eat.

Mothers who have young children know the syndrome well. There are always good intentions about getting out of the house in a timely manner. But then one toddler has to go to the bathroom, one kid can't find a shoe, and the third has thrown a hat under the bed. The same principles apply to organizing and mustering out twenty-one high school football players. It's always something. The vans eventually pull away, but destinations are not always reached with precision timing.

Coach Voss had scoped out the circumstances and happily discovered that there was a Friday night lights football game that evening at nearby Colony High School. Colony was playing South Anchorage in a large-schools game and he wanted the Whalers to watch.

"I wanted them to see the 'big boys' play," Voss said. "When you think about it, a lot of these guys have never seen a game they haven't played in."

He was right. In person, that is. The Mat-Su Valley, where the Whalers were roaming this day, had football-playing schools Palmer, Wasilla, Colony, and Houston within a dozen or so miles of one another—unlike Barrow, where the closest team was four hundred miles away. There would be no drop-in game watching on the North Slope. And the players were so new to the sport, outside of television, the majority of them had never seen an official game played involving other teams.

Colony had a real stadium, with fences and about two thousand fans in attendance. Admission was charged at the gate, though the players—who again received much attention from fans once it was realized they were in the house—got a student rate of $1. Sure enough, by the time carpooling Barrow arrived, the game was underway. No matter. It wasn't as if any of them were keeping play-by-play statistics. Voss just wanted his guys to see football.

Both clubs were solid teams. Not the best in the state, but early in the season they seemed to be contenders for league championships.

South Anchorage had an exceptional running game and worked over the Knights on the line of scrimmage for a while. They played on a real grass field, not something that would have thrived in Barrow. Voss took notice of the field's bright green sheen right away.

"I wonder how their field looks from the air," he said.

Well, not bright blue and yellow and probably not shiny new.

It was amazing how much attention the players got. Good wishes were collected everywhere they went, from the Fair to the field. Compliments on their new field were sprayed around generously. Alaskans know Barrow is the northernmost settlement in the country. The status is a special cachet, and not just for tourists. Even in many sections of Alaska, Barrow remains a somewhat mysterious place. Alaskans don't drive there, the key obstacle being no roads. Alaskans don't jet in just for the heck of it. Instead, they use vacation time to see relatives in big cities of the Lower 48. But Alaskans understood the challenges cold weather and distance presented to starting up a football team, and they were rooting for the kids from the Far North.

The Whalers cleared out before the final gun, anxious to miss the traffic, and finally to make it into their beds in their makeshift hostel in Houston. One vanload of players stopped at a convenience store off the Parks Highway between Colony and Houston, and the players raided the snack area for the usual cold drinks, chips, and cookies.

Forrest Akiviana, however, chose his own path, scooping up whole grain Power Bars. For the first time all day, one of the Whalers discussed nutrition. "I don't care if it tastes funny," Akiviana said, pointing to the Healthy Heart symbol on the wrapper. "It's good for you."

With an attitude like that, Akiviana could put the State Fair out of business.

## CHAPTER 19

# *Houston Hospitality*

GETTING OUT OF TOWN was good for the Whalers' egos. Whether it was the State Fair or the Colony football game, enough strangers approached for them to realize people around Alaska were following their story.

"Big John signed his first autograph today," Coach Mark Voss said aloud, half to tease his gentle giant.

"I didn't have a pen," Big John said.

Even if his job is to be fearsome on the field, intimidate with his size, and bash opponents with his muscle, left to his own nature Big John would probably never engage in contact except for hugs. Some people sense that trait in him immediately.

"Little kids love Big John," said Colton Blankenship.

Some people Cody Gleason bumped into on the day's journey were really into Barrow football. "They said we were famous," Gleason reported.

The accommodations at Houston High School consisted of a weight room off the main gymnasium. Athletes traveling in Alaska gain insight on their first trip. They know there is a trick to packing right. The floors are invariably going to be as hard as sidewalks, so it is important to not only carry a sleeping bag, but a sleeping bag cushion soft enough to ward off a backache. The truly wise understand that the best cushioning is provided by air mattresses.

Voss transported a double-wide air mattress that when pumped full of air stood a couple of feet off the floor. It looked big enough to use for floating the Mississippi River. By Bush travel improvisational standards, it was a piece of furniture fit for a palace.

Although there were only guys on this trip, a certain measure of modesty outside the shower room was called for. There was a creative bent to current teenage boys' sleepwear. Blankenship wore pajama pants paying homage to the University of Wyoming Cowboys, the main college in the state where he previously lived. Jim Martin had Simpsons pajamas. And Justin Sanders wore Snoopy pajama pants. It wasn't exactly *GQ*, but the fellows definitely showed off some color in their choice of trousers.

Voss said he imparted one general policy of wisdom that covered both attire and behavior. "If your grandmother wouldn't want to see it, don't do it," he said. "Like wearing butt-crack jeans."

The players set up their personal mini-camps around the room, mostly hugging walls. Some read. Some played computer games. Some blabbed with their neighbors. Robert Vigo tossed a football up and down while seated.

"I can't wait till tomorrow," he said. "Because it's game day."

Daniel Thomas revealed that since the season had begun, on each night before kickoff he dreamed about the game. "We always win the game," he said.

As those around him changed into pajamas, Blankenship was spied walking around the room in his No. 78 Whalers game jersey and pads. "No, no," he said. "Not to sleep in. I'm just getting them situated."

The coaches had claimed what they considered to be prime sleeping spots, clustered together along the walls and near a corner, giving the players a little space. "Don't sleep near me," Coach Houston warned.

Not many players wanted to, since the coach had the reputation of being an earthquake-instigating snorer. The goal for the night, Blankenship said, was "to fall asleep before Big B." Someone mentioned a need for earplugs.

Whenever he was around the Whalers, or attended a football game as he had earlier in the night, Houston's thoughts drifted back to his own playing days. He examined what had gone through his own mind when he was playing, and how to apply the lessons to this group of young men. When he was in college at New Haven, he said, one year the team advanced to the NCAA Division II playoffs. In a game against Jacksonville State, they trailed by a touchdown at halftime, and there were tears in his team's locker room.

"That's the kind of hunger I want to see from these guys," Houston said.

Lights-out came at 11:00 P.M., but there were still stirrings, still treks to the men's room, still giggling. "How long does it take for you to lie down?" Voss said to Mike Gonzales, sounding very much like a camp counselor.

There were whispered conversations, the rustling sounds of players turning over in their sleeping bags, the occasional cough. And then all was quiet except for some low-key mystery music of unknown origin and the electrical nighttime sounds of the building.

The coaches let the players sleep in, with a wake-up call for 9:00 A.M. Energetic from the get-go, some players ran pass routes in the gym. Others fooled around with a volleyball. Alastair Dunbar smacked a volleyball off the wall. Going to the pro circuit?

"I wish," he said, laughing.

Dunbar, a sophomore, was a wide dude appropriately stationed on the defensive line. He was usually smiling, and was the type of player characterized as a "locker room guy," meaning he was good for team chemistry and interacting with different groups. It was easy to see that he might emerge as a full-fledged team social director (currently a Gonzales specialty) as he moved up in grades. He had long been passionate about playing basketball, Dunbar said, but that was changing. He was probably the slowest runner on this team, but his body seemed more cut out for football.

"I was thinking about basketball and football in college," he said, "but basketball is a dying dream."

There was much horsing around. Players did not have game faces on yet. Luke George put Zac Rohan in a headlock and announced, "I want to be a tackle today." Then he went into a rap of sorts. "I'm not a tackle. I want to be a guard today. I'm not a guard. Maybe a nose guard." Whatever, the words were not exactly poetry.

Coaches Houston, Igou, and Arnhart huddled on one side of the room reviewing game strategy. Arnhart had every Barrow formation and variation in his laptop. Igou wrote things out by hand. Houston kept information in his head.

Gonzales and Keifer Kanayurak grappled in an impromptu wrestling match. That seemed like a senseless pregame injury waiting to happen.

"You guys should stop," Dunbar said. They disengaged. "Thank God."

Forrest Ahkiviana reclined on his air mattress reading a science fiction book. Not everyone was completely alert yet. Mike Olson angled for every moment of shut-eye. Quarterback Albert Gerke still huddled under the covers. Gerke, who had made the varsity basketball team as a freshman the year before, was very used to roughing it on hard floors.

"I finally got a mattress," Gerke said. "I had trouble sleeping a lot last year."

The late snoozers perked up for meal call. Houston volunteers, mothers or Hawk boosters, provided breakfast. The menu wiped the sleep right out of the Whalers' eyes. There were eggs, biscuits and gravy, burritos, bagels, muffins, corned beef hash, cereal, watermelon, donuts. "That's a serious breakfast," Voss said.

Dozing in comfort only moments before, Olson smiled. "They have everything," he said. "I'm happy."

Ahkiviana lobbied a teammate to use a plate for his eats, praising the merits of etiquette. "We don't want them to think we're savages," he said.

"We do!" chimed in Tim Barr, thinking that maybe the Whalers could psych out the Hawks players with uncivilized table behavior. Not that there were any opposing players present. "Rumors spread," Barr added.

After breakfast it was time to focus the team on business, to get those wandering minds concentrating on football. The coaches gathered the players in an empty classroom near the gym. Most of the players were seated by the time Olson walked in the door.

"Hello, class," he said.

It was class. Coach Igou pounded on one point as if he were driving nails. Over and over he had tried to get the message through since two-a-days, but it was still a problem. When the ball was hiked, the Whalers did not react quickly enough. They did not pay the price in the win over Seward, but they got smoked by Eielson at least partially because they were slow at the snap and maybe lacking confidence beneath a sheen of false bravado.

"We started believing the hype after Seward," Igou said. "But we need to believe in ourselves. You need to come off the ball. And you guys have got to go until the whistle blows. You've got to keep pursuing."

Really, cutting through the verbiage, much of the problem was fundamentals and experience. Line up correctly, fire off the ball swiftly, don't let up. Basic stuff really, but a point to hammer for a new, young team.

Arnhart had the scouting report on Houston's tendencies. The Hawks also seemed as if they would be one of the Greatland Conference's most formidable teams this season.

"They pass the ball 70 percent of the time, but they can run," Arnhart said. "We've got to start hitting people every play. We can't be passive. We are going to run it down their throats. We are bigger and stronger than they are."

Arnhart summed up Barrow offensive keys: "Run—Come off the ball. Pass—Give the quarterback time."

There was still time to kill and chill. Huddling in a corner, Anthony Edwards pulled the hood of his gray sweatshirt over his head and put on his game face that said, "Leave me alone."

Some players finished dressing and participated in an informal walk-through of plays on the field, which was just outside the door to the gym.

"Justin," Igou said to Sanders, eyeing his uniform. "Where is your belt?"

The trademark yellow Barrow belt was not around Sanders's waist holding his pants up. "Ah," he said, "no wonder if felt funny."

Some Barrow parents who had flown into Anchorage, and just driven into Houston, showed up at the school. Dunbar's relatives arrived. Trent Blankenship, who had been in Anchorage on school district business, appeared.

"Coach," he asked Voss, "how can I help?" Voss faced the superintendent with a deadpan look and said, "Shoot a couple of theirs with a tranquilizer dart."

Blankenship was unarmed, except with philosophy. Given that he had initiated the program and that he had a son on the team, he was probably the most devoted Whaler fan. He got excited on game days, and he was ever ready to defend the program if anybody raised the issue of it being too expensive. The gift of the field, the nationwide publicity from media outlets like ESPN and *Nightline,* and the by-all-measures successful Seward game celebration had solidified his confidence.

"The amount of money is really not any more than we would spend on any other sport," Blankenship had taken to saying, explaining that was because the football team was scheduled for what turned out to be seven games, compared to the twenty-something for basketball.

"It's the same cost per kid," he said. "It's a plane ticket. We've got Title IX covered with girls volleyball, basketball, cheerleading, and running cross-country. Flag football, that might be something we'd like to look at. Football is successful. If (critics) can't see it's been good for the kids and if they can't see it's been good for the climate of the school, I don't know what else I can say."

He could say, Are you ready for some football?

Voss was succinct in his final message to the team. "Gentlemen, you've got a good opportunity right here," he said.

It was a league game that, dare-anybody-say-it, could position the Whalers nicely in the standings for playoff consideration.

Houston had more to say. He went into his big-picture act. His messages would seem equally at home coming out of the mouth of Vince Lombardi or Billy Graham. He stressed motivation to the Whalers.

"Motivation is the will to do something to the absolute best of one's ability," Houston said. "Motivated men are fearless. They never compromise. Motivation is about taking pride in being a Whaler. Motivation is about taking pride in being an upstanding member of our community. They invited us for homecoming today. You know they always invite teams to homecoming they think they can beat. They invited the wrong team today."

The crowd was sparse for the 2:00 P.M. kickoff. The weather was mild compared to Barrow, but it just might have been that Hawk supporters thought Saturday afternoon was better invested at the State Fair. That was probably true—for Barrow fans.

If anything the players learned all week in practice or had instilled in them during chalk talk that morning had been absorbed, it did not do any good. The Houston Hawks took a 7–0 lead in the first quarter and kept building on it. 14–0. 21–0. 27–0. 34–0. Most of the damage was done in the first half. Once again the Whalers on defense looked more like matadors waving the bull past, rather than digging in for solid hits.

The bright spot in the score changing to 34–7 was a leaping catch in the end zone on a fifteen-yard completion, Gerke to Justin Sanders. Sanders has good hands and good hops, and if the ball is in the air near him the chances are good he is coming down with it.

There was some enthusiastic pursuit, as the coaches had requested—but there was way too much pursuing necessary, as Hawk ballcarriers burst into the clear to set up touchdowns. At one point, Romine caught a pass for a good gain, was hit hard, and didn't get up. Eventually, he was helped off the field by Voss and Igou, favoring his right leg. Although Romine went back in four minutes later, he had a freshly sprained ankle to contend with.

Whether it was because he was so immersed in the game, or because his frustration was mounting—or both—six-foot-five, 280-pound Colton Blankenship began issuing guttural growls as he made hits. In a brief moment of levity in a generally hopeless cause, Voss found himself standing next to Trent Blankenship on the sideline as Colton briefly spoke bear language.

"Whose kid is that?" Voss said.

"That's new," said father Blankenship.

Later, Colton Blankenship explained.

"I just do it out of fury in the game," he said. "I get angry."

It was 41–7 with about three and a half minutes left in the fourth quarter when the Whalers pulled off what would stand as one of the sweetest plays of the season.

The snap went to Gerke, as usual. He flipped a lateral to Austin Fishel, but instead of racing downfield, Fishel grabbed the ball and flung a twenty-yard touchdown pass to Jim Martin. It was a beauty of a play to take satisfaction from, but the final score was 48–13, not so dissimilar from the Eielson romp.

Gerke was under considerable defensive pressure all day, and took some sacks and hits just as he released the ball. His uniform was marked with grass stains, something he did not experience on the artificial turf in Barrow.

"I'm going to be sore tomorrow," Gerke predicted.

During the postgame team huddle-up on the field, the spirit seemed sapped from the players and the coaches instantly sensed this was not the time for criticism. "Good job in the second half," Arnhart said.

Voss said despite the outcome he saw good things, especially in the second half. "Hold your heads up high," he said. "You started coming together as a team."

It is always more fun to overcome mistakes within games that are won than to take lumps in games with scores that register sound beatings. The Whalers had only been gone from home for two days, but the thoroughness of the beating magnified emotions.

Suddenly a little bit teary-eyed, Voss thanked the team for being so supportive of him over the last couple of days since his grandmother passed away. It had been a tough time for him, he said. He knew it was a tough time for the players, as well, losing big like this.

Then Voss blurted out, "Just hug each other and me." The entire team rushed him at once, creating a multicar pileup as much as a group hug and then when he realized what he had instigated, Voss said, "Oh, crap."

The Whalers were 1–2 and they were flying home to Barrow, Chinese hats in hand from the State Fair (hoping they didn't get crushed as carry-ons). It is often said that until a team travels together it is not yet really a team, that the bonding pays off with shared experiences.

The Whalers would find out if the road helped them or not. The Whalers would find out if the players left behind in Barrow still felt part of the team. The next game was at home against Nikiski. Although nearly twenty years had passed since the debacle, Nikiski was the team on the receiving end of the most humiliating score in Alaska football history during its first season of varsity play, that 89–0 mashing at the hands of Soldotna.

Nikiski was not a preseason Greatland title contender, but the Bulldogs were a solid team. They clearly posed a threat to reeling Barrow. But the Whalers didn't want anyone else jumping into their ocean in victory.

CHAPTER 20

# *Home on the Tundra Again*

WITH LUCK, AND A TOUCH OF WHIMSY, the Barrow football minibus will become an icon of Whaler football. It is on its way. With a little bit of time, effort, and public relations, it may emerge as one of the most identifiable football support vehicles in the nation.

Bill Rohan, father of player Zac, may not yet be mentioned in the same breath as Henry Ford, but he is at least deserving of comparison to John DeLorean. The Barrow Mobile is a work of heart and a work of art.

Rohan converted the easily parallel-parked four-wheeler into an imitation bus smaller than a Hummer. The vehicle is yellow, has the words "School Bus" written on the front, has a sign on the driver's side reading "Stop" that pops out, but it has an open air top where the driver can stand up and cheer at a game. Oh yeah, and the faux "driver" is a fully dressed dummy in a yellow jersey masquerading as a Barrow football player. It is as if the phony player is dressed in a Halloween mask under its football helmet.

Rohan, who drives the bus to home games, gives rides to fans and roots for the team from his perch above the dummy. It is also far from a finished model. Rohan said he plans to enlarge the bus to accommodate several players at once and to decorate the tinted side windows.

"I'm going to put pictures from this season on the windows," he said.

Given that the bus has the horsepower of perhaps one Budweiser Clydesdale and doesn't have heat, the chances are slim that despite any temptations, the bus will ever make a road trip of four hundred miles or so across the tundra.

"Uh, no," Rohan said.

The calendar had just spilled over into September, but already the Whalers were facing their fourth opponent. School was open and underway, and Trent Blankenship was pleased to report that enrollment reached 297. Did that mean Barrow was retaining more high school kids, that there were more kids willing to keep trying, or that there were simply more kids coming of age for high school? Blankenship didn't know. He only knew one thing for sure on that topic at the start of the school year.

"It's the highest we can remember," he said. "And tardiness, disciplinary actions, and absenteeism have declined."

After traveling with twenty-one players, Coach Voss wanted to make sure his numbers were back up at practice. There did not seem to be particular resentment among players left behind for one reason or another. Many understood and did not dispute where they ranked on the depth chart.

Freshman linebacker Joe Burke said he had not expected to make the travel squad, and spent some of his idle time on the preceding Saturday trying to find out what had happened in the Whalers' game.

"It's my first year. I don't really know all the plays," Burke said of one thing holding him back. "I was wondering if they won, but I never found out. On Sunday my brothers told me."

Dane Enoch, seventeen, the younger of the Enoch brothers, did not make the journey, either. As someone whose family has moved around a lot—he spent half the preceding school year in Germany and half in Barrow—he felt he was still getting used to the sport, and that after attending several small schools that never would have fielded football teams he was lucky to be able to play at all. Staying home from a game was something he could cope with.

"It didn't bum me out all that bad," Enoch said. "I thought of it as a win–win situation. Either I got to go or I could hang out and spend time with my girlfriend. The coaches told us that if we didn't make this road trip there would be other opportunities."

Enoch said his brother Denver had one goal for them to complete that could make a lifetime memory. "Denver's biggest dream is for us to sack the quarterback together," Dane Enoch said. "I would love to do that."

Sophomore Mikey Stotts was a third player who had to stay in Barrow rather than play in Houston and he, like Burke, exhibited the type of attitude the coaches wanted to see. He was another football novice and he hoped to grow into the game, both in size and knowledge, and force his way onto the travel team.

"It didn't really upset me," Stotts said. "I just wanted to know if they won or not. I didn't find out the score until later that night."

Freshman Nathan Snow, fourteen, another stay-at-home player, whose previous involvement with football was in a middle school physical education class, was still adapting to the sport.

"It just seemed like it would be fun to play," Snow said. "But everything is faster in a game. You have to work harder."

The gang was back together for practice the afternoon before the Nikiski game. Once again it was sunny and unseasonably warm. A heat wave in Barrow at the beginning of September meant the thermometer was cracking 50°F with an arrow pointing up.

"Every Friday it's warm before our games and then Saturday it's not," observed Burke, who apparently had a little meteorologist in him.

He was right, though. That seemed to be the pattern. Barrow couldn't stand more than one nice day in a row without reverting to form. Just about anything could be expected from Arctic Fall, even if it was still summer on the calendar. The odds were probably about the same that the Whalers would wake up on game day on the first Saturday in September with a temperature of 32°F, or freezing, as residents of, say, Los Angeles or Atlanta would wake up the same day and read 90°F on their thermometers.

But hey, for the moment it was nice out.

"Eskimo summer," Voss said sardonically.

While Romine had toughed it out by returning to the Houston game after twisting his ankle, it was a lingering problem. After the game, that night in an Anchorage hotel room, it took two hours for him to fall asleep because it was throbbing. Back in Barrow, after a couple of days of practice, the ankle acted up again, waking him in the middle of the night.

"It just hurts all of the time," Romine said, shrugging.

Then he jumped back into practice. The football warrior mentality is either innate or influenced nationwide at all levels of the game by televised pros who suck it up after injury and return to the field.

During some of the drills at Cathy Parker Field, about a third of the team watched. But teens being teens, they were not rapt pupils for every second. Sometimes they behaved like kids in a classroom with the teacher out of the room, acting silly for no real purpose.

Slightly built Van Edwardsen twirled a football up and down in front of him. Twice-as-large Alastair Dunbar said, "The ball." "No," Edwardsen replied to the demand. Dunbar drew himself up to his full 265 pounds and stared at Edwardsen and his 135 pounds. Edwardsen kept the ball. What we had here was a failure to intimidate. Suddenly, Dunbar reached over and poked the ball free of Edwardsen's hands, stealing it using guile rather than power.

Robert Vigo, looking for a play-catch partner, threw a ball to Cody Gleason. It hit Gleason in the leg. "It's sunny," Gleason said. "I can't see."

It was like a baseball player claiming he lost a ground ball in the sun.

Watching the ball ricochet off Gleason's leg, Dane Enoch felt compelled to add a sarcastic observation: "Cody, I don't know how you catch, but I use my arms."

Ganina Pili watched the goings-on with a slightly removed look, as if to say, "Don't lump me in with these immature boys." She was asked if girls were just as goofy as guys on the sidelines of their games. "No," Pili said. "Just different goofy."

Probably so.

Vigo spit some sunflower seeds in her direction. After trying to ignore the gesture of affection, Pili just said, "Quit it."

Pili admitted that she was having fun playing football, even if she was the only girl, but that her girlfriends still thought she was a bit loony for throwing herself into this mix.

Big John, who often seemed to suffer some minor injury indignity, came off the field suffering from stomach problems and had trouble swallowing. It was hard to tell if this was early warning signals of the flu or some passing intestinal disorder.

The regular postpractice gathering at midfield included a fuel advisory from Voss, who urged his players to wake up at 8:00 A.M. and eat smartly. Oatmeal, pancakes, waffles were on the highly recommended list.

"Just make sure you've got some fuel," Voss said.

The event was being hailed as Homecoming, another Lower-48 tradition that Barrow was importing. So it seemed cool to host a bonfire on the beach. Fire, however, was not the type of fuel Voss was endorsing interaction with the night before a game. Well aware that he had a team of frisky, fun-loving players who were just as susceptible to foolish, unthinking dopey acts as any other teenagers hanging out with friends, Voss wanted to set some parameters.

Voss knew that without a football team there would be no Homecoming. Heck, center Mike Gonzales was a candidate for Homecoming King, so it wasn't as if the players were aloof from the festivities. Voss knew without football there would be no bonfire, either, and that both events could engage the student body and the community at large. Voss did not want his players to be reclusive, since this was a way of bonding with the rest of Barrow in a highly visible manner that could increase team support.

Voss looked around at the players spread out around him, some on one knee, some sitting down.

"You should be home warming your tootsies up by ten o'clock," he said.

Being wiseasses at heart it was inevitable that someone ask, "Or else?" But knowing that was coming, Voss cut off the question before it was issued.

"Being on the beach fooling around is a no-no," he said. "I don't want somebody spraining an ankle on the sand. If that happens, Coach Igou might have to put a foot up some part of your anatomy."

Justin Sanders, who earlier in the season had been singled out by the coaches as the model hardworking player and served as a cocaptain, wanted a rare turn at the microphone for a minute.

Sanders is dark-skinned, with slightly wild hair. Sanders is sleek, but not necessarily in a football way. He seems too thin, but he has football instincts that put him in the right place and keep him around the ball, and is both well-liked and respected by his teammates. If Sanders had something to say, they were going to listen. If he wanted to say something to the team at the end of practice, the players knew it was because he felt strongly about it, not because he wanted to get in the last word as a joke aimed at the coaches.

"Play your hardest," Sanders said to a quiet crowd recently stung by demoralizing, take-them-down-a-peg defeats to Eielson and Houston. "I'm tired of losing. Aren't you tired of losing? I don't want to lose at home."

It had gone unmentioned that because of Barrow's location the schedule had been made top-heavy with home games to avoid the chance of intersecting with the worst possible weather. As a by-product of being situated at the Top of the World, where winter might start tomorrow, the Nikiski encounter was the last home game of the year. It was crazy that that could be true on September 8, but there it was. The high school powers-that-be in the Greatland Conference didn't mind including Barrow in the league, but they were not anxious to play in games when it might be twenty degrees, windy, and snowing.

Yet for all of the genuine worries about cold in Barrow, the fact was that residents were still wondering if global warming was warming up their region. There was no sign that the Arctic Ocean was freezing over yet. And with the price of gasoline rocketing over $3 per gallon in the Lower 48, once again attempts were percolating to try to open up drilling for more oil in the Beaufort and Chukchi seas. That was really close to home. How would that affect the return of bowhead whales? The seals? The fishing?

Shell Oil owned offshore leases in the Beaufort Sea and was poised to invest hundreds of millions of dollars to drill. Opponents fought back based on the endangered nature of the bowhead. A court order had been issued a couple of weeks earlier to prevent the exploration temporarily, but it was still a live issue and very much on the minds of wary Barrow residents.

There had been much more attention Outside focused on the Arctic National Wildlife Refuge and the migration of caribou herds, but for the people of Barrow an oil spill that washed up to their beach could be even more tragic. And it might not even take a spill to disrupt bowhead whale hunting.

"We just don't know what would happen," Big Bob Aiken said.

The oil exploration was seen as a financial bonanza by some and as a threat to a way of life by others. Aiken was correct. There were no guarantees of what would happen. What would the future of the Iñupiat people be like if they woke up one spring day and discovered the bowhead whale was never coming back?

Maybe Jim Martin was right after the Eielson loss, when the Ravens jumped in the water, that the Arctic Ocean was worth defending in all ways.

Voss took up the theme of defending homecourt, winning for the home fans, and yes, keeping the Bulldogs out of the Whalers' Arctic Ocean.

"Not in our pond," Voss said, modifying the often-uttered sports phrase "not in our house," used by so many teams as motivation for home victories. "There aren't going to be any more dips in the ocean celebrating from anyone not wearing blue and gold."

The beach where the bonfire was lighted for Homecoming later on that surprisingly cozy night was littered with bleached whale bones left over from the harvest that were the size of wooden ceiling beams, and the shells of umiaqs minus their sealskin coverings. They were remnants of the hunt. The pieces of the bowhead dispersed on the beach were reminders of why the football team was called the Whalers.

No one got into trouble at the bonfire.

CHAPTER 21

# *Making It All Work*

STANDING AT THE GREASEBOARD in an empty classroom down the hall from the makeshift dressing facilities, inside otherwise abandoned Barrow High School on the sharply cold September morning, Coach Igou drew up plays.

"If you play the game the way you played the second half at Houston last week, we'll kick their butts," Igou said. "Hit 'em in the mouth every single time."

This was good advice for the Whalers, who seemed a bit yawny and sluggish at the 9:30 A.M. gathering. Being slow off the ball at the snap meant that the Whalers often did not make initial hard contact blocking or trying to tackle. The hit-them-in-the-mouth theme was not literal, but reminded the players you don't get anywhere in football without collisions with the other guys.

It's not that Nikiski, on the Kenai Peninsula, about 160 miles south of Anchorage, is located in the banana belt, but the Whalers at least subconsciously felt that crappy weather of 35°F, windy and misting, would aid them.

Coach Arnhart took a turn.

"Today, let's have four good quarters," he began. "They blitz a lot up the middle. Let's protect our quarterback."

This was Coach Houston territory. They were putting responsibility on his linemen.

"You know they're going to blitz," he said, emphasizing his booming voice with a pointing finger as he often did. "You have to communicate. You have to be the baddest ass and the biggest dick on the block."

Pili excepted, of course.

Arnhart modified the direct talk.

"You've got to be a man," he said. "Go 100 mph all day."

Coach Voss took over. His talk was philosophical more than specific.

"Ain't gonna be any hoppin' in the water today," Voss said of Nikiski. "Get your mind right, boys."

There were still two hours to kickoff, and the coaches let the players mingle quietly. Cody Romine put on earphones and lay on a table facedown. Luke George lay down on the next table. Robert Vigo lay facedown on the thinly carpeted floor. Daniel Thomas sat in a corner with his headphones on. Trevor Litera chewed sunflower seeds.

This was all inner sanctum stuff, preparation that should have been unfolding in a locker room. But since there was no locker room, this classroom would just have to do. There was another peculiarity: the season was only half over, and it felt odd for this to be the last home game.

The players chilled, but the coaches talked among themselves. Their minds were right.

"They run that little Statue of Liberty play," Arnhart warned Houston.

"We should tackle everyone in the backfield today," Houston answered. He was not above playing little psych games to get his men mentally prepared.

"It's nice out!" Houston announced to the room.

"No, it's freezing out," Mac Rock said.

Houston wouldn't let him get away with that attitude.

"Today is the perfect day," he said.

How so? Well, because it was game day, and every game day was the perfect day because you were playing football.

Rock helped Forrest Ahkiviana adjust his shoulder pads just so. Some players tossed a football back and forth in the narrow hallway.

During the week you could probably get detention for doing that. Now it was just burning off nervous energy.

John Wilson walked in wearing a jersey and blue jeans. He was off crutches, but still couldn't play. Wilson said he still needed six more weeks of rehab. His season was definitely over.

"I miss putting on my pads," Wilson said.

Mark Gonzales worked diligently to cut out the palms of a pair of gloves. The adaptation provided a better skin grip while still protecting the knuckles. Colton Blankenship studied the creative cloth work and said, "You'll work for Nike some day."

Houston returned to work at the greaseboard. While holding a dictionary he wrote: "CHARACTER, a man of sound moral excellence and firmness." That was the definition according to *Webster's*.

Unfortunately, down the hall, Big John Lambrecht was throwing up into a trash can. It would be easy to write off the reaction to simple nerves—after all, Bill Russell, the leader of the Boston Celtics' dynasty of champions in the 1950s and 1960s, vomited in the locker room before every game. However, this was more likely a case of stomach flu. That is not the ideal condition to take into a football game.

The players gathered again.

"We saw you guys turn a corner last week," Houston said. "We need to see some true character today. Today is our day. I know it. I feel it."

A guest pastor stepped into the room and, choosing a familiar, but totally inappropriate topic for a mini-sermon, talked about a house divided against itself. Huh? There were no divisions on the Whalers. He talked about a kingdom divided being destroyed and a team divided being already defeated. All well and good, but none of that had anything to do with the unified Barrow team. It wasn't as if the Whalers had a Latrell Sprewell on the roster.

Once again it was left to Coach Voss to pull together all of the verbiage. He talked of having a football dream about a team that went out on the field and made no mistakes. "No mistakes," he said. "No mistakes. That's what's going to win the game for you today."

Romine was still lying down.

"Did he sleep through the whole thing?" Ganina Pili asked.

Maybe so. Or at least he did a good job of faking it.

In full uniform, the players marched from the building to the bus. Mike Olson had headphones on and was bopping to the tunes. A blue truck was parked near the door and someone had written the words "El Gonzo" into the dust coating it. You didn't need to read the registration to know it belonged to Mike Gonzales.

"We mess with him all the time," Wilson said.

At 10:45 A.M. the bus rolled into a foggy morning. The landscape looked bleak on the gray day.

"Hush!" Houston ordered, wanting players to stop joking and to start thinking football only.

When the Whalers pulled up to the field and exited the bus, George paused to hand Houston his asthma inhaler. It was one of the patterns the team always followed. Big John's glasses lived on Voss's dashboard, and George's inhaler lived in Houston's pocket just in case it was needed during the game.

The "other" Barrow bus, Bill Rohan's creation, naturally was on the scene. One thing that vehicle would never do was get into a drag race.

"I can only do about twenty," Rohan said.

There had been a lot of talking this season, a lot of planning, a lot of drilling. But all of the scrimmaging and studying had not added up to a lot of victories. Coach Houston was right, though. This day felt different.

Quarterback Albert Gerke was the engineer as Barrow paraded down the field on its first possession. With running back Anthony Edwards dashing left, the Whalers culminated the drive with a twenty-five-yard touchdown run. 6–0. Being ahead felt good.

Nikiski, which brought twenty players north, including one on crutches, made its own offensive push, scoring a touchdown. Barrow got the ball back and discovered that Edwards was just as open this time as the last. He scampered sixty-five yards for another six-pointer, and at the end of the first quarter the Whalers led, 14–6. Things were clicking. Things were translating from the coaches' mouths to the players' feet.

Fans, from the elders bundled up in the bleachers, to the students dressed too skimpily because they were teenagers and believed they were invulnerable to the cold, cheered and clapped. Shouts of "Aarigaa!" mixed with howls. How nice, indeed.

One antsy spectator was Taylor Elbert, like Wilson exiled to the disabled list, because of the balky ankle.

"Sitting on the sidelines is killing me," Elbert said. "Next season I'll be ready to go."

The Whalers were ready to go right then and there. The Bulldogs fought back and claimed a 15–14 lead in the second quarter. There were some key fumbles, and that was the only indication the players were bothered by the cold, though it's never easy to tell exactly what causes a fumble outside of a direct hit. As a courtesy to fans, school buses ran out to Cathy Parker Field from downtown, but even better, the buses stayed at the game and kept their engines running. If fans got too shivery, and they didn't mind missing a few plays, they could retreat to a bus to warm up for a while. Behind the orange fencing, behind one end zone, fans who had arrived early and planned ahead sat in their cars watching. But hundreds of fans sat out in the wind and just accepted the conditions. Windchill hassles in early September? It was just Barrow being Barrow.

Anyone who could not wait out the clock and fled to a bus to warm up before the half, however, missed the most important play of the game. Nikiski was deep in Barrow territory, trying to put one more touchdown on the board before the intermission, when a Bulldog player fumbled. The alert Edwards, showing he could handle the pigskin just as well on defense as offense, scooped up the loose ball and legged it seventy-seven yards for a Whaler touchdown. The play gave Barrow a 20–15 halftime lead.

A perfect momentum setter. Barrow players charged off the field with fresh enthusiasm, climbing onto their own bus serving as a half-time locker room. All but one Barrow player, that is. Mike Gonzales hung around for the halftime Homecoming festivities. Sure enough, Gonzales had been elected Homecoming King.

Standing on the field, next to his dad, Chato, Gonzales held his football helmet in one hand while a soft, blue velvet crown was placed upon his head. Factoring in the State Fair Chinese hat and his helmet, Gonzales was definitely a man of many hats.

Spectators applauded, Gonzales posed for pictures with the Homecoming Queen, then shed the crown, handed it to his dad, said, "I've got to go," and ran for the Whalers' bus to be with his teammates.

The ceremony didn't last very long. Barrow Homecoming was not to be confused with either the pageantry or length of the Orange Bowl's halftime show, the longest in captivity. Maybe with a little bit more practice.

On the bus, Voss told the players to be ready because he expected Nikiski to try to pass more in the second half. The sky spit intermittently during the first half, but not enough to really bug a quarterback. *Where was the rain when he needed it?* Voss mused.

Fans who watched the game from their cars developed an interesting way of showing their appreciation for a good play. They beeped their horns. Either the officials or Nikiski took exception to the practice, because the public address announcer asked drivers to refrain from repeating their beeps—as if that was more annoying than smacking together thundersticks.

On Nikiski's first possession of the second half, the Bulldogs did indeed, as Voss predicted, show pass. Only Gerke was better positioned than the receiver and intercepted the ball. The next time down the field, Nikiski tested the Whalers' defense every way possible. Repeatedly, as the Bulldogs' back dove toward the line, he was met by defensive tackle Jason Ruckle. Ruckle, a soft-spoken member of the team whose own mother can barely get him to talk, brought a singular ferociousness to this game. His contributions, as many linemen's are, were subtle to the average observer, except when he figured big on a goal-line stand.

Meanwhile, the Whalers could not duplicate their offensive success of the first half. They reverted to committing too many rinky-dink penalties. Or at least they were whistled for illegal procedure and offside more often than fans yelled, "Let's go!" This development drove the coaches batty.

After a second five-yard penalty in a row, Houston yelled, "Are you kidding me? Are you serious?" It was not immediately clear if he was venting at the officials or his own players, and he didn't seem approachable at the moment to find out.

There was almost no smooth ball movement in the third quarter, and Gerke ended it with another interception. The fourth quarter evolved into a circus of turnover trading, a fumble here, an interception there. Gerke dropped the ball on one play, and on Nikiski's first play from scrimmage after that, intercepted it right back, his third pick of the game. Romine made an interception. Edwards committed a fumble. As the game wound down, with the Bulldogs seeming fully capable of pulling off a last-minute snatch of the result, one more fumble ruined them.

Forrest Ahkiviana grabbed the bouncing ball and rumbled fifty yards for the game-clinching touchdown. Barrow 27, Nikiski 15. Boy, that score sure looked pretty. As the final seconds ticked off the clock, Whalers jumped up and down on the sidelines and roared.

"I love it!" shouted Houston.

"Excellent job," Igou said.

Lots of kudos. Vigo came up with two quarterback sacks at crucial times that ruined Nikiski's drives. Edwards, who took over the extra point kicking, scored twenty-one points.

"It feels so much better than losing, doesn't it?" Voss asked his team.

Cornered, Ruckle talked briefly about halting Nikiski inside the 5-yard line.

"The defensive stops were big," he said. "That just turned the game around. I'm very satisfied."

Everyone in Whaler Nation was.

Gerke had not played a perfect game on offense, but more than made up for it on defense. He caught as many Nikiski passes as any intended Bulldog receiver. He said he just had the mind-set on coverage that, "It's my ball. It's my ball."

It was really Ahkiviana's ball, actually. Glory for linemen, even on the defensive side, is rare. Touchdowns are for running backs, quarterbacks, and wide receivers. A lineman can play football for more than twenty years, through high school, college, and the NFL, and even be chosen for the Hall of Fame, without ever scoring a touchdown.

Imagine Ahkiviana's glee when he found the ball in his hands and an open field in front of him. His first thought was, *Oh, my God. What is this? Where did this come from?*

But he knew which direction to run in.

So did Edwards, all day long. Still only a sophomore, having just turned sixteen, Edwards flashed the mix of power and speed packed in his 208-pound body that promises to make him a future star. He never pictured himself scoring so much.

"I'm shocked," Edwards said. "They (the line) opened holes and just led me to the touchdowns. I was just reading their plays over and over and thought, 'I know what you're doing.'"

For once, the Whalers skipped jumping into the water after a win. So many of the players, from Big John (who endured through the game) on down, were sick, getting sick, or afraid they would get sick, the last thing they needed was catching a chill after a dunk in the frigid Arctic Ocean.

Instead, players called for a rendezvous later that night at Arctic Pizza. Over pepperoni, cheese, and sausage they could replay the big plays and celebrate victory. They did not want to let the day go.

CHAPTER 22

# *Delta Force*

AS THE CELEBRATING COMMENCED following the Nikiski win, Colton Blankenship paused. "We got Delta next week?" he half-asked, half-stated. "Awesome."

Coach Arnhart confirmed and noted the significance. "Revenge," he said.

The year before, when Barrow introduced football, the first-ever opponent on the schedule in the first-ever high school football game played above the Arctic Circle was Delta Junction. The result was a 34–0 bruising. The topic is still a little bit raw.

Delta Junction is a speck of a town on the Alaska Highway about a hundred miles south of Fairbanks. Things looked considerably different entering this game. Delta players had graduated, players were hurt, and there had been suspensions. The coach was fired. It had been a plagues-of-Egypt season for the Huskies.

Two weeks before the Barrow game, Delta Junction forfeited a game because in the minds of its coaches it didn't have enough players to safely field a team. The team resumed competition a week later, but really, almost until the Whalers boarded planes to leave Barrow, there was a little doubt that the game would come off.

In the interests of the budget, Barrow High worked out parallel travel plans with Fairbanks-based Frontier Airlines instead of Alaska Airlines. One group flew directly to Fairbanks. A smaller group rode a smaller plane and made a stop in picturesque but very remote Anaktuvuk Pass, a beautiful community in the foothills of the Brooks

Range. Voss had once taught there. The combo plan allowed the coach to take twenty-five players on the road this time, though he waited till the last moment to announce who was going.

"I was real happy," said defensive back Forrest Enlow II with a big smile. "I didn't know it."

Mac Rock, who didn't expect to make the journey, either, stayed up late hustling to wash his slightly moldy game equipment and to pack. He also had to get parent approval papers signed. The guy barely slept scrambling to get ready for the Thursday morning flight.

Voss was glad he could bring some fresh faces on the trip. It was always good to have a couple of extra players if things went haywire with injuries or something. But more importantly, it was better for team camaraderie, and good to give young players experience. "I want to keep their interest up," Voss said. "This allows me to bring some kids who are a little marginal in their playing time."

Participation is supposed to be the point of it all in Barrow football, so upping the travel list slightly was just part of that big picture. Voss worried that without any more home games, if some kids knew they wouldn't make the travel cut for the rest of the season they might quit. Yet he couldn't honestly choose inferior players over more deserving ones. That would impact the team's ability to win and it would be unfair to the more talented players. So taking a few more players was a win–win deal.

"For kids who have been on the sidelines, this time I get a chance to give them a little expanded playing time," Voss said.

The wild card in the travel arrangements was Ganini Pili. The lone girl on the team made the travel roster for Delta Junction. While this was a testament to her athletic ability and a reward for her steady practice and play, it created logistical dilemmas. This was a sixteen-year-old girl taking a two-day overnight trip with twenty-four boys of her age, and under school auspices.

Voss was not winging it. He was a stickler on the preplanning. First, he telephoned Pili's mother, Seesei, and talked about the situation. He pretty much pledged his life to protect her little girl. He promised mom that Pili would have private quarters if she wanted them; otherwise she could set up her bedding with the coaches, away from the boys.

"Her mom is OK with it," Voss said. "I needed to be able to tell her parents she would be in a secure place."

Voss telephoned the principal at Delta Junction and explained the deal. He said he needed to have an extra room where the door could be closed and locked. The school officials said no problem.

"She deserves to go," Voss said. "She deserves to be here just like the guys. She's missed one practice all year."

A more surprising good-news traveler was linebacker Jarid Hope. His leg healed, he rejoined the team for practice in midweek, and Voss said it was as if he had never missed a day working out. Hope said that the first couple of weeks on crutches he felt hopeless, and now here he was, back with the team, on the road to Delta Junction.

"I didn't think I was ever going to play again in high school," Hope said. "I'm pretty happy. And I'm hoping for it," referring to payback to Delta.

Voss seemed to have mixed emotions about how much of a grudge match this game was with the Huskies. Given that the 2006 contest was Barrow's first ever, losing by thirty-four points was not totally unexpected, yet he also wanted to show how far the Whalers had come.

"They were gentlemen," Voss said of Delta the previous year. "They didn't take it easy on us, but they didn't run up the score. But, ah, I want to go beat Delta."

How much could you really despise a team that, after visiting Barrow, wrote a letter to the *Arctic Sounder* lavishing praise on the community for how well it had been treated?

Delta Junction is a landlocked town. Minus-forty is a common enough occurrence in winter that if you own a vehicle you definitely want to have plug-in capability to electricity in order to heat the engine.

Autumn might be poised to change to winter on a moment's notice, but the forecast for the game was sunny and pleasant, maybe 50°F.

Not so in Barrow. The day before the team evacuated, practice at Cathy Parker Field was highlighted by 35 mph wind gusts and temperatures in the 30s. "I had on three coats," Voss said.

Winter was coming to the north. Voss said he doesn't mind −30°F temperatures, but when it drops to −45°F he doesn't want to even mess with his own car. He calls a cab if he has to go anywhere. Actually, the taxi cab business in Alaska, even in Anchorage, does a booming business in jump starts. You can telephone a taxi driver and have him come over to the house with his jumper cables to get you going. It's cheaper than towing.

At baggage claim, Vigo insinuated himself into the crowd straining for suitcases with a flirtatious move toward Pili. "Let me go to the woman I'm gonna marry," Vigo said.

Leaves on trees were changing colors along the not terribly heavily trafficked highway between Fairbanks and Delta. But on the night ride from the airport, the view wasn't quite so pretty. It was downright dangerous. The Barrow vehicles spotted four moose along the road. Sometimes moose run across the road, heedless of approaching vehicles. Sometimes they just keep on chewing whatever foliage interests them as cars pass. Sometimes they run away. And sometimes they rather haughtily and casually stroll away. But nobody knows which behavior pattern will be followed during each encounter. Voss was very much spooked by the negative possibilities.

Moose–car collisions are greatly feared in Alaska. While deer–car crashes are counted in the tens of thousands in the Lower 48 in places like Wisconsin, Michigan, and Illinois, most drivers walk away from them. In Alaska, moose, the largest member of the deer family, can weigh 1,200 pounds rather than 120. A driver who hits a moose at 50 mph might flip the moose over the hood and through the windshield. Deaths do occur this way. So the ride was nerve-racking for Voss and the others as they cautiously drove to Delta Junction, where they would again sleep on the floor.

Driving into the town from the north, motorists are greeted by a sign reading, "Welcome to Delta Junction, Alaska's Friendly Frontier." This is the northern end of the Alaska Highway. At a visitor's center a permanent chart is posted listing some special, zip-up-the-coat and throw-away-the-key freezing cold days in town history. On January 16, 1975, the temperature bottomed out at –70°F. That's not just cold, it hurts.

Forrest Ahkiviana said it had been an interesting week. He was the toast of the student body for running back the fumble for a touchdown, but he detected a bit of jealousy from his fellow linemen in their teasing. "Everybody on the line is mad at me," he said with a grin. "They say, 'I hate you for doing that.'"

Those with long memories and vengeful natures were not thinking about the Delta Junction visit as a renewal of friendship. The 34–0 score was etched in some minds.

"It just sucked," Cody Romine said. "We didn't know what to do. We're going to murder them this year."

Van Edwardsen had a prediction. "It's going to be the opposite score this year," he said.

At one time or another this season, it seemed, Daniel Thomas, Mike Gonzales, Colton Blankenship, and who knows how many more reticent players, had dreamed about football, sometimes in startling specifics. In his dream, Blankenship said, it was him, not Forrest, who scored a touchdown with a recovered fumble. Ahkiviana was right. The linemen were jealous.

Kickoff was scheduled for late Friday afternoon. The game was neither a true Friday Night Lights event, nor a typical Saturday afternoon game. Once they woke up, goofed around, and ate breakfast, the Whalers still had time to kill. The coaches worked their darnedest to focus their minds on football, but it was a tough challenge for eight straight hours.

"Rest and start thinking about the game," was Coach Igou's sound advice.

Pili had not wanted to be segregated in an adjacent room. She set up her sleeping bag arrangement against a wall a short distance from the coaches. That was it. No hassles. In the downtime, Pili and others on the team read books, listened to music, and even watched movies through the magic of laptop technology.

Although they prepared diligently, followed usual procedures, and didn't say anything aloud to the players, there was a minor undercurrent of worry among the coaches that Delta Junction might not have enough able bodies to play. It was peculiar to be such a new and young program and yet have to worry about being careful not to run up the score on somebody, as Voss did. It was kind of soon and kind of weird to potentially be the bullies in a game.

Soon enough after relaxation, it was time to talk business. Coach Arnhart wanted the offense to take care of the ball better, to avoid penalties, and to hit people across the line in a knock-down, drag-out, take-no-prisoners, smash-'em-so-hard-their-family-tree-shivers performance. But to do it honorably.

"Drive, drive, drive," he said. "No fumbles. You guys go 100 mph and hit the holes hard."

Perhaps mindful that Delta Junction would be outnumbered and could definitely become fatigued by an aggressive, crisp defense, Coach Houston began his pep talk succinctly. "You can take the wind out of these guys," he said. "And I mean early."

After preliminary talks there was more time to fill. Mac Rock and Van Edwardsen began advocating the use of trick plays the likes of which they had seen in the recent remake of *The Longest Yard.*

Arnhart, whose laptop was filled with offensive play possibilities, though maybe not the ones they were pitching, said, "You guys watch too many movies."

As an Eskimo from Barrow, Robin Kaleak, who was shooting baskets, had had little interaction with fall foliage in his life. Barrow did not have trees, and Kaleak said he didn't miss them. And Mike Olson had just seen fall foliage, leaves changing colors, for the first time.

"It's pretty weird," he said. "It's my first time seeing an orange tree. I don't even think about us not having trees. I like looking over the landscape and being able to see far away."

Vigo couldn't sit still. He was practically jitterbugging, though he didn't know the dance. He chattered and joked until Voss, hoping to see some game faces, instead of games being played, ordered Vigo to sit down by him.

"Coach," Voss said to Igou, "remind me not to play Robert today."

The perpetually sunny Vigo frowned, but had a comeback. "Coach," he said, "don't crush my spirit."

About an hour before game time, Houston gathered his two-way linemen in one corner of the gym and unleashed some of his best FDR oratory on them. He might as well have been talking about nation building as football. He seemed to put the weight of success on their shoulders.

"You are the heart and the soul of this team," Houston said. "Nothing happens without you guys. Let's go bury these guys quick so everybody gets to play. Let's put three quick scores on the board. We owe these guys. We owe them from last year."

Almost in a whisper, Gonzales recalled that result. "It was bad," he said.

"They cannot stop us!" declared Houston.

Powerful Keifer Kanayurak believed him. Kanayurk wore a gray, sleeveless T-shirt and written across the front were the words, "Built Tough." As he stood up, Kanayurak said, "Boys, let's do it."

One thing about lodging in school gyms is that usually no bus is needed to get to the stadium. The players just run out the back door, and within yards they are on the field. The Whalers took to the field for warm-ups nearly an hour before kickoff. Time passed. No Delta Junction. Fifteen minutes after the hour, twenty, twenty-five. No Delta

Junction. About half an hour before game time, the door to the far end of the gym opened and players in uniform jogged out. One, two, three, four, five. Here come some more. Six, seven, eight, nine, ten. Gap. Eleven, twelve. Gap. Long gap. Player on crutches. Gap. That's it. Delta Junction was suiting up twelve men.

Not since the days of leather helmets had teams regularly fielded so few players. Needing eleven men to play offense and eleven to play defense, Delta Junction barely qualified a starting lineup, and needed almost all of its guys to go both ways in the forty-eight-minute contest. The coaches were right to worry about whether the game would actually take place. Whew. At least it would start, but everyone knew that if Delta Junction had an injury or two the game might be called off in the middle.

It was actually a spectacular, perfect fall day for football, with the sun out and the temperature climbing into the 50s. The trees surrounding the field were changing colors.

"We believe!" shouted Barrow players.

Delta Junction opened the game offensively in the shotgun formation, allowing its quarterback to receive the snap a few yards behind the line of scrimmage. It represented a hope that Barrow's size advantage on the line would be slightly negated. The Huskies didn't move the ball, though.

About midway through the first quarter, the Whalers got on the board when Albert Gerke ran a bootleg five yards around right end for a touchdown and Anthony Edwards kicked the extra point. In the second quarter, the Whaler lead expanded to 14–0 on a Gerke ten-yard TD pass that was tipped but that Austin Fishel grabbed.

A little later Edwards caught a screen pass and darted sixty-three yards down the left sideline for a touchdown. But it was called back for a holding penalty. That was the type of mistake that kept the coaches' blood pressure high. Fishel retaliated with an interception on the Huskies' 33-yard line, and quickly Edwards got his touchdown on a two-yard run. He added points on the two-point conversion and Barrow led 22–0.

Things started to get out of control after that. Dave Evikana, also on his first road trip, made a big fumble recovery on the kickoff and Edwards scored on a sixteen-yard screen pass, then booted the extra point. 29–0.

As the half ended, Fishel observed, "This is a lot like they did to us last year."

The lead expanded to 36–0 when Edwards slashed right for twenty yards and another touchdown and extra point. Luke George intercepted a pass and ran it back thirty-four yards for a touchdown. And Vigo, operating out of the backfield instead of Edwards, burst through the line on a sixty-four-yard breakaway run. It was 48–0 Barrow with 5 1/2 minutes remaining in the third quarter. By agreement of the coaches and the officials, the clock shifted to running time for the rest of the game, a mercy rule.

With just a bit more than a minute remaining in the quarter, Delta Junction's freshman quarterback Anthony Bricker went down on a play and didn't get up. Injury. There was a delay. Eventually he was helped off the field. Delta Junction had eleven healthy players and more than twelve minutes to play.

The Huskies stuck with it and Barrow scored no more. 48–0 final. The lights on the scoreboard with the final numbers were turned off before the two teams completed the handshake line, as if Delta Junction was already trying to erase the memory of the rout. And it was a short handshake line, at that.

"Those guys played their hearts out," Voss said of Delta Junction's undermanned squad. He liked what he saw from his own team, too. "I thought they played a tough, scrappy game."

There was a lot of whooping it up afterwards. Victories were precious, the Whalers had learned over the last couple of weeks. They had taken their own lumps and now they had delivered some. They deserved a few moments of frivolity.

Jason Ruckle was wearing a Reese's Peanut Butter Cup T-Shirt under his uniform jersey and was asked if the candy treat was the true breakfast of champions.

"Of course," he said.

Romine proclaimed his happiness at the vindication. Fishel said the defense stepped up all game and as the Huskies tired, it got easier and easier to stop them in the late going. Everyone was giddy. Even Arnhart seemed to have lost his prudence temporarily. He mentioned the prospect of the playoffs—that somehow, despite getting clobbered by Eielson and Houston, they might still finish in the top two in the Greatland Conference.

Playoffs? Why not? At the moment, anything seemed possible.

"We've got to take care of business, though," he said.

Back to pragmatism immediately.

CHAPTER 23

# *The Pipeline Bowl*

THE OIL PUMPED FROM THE North Slope fields in Alaska is unearthed from Prudhoe Bay and loaded into the Alaska pipeline in Deadhorse. It flows southward across the tundra, the mountains, and the wilderness to the pipeline's terminus in Valdez, eight hundred or so miles as the raven flies.

The Port of Valdez was named after a Spanish naval officer, Antonio Valdes y Basan, in 1790, and modern-day Valdez is actually pronounced *Val-deez.*

Valdez was a mind-your-own-business town that practically nobody knew about in 1964 when the United States' largest earthquake ever shook up Alaska with a 9.2 Richter Scale reading on Good Friday. The cataclysm was so violent that people in Oregon died from a tsunami 1,500 miles south. The epicenter of the quake was forty-five miles west of Valdez and the force of it triggered a mudslide that roared down a mountain on top of the town. The earthquake killed thirty-one people in Valdez and caused $15 million in damage.

Downtown Anchorage streets were shaken to bits. Land areas along the Seward Highway abutting Turnagain Arm dropped. And the town of Valdez was flattened. Over the next couple of years Valdez, now with a population of 4,300-plus, was relocated and rebuilt several miles from its original location. When it comes to worldwide attention, the pipeline and the earthquake pretty much make up Valdez's history. That, and the fact that Captain Joseph Hazelwood steered an oil tanker called the *Exxon Valdez* into a charted reef and split open its hold to create an eleven-million-gallon oil spill in 1989 that is still being fought over in the courts. But that was a ship, not the place.

College football is loaded with intense, long-term rivalries in which the parties fight over annual possession of a trophy emblematic of their relationship. Purdue and Indiana compete for the Old Oaken Bucket. Washington and Washington State wrestle over the Apple Cup. Bowling Green and Toledo engage in the Battle of the Peace Pipe. Minnesota and Wisconsin go after Paul Bunyan's Axe. And there are loads more, so why not start your own chase for a coveted piece of hardware when the program is young?

When Barrow coach Mark Voss said the Whaler-Valdez showdown was for Pipeline Bowl bragging rights, it sounded like a joke at first. However, after the schools played in 2006 during Barrow's quickie first season, a trophy was established (Voss had never seen it). Henceforth, the schools really would contend for the Pipeline Bowl crown.

Valdez's participation in the Greatland Conference is not as well known as Barrow's, especially outside the state. But Valdez was hosting Barrow in a pivotal football game for the Whalers. A win, and the Whalers' record would be 4–2, and they could genuinely hope to sneak into the playoffs, provided other results in other games fell into place. Houston had not been so overpowering against the rest of the league and the Hawks were catchable in the standings. A loss, however, and the Whalers could pretty much forget about playing in October.

"This is our game," proclaimed Colton Blankenship, who by this time had trimmed his hair so closely he was sporting a warrior's cut.

In terms of access, Valdez is in a quirky spot. It is three hundred miles from Anchorage by car, but that's only because the road winds through the mountains. It is a much more direct trip by airplane, but getting from Barrow to Valdez by air on regular commercial flights entailed switching planes and airlines and long layovers. Voss debated the method of travel for a long time, but the Whalers ended up flying into Valdez in turbo twin-engine prop planes that refueled in Fairbanks. Lord knows how long it would have taken via commercial jet from

Barrow to Fairbanks to Anchorage and then busing it. Two days? Instead the Whalers arrived in Valdez at midday on the same day they departed from Barrow. Besides the players, about a dozen cheerleaders were on the trip, too. With the surprise weather, the cheerleaders would be able to prance around and yell in normal cheerleader garb without parkas, without four layers of clothing.

It was a picture-perfect sunny afternoon in Valdez, with sunshine glistening off the surrounding mountain tops and the water in the harbor that led to Prince William Sound. This was a gift, a Chamber of Commerce filming day, since Valdez's weather, at least in terms of precipitation, is even worse than Barrow's. It seems to rain all of the time in Valdez—except when it is snowing. And when it snows it snows in feet, not inches. Nearby Thompson Pass, on the outskirts of town, has set records for snowfall. You don't want to be commuting to Valdez by automobile in the winter. You could run off the road, be buried in snow and not be found until spring.

Each winter in Valdez, when the overworked plows clear the streets of snow, virtual mountains of snow are constructed. The residents, making logical use of one of their natural resources, host a Snowman Festival. Some four thousand snow sculptures have been built at a time, many larger than the linemen on the Buccaneers' football team.

The day before the Whalers left Barrow, their final home practice took place with the thermometer nicking 35°F, but accompanied by a 24°F windchill. Voss brought twenty-one players on this road trip and it was a changing cast of characters. Wide receiver Jim Martin had been out for two games with a hamstring muscle strain, but was recovered and back in the rotation. Cody Gleason, it turned out, had broken his hand in a practice before the Delta Junction game.

"He didn't bitch and he didn't moan," Voss said. "He put an ice pack on it."

And played against the Huskies. Only the pain didn't go away so he eventually saw a doctor. The kid played a game through a broken bone, but now he was out. Gleason gave up boxing and broke his hand anyway.

The Whalers were very happy with the result against Delta Junction—heck, they were happy enough to get the game in at all because of the Huskies' manpower shortage. But because of that thin lineup, the coaches, upon further review, weren't 100 percent sure what the victory meant.

"It was so hard to gauge," Voss said. "We should have looked crisper against Delta."

Valdez was a tougher opponent. It seemed like a pick-em game, a toss-up between two teams fighting for the same thing in the same league—a chance to be in the hunt at the end. Barrow was 3–2, Valdez 3–3. Eielson was still humming along, 3–0 in conference, so they could forget about the Ravens.

"We're at a place right now if we win, we will have fulfilled as much of our destiny as we can," Voss said.

The Valdez football field, once again just out the door from the gym where the Whalers parked their gear and bodies, was more comparable to Bobby Fischer Field than Cathy Parker Field. That meant the gravel layer gave like sand when someone ran on it.

"Like home," Forrest Ahkiviana said, comparing the field to Bobby Fischer. "You sink in more."

The texture could slow down running games. After backs received the handoff, their plant foot might slide backward and throw them off.

On a marvelous, sunshiny day, with the temperature sneaking past 60°F, the players wore shorts. Which meant that their legs got battered when they hit the ground, rubbing against that good old gravel.

"It wouldn't be so bad if we had our practice pants on," linebacker Tim Barr said, "but whatever. This is all gushy. It makes it more work to be explosive."

The mountains behind the field provided the type of scenic backdrop that TV cameras love to pan when professional football games are being played in Denver or Phoenix. Most of Alaska's topography features mountain ranges, from the Chugach Range adjacent to Anchorage to the Alaska Range with towering Mount McKinley, at 20,320 feet, the tallest peak in North America. But the tallest mountain in Barrow is either a trash heap or a tuft of tundra sticking up near the ocean.

Houses with picture windows just behind the stadium, and beneath those mountains, offered outstanding views of the action if anyone wanted to watch. It was almost like being at the hotel that is inside the Toronto Blue Jays' Sky Dome–Rogers Centre, where you can get room service and watch a ball game.

Defensive tackle Alastair Dunbar liked the image of viewing football with all of the comforts of home at your fingertips.

"It's so cool," he said. "You can sit in your house and watch the game."

Fresh in the news was how New England Patriots coach Bill Belichik had been nailed for spying on the New York Jets. The Barrow players decided that the houses facing the field would be ideal for video surveillance, and Valdez players right then were probably watching practice and stealing their signs from someone's living room. Or maybe from the roof of the school. Or maybe from that mechanical gizmo mounted on that pole. For those on the sidelines during practice, it became a game, trying to figure out the best place Valdez could put the sophisticated electronic taping equipment that would record all of Barrow's secrets.

"They've got somebody on top of that green tower," Barr said, pointing, and suggesting a previously unthought-of vantage point.

Oh yeah, there was a shed at the end of the field, too. Could be there. Or maybe something was mounted on top of that flagpole. For a generation raised on electronics, this wasn't just James Bond stuff: the players could envision how someone could pull it off. Not for a second, though, did they think anyone would go to the trouble. The joke had legs, however.

"Cloaking devices on," Martin said.

Now they were on to Star Trek technology.

Meanwhile, a few yards away, some serious work was taking place with drills focused on special teams. Coaches urged the players to sprint off the ball on the kickoff for good coverage and to fill blocking lanes for their own return man.

"We cannot come halfway!" Coach Houston yelled.

Suddenly, Blankenship, who was wearing a cutoff mesh jersey over his shoulder pads, jumped up squirming, twisting, and shaking, as if some mysterious music beat that only he could hear had invaded his head. Eyes turned toward this spirited dance.

"I have a bee in here!" he shouted.

Someone with a fine sense of humor said, "ZZZZZZZZZ."

Blankenship calmed down, but didn't see any bee fly away.

"Maybe you killed it," Dunbar suggested.

The players realized that the softest parts of the field were in the middle, and the footing was firmer going around each end. Someone suggested that the offensive game plan be modified so that all plays avoided the middle. Coaches ignored the comment. The grass portions of the field were outside the white lines, along the bench areas.

"Nice grass over here," Coach Igou noted.

Blankenship's bee started a fresh discussion among players waiting their turn to be invited back onto the field. A Barrow student who collected bugs was mentioned. Big John Lambrecht, someone recalled, once stomped on a lemming. Players who had grown up in a place in which providing for the family meant shooting seals and caribou, in addition to whaling, discussed the challenges of hunting and shooting accurately.

Igou drifted over, caught the drift of the anything-but-football conversation and groaned. "You need to be focused on the task at hand," he said.

On the field, Houston stressed fundamentals again. It was one of those basics he hoped his defensive lineman would have so ingrained in them that they would never forget it and he would never have to mention it again. Yet one had the sense that no matter how instinctive the players became, Houston would never stop mentioning it.

"If you use the technique and stay low—and I know this is sluggish stuff to be hearing," Houston said, "but if you stay low, we win the game."

The whistle blew signaling the end of practice and players started to walk toward the sideline. "I don't want to see anybody walking!" Coach Arnhart boomed. Make that *running* toward the sideline.

The coaches had scouted Valdez as thoroughly as possible and pinpointed a handful of players for the Whalers to watch. Number 72—they didn't bother with a name—was a solid player, a tough lineman who could hurt Barrow in more ways than one, blocking or tackling. On defense, the coaches wanted Blankenship to be so zeroed in on him that he would know how Mr. 72 likes his pancakes.

"This is the biggest game of the season for us," Igou said. "It's the biggest game in Barrow football history."

Such as it was. That line didn't exactly wake up the echoes, given that Barrow football history wasn't nearly as old as some of the blue jeans the players brought on the trip.

After cleaning up, the players ate dinner at the Alaska Halibut House. The operators of this establishment were on the ball. They served twenty-one players, plus coaches, at the speed of light. It was a dramatic contrast to a McDonald's the team stopped at in Palmer on the State Fair day that had the slowest service in the universe.

Halibut is only periodically found on menus outside of Alaska, but it is one of the tastiest game fish around. Living deep in the ocean, the fish can exceed four hundred pounds (though that's rare), and ordinarily wouldn't be considered high on teenage boys' list of favorite foods. But seafood is common and popular in Alaska, and kids are brought up eating more of it than in many places. Not that these guys were about to give up on McDonald's after one bad service experience. The absence of McDonald's in Barrow meant that they would forever flock to the franchises on road trips.

In many instances when high school and college sports teams take road trips, their athletic departments and coaches include as benefits from the travel being exposed to different cultures. In Barrow's case, the benefit worked backward: they are from the exotic culture, and when they visit other cities they try to soak up as much mainstream American culture, usually only seen on TV or in movies, as possible.

True to his word to evaluate and make considered decisions about the travel roster each week depending on health, practice attendance, and hard work, Voss surprised Joe Burke when he told him he was on the squad for the journey to Valdez.

At the end of practice, Burke ran up to Coach Houston and asked for clarification on his special teams assignments for the game. After the drills, he wasn't clear just where he was supposed to line up in which formation. Those are the types of questions coaches like to hear and answer. It is evidence a player is trying, is thinking about what he is supposed to be doing, not just responding by rote.

"Not bad for a freshman," Houston said.

CHAPTER 24

# *Pivotal Moment*

A LITTLE BIT MORE THAN TWO HOURS to kickoff, the coaches conducted a run-through of the plays as a refresher. The workout was conducted inside the gym, with players still in their pajama bottoms, shorts, and T-shirts, some still in socks, surrounded not by metal bleacher seats, but by portable mattresses.

Did the Jacksonville Jaguars do it this way?

Jarid Hope yawned. Dave Evikana pulled the hood on his sweatshirt over his head and lowered his chin as if he might be able to get lost in his clothing and sneak a nap. Austin Fishel yawned.

Albert Gerke couldn't disappear because he was running the offense. Without a uniform, without shoulder pads on, he seemed like the skinniest kid on the block. He had the waist of a super model and a slender upper body. Where did the arm strength come from to throw a football fifty yards in the air?

To say that most of the players' heads weren't in the game quite yet was an understatement of major proportions. Half of the guys were still in la-la land. Out of the blue, related to nothing going on, suddenly Forrest Ahkiviana performed a ballet pirouette, hands above his head. Coach Igou glanced over and caught the movement.

"Are you kidding me?" he said. Igou shook his head in disbelief. Football, he reminded himself. This was football.

Ahkiviana tried to explain himself. "I was just bored," he said. "And I was wearing really tight pants."

Ah, there was the connection, overlapping wardrobe between football pants and ballet tights. Wonder if Mikhail Baryshnikov shopped at the Sports Authority.

Coach Voss explained some of what went into his personnel selection for this road trip when he was limited to twenty-one guys, but Joe Burke's presence was partially about giving all of the freshmen hope that if they kept at it they too could work themselves into the rotation and onto the plane.

"I wanted to reward a ninth grader who worked hard all season," Voss said. "You have twenty-one seats. Someone is always left behind."

So what was Burke's reaction when informed by the coach that he had better pack? "Shock," Voss said.

Burke said he got the word after Thursday practice and that sent him into a packing tizzy. "They told me I've been working hard," Burke said. "I didn't mind whether I played or not. It was about coming out there and being with the team and having fun."

One reason there was a seat available was the absence of Mike Gonzales. His brother was graduating from that Air Force program over the weekend in San Antonio and his parents insisted he accompany them to Texas instead of going to Valdez with his teammates.

And Mike Olson, the chatty, friendly, large dude who was proud to wear number 75 in his hair, was missing, too. There was a death in his family and he stayed in Barrow to attend his uncle's funeral.

Ekivana scooped up a copy of the *Anchorage Daily News* sports section from the day before that was lying on an inflated mattress, and had about one second to look it over before a play started. It was a pass. Running a route that took him past a sleeping bag and called for him to weave in and around loose shoes, Justin Sanders grabbed a Gerke toss.

Barrow's preparations for the Pipeline Bowl ceased and the players scattered to their rest spots. After the game was decided, there was going to be a luau, at $17 a pop, as a fund-raiser for the Buccaneers football program, though the Whalers wouldn't have to pay.

"I hope we make it out of here with the trophy," Coach Houston said, "but I'd like to see them raise some money. I'd like to see these guys get a field, too. It's a tough field to play on. It's going to be like beach football."

As a black man working in Barrow, Houston sometimes marvels at the overlap and mix of cultures that brings together Eskimos, black music, and white pop culture. The kids know all about rap music, Britney Spears, and Jessica Simpson, some of which he lumps together as "pollution." Houston was amazed to come across an Iñupiat rapper—not a football player—singing about big city streets. He took the young man aside and asked, "Why don't you sing about hunting, or your culture?" Houston shook his head. "You want to be believable."

During the downtime, Alastair Dunbar built his own football player by his sleeping area. Dunbar pulled together his number 66 white game jersey with shoulder pads, blue football pants with their yellow belt, blue helmet, gloves, and shoes and created a ghost player sitting up on its own. In a cornfield it would have been a heck of a scarecrow.

Luke George took a hit off his asthma inhaler. He has not needed to borrow it back during a game yet, though once he needed to use it during a practice. "I'm good for four hours," George said.

Tim Barr had a huge empty Arizona Green Tea bottle, forty-two ounces, that he filled with water. "This is my Super Server," Barr said.

This was a meaningful game, with something at stake. The Houston Hawks had dropped by the wayside and the winner between Barrow and Valdez would ascend to second place in the Greatland Conference behind Eielson. The winning team would have the inside track for advancing to the playoffs, an accomplishment that would be as extraordinary as it was unlikely for such a young program.

"We've got the keys to the door," Coach Houston said, warming to his psych-'em-up task. "We can go to the playoffs. It's up to us. This is the biggest game of our season. This is our day."

Each coach took a turn trying to boost the team's spirit, energy, determination, and commitment to victory, sometimes in a serious way, sometimes in a humorous way. "You need the heart and the desire and you can compete with anybody," Coach Igou said.

Voss cleared his throat. "In your short time playing football, you have not had many opportunities like this," he said. "You do have your destiny in your hands. People around the state are watching to see what happens today. You can pretty much ignore them. The only people who matter are the people on the field. We're gonna have a good time today. The best way to have a good time is to win."

That was practically Lincolnesque compared to Coach Arnhart's short, but sweet follow-up message. "Kick ass and have fun," Arnhart said.

"Yes, sir," replied Daniel Thomas.

Then the Whalers formed a circle in the gym, held hands, and were led in the Lord's Prayer by Houston. But that was not the last word. "Valdez beat us last year," he said. "We owe them. We've got a trophy to take home."

In what was a bigger upset than Barrow contending for the playoffs, the sun was brilliant in a blue sky in Valdez for a second day in a row. Walking onto the field an hour before kickoff, Voss reflected on the unlikeliness of the situation. He couldn't believe his team was about to engage in a game that might put them in the playoffs. How did that happen so fast?

Of course, given the nature of the field, things might not happen so fast this day. "It's going to be awful by the end of the game," Tim Barr predicted of the footing. "Maybe the quarter."

Cody Romine was ready to play. Sort of. His ankle still bothered him, but he persevered with "like eight pounds of tape" on it.

Number 72, who the Whalers had been warned about, was a flesh-and-blood person. At six-foot-one and 245 pounds, lineman Nate Rogers, the conference's player of the year for 2006, indeed was made up of large amounts of flesh and blood.

According to the public address announcer welcoming the hundreds of fans who trickled in to fill the few rows of bleachers and the sidelines, the game had taken on a more formal status. It was called the "Pipeline Pigskin Bowl."

Shortly before kickoff, Trent Blankenship appeared on the Barrow sideline. He had flown to Anchorage the night before, rented a car, and just completed driving the three hundred miles to Valdez. Sometimes, as parents do, he wore a replica of son Colton's number 78 jersey.

Blankenship was at least as surprised as Voss that this game might produce a playoff berth. "I knew they had improved a lot," he said, "but it's cool."

Then he invoked the Whalers favorite chant: "We believe!" So did the Whalers, bursting out of a sideline huddle. "We believe!"

It didn't take very long to see that the Buccaneers did, as well. A sixty-seven-yard sweep around the left side burned Barrow for a touchdown and a 7–0 lead.

Occasionally, at small school games around the state, parents or spectators who came simply to root, but knew the sport, were pressed into game service. Blankenship had helped move the chains measuring the distance for a first down at one game. Valdez had more experienced crew members than other places, mostly concerned with the fortunes of their own team, but loosely familiar with the Barrow story and the Arctic's new field.

"Was it a rich Floridian?" a woman on the crew asked. "Or was it a rich Texan? That's what we need."

Some of the blanks in her comprehension of how Barrow actually acquired the field were filled in. The chain crew was about the friendliest and chattiest in the league. All of a sudden the scoreboard made a buzzing sound and went blank. One body of opinion said there was 5:04 left in the first quarter. The officials said 4:00. The chain gang was asked if such fritzes occurred regularly. "Sometimes cell phones knock it out," one guy said, perhaps serious, perhaps not. "Someone must have phoned for pizza."

The Whalers were not as sharp on offense as had been planned. Number 72 did have something to do with that, proving his reputation was genuine. As the second quarter began, Coach Igou correctly observed, "We've got to maintain a drive here."

The wishful comment apparently pushed the right buttons. A few minutes later, Gerke raised his arm, fired, and found a leaping Austin Fishel in the end zone for a twenty-yard touchdown pass. The extra point failed, so the Whalers still trailed 7–6, but they had made some confidence-building noise.

On Valdez's first possession after the kickoff, Robert Vigo, using his gift of speed, dashed into the backfield from defensive end and caused a quarterback fumble. The ball was recovered by Colton Blankenship. The Whalers had first down on the Buccaneers' 24-yard line, a golden chance. Only Barrow fumbled the ball right back.

Usually, turnovers represent the big mistake that can cost a team the game in a close contest, but there were several tradeoffs this day. Nonetheless, Romine showed how devastating a turnover can be when he intercepted a Valdez pass and ran it thirty-two yards for a touchdown and a 12–7 Whaler lead.

A little later, midway through the second quarter, the scoreboard suffered its second eclipse. Trent Blankenship chuckled. The biggest problem with the tiny, temporary scoreboard and clock at Cathy Parker Field—besides its size—was the fact that when the sun fell on it the lights became invisible to the viewing audience.

"Ours works," he said, "but you can't read it."

At halftime, a female streaker sought to lighten the mood. Wearing an orange bikini and a black football helmet, she was in partial disguise hiding her face pretty well, if not her other assets. The girl dashed past the Barrow sideline and exited the field onto a path and into the woods, not to be seen again. A minimally impressed Barrow fan recalled the Seward game streaker incident at home.

"Our streaker was nude," he said. Then paused, remembering the result. "His bail was higher than the bet."

After the coaches' skull session dissecting the first half of play, Gerke bent over coughing as if he might puke. "I'll do it on their field," Gerke said. "It's already crappy." He did not spew.

Zac Rohan sat down on the bleachers on the Barrow sideline, took off his left cleat and shook it. "I have a rock in my shoe," he said. Then he repeated the process with his right shoe. Shades of Bobby Fischer Field.

It was not entirely clear under league rules—with the games remaining, and whatever all the tie-breakers were—whether winning this game meant that Barrow was automatically in the playoffs or not.

"What do we know?" Trent Blankenship said. "This is our first rodeo."

In the third quarter, Valdez drove downfield into the Barrow red zone. Justin Sanders tracked a pass into the end zone, employed his impressive vertical leap to latch onto the ball for an interception, and then fell awkwardly and lay still on the ground.

Barrow coaches and a Valdez trainer ran to his aid. Sanders didn't move. Each team retreated to its bench and watched anxiously. The Whaler players prayed for Sanders. Time ticked by.

"He's moving," Jason Ruckle said.

From a distance, though, nobody could see Sanders moving right then. Within fifteen minutes, a Valdez Fire Department ambulance arrived and drove onto the field. Sanders was rolled onto a stretcher bed and carefully loaded into the ambulance with Voss and Houston helping. As Arnhart came back to the bench, Romine said, "Can he move?"

"Yeah, uh-huh," Arnhart said. "He can move. He can talk. His neck is going to be real sore."

The ambulance rolled slowly across the end zone and outside the playing field, then out of sight.

"He's gonna be OK," Houston said. "I sat there and said a prayer with him."

During the unscheduled break, Voss trotted back to the gym and delved into the paperwork he carried to every away game, then he dialed Sanders' relatives in Barrow to inform them that their son had been injured.

The game resumed after a break of about twenty-five minutes.

There was no way to quantify how much Barrow missed Sanders, a key leader and one of their steadiest players, but Valdez took the lead at 14–12 on a twenty-two-yard run in the fourth quarter, and then upped it to 20–12 on a twenty-nine-yard run with four minutes, twelve seconds remaining.

Barr was so frustrated by the second score that he angrily flung his helmet, and the Whalers were slapped with a fifteen-yard unsportsmanlike conduct penalty.

With a few minutes left, Ruckle stayed down on the ground at the end of a play holding his left knee. He limped to the sidelines. Voss went over to Ruckle as the game continued, ruffled his hair, and said, "Hang tight."

The final score was 20–12 Valdez.

It was a tough game, pretty evenly matched, and the Whalers poured themselves into it. They just weren't good enough to win this day. The disappointment was written on their faces. They were a little bit dirty from the contact, a little bit sad from the result, but not crushed in spirit. They didn't harbor the belief that something had been taken from them that they could never recover. This was a team that had barely earned its stripes. It wasn't old enough to suffer lingering heartache, but was old enough to learn lessons for the future.

"We're going to keep our heads up high," Coach Igou said. "And shake hands and show good sportsmanship. In close games you can't have breakdowns. I thought you brought it to them the majority of the game."

Voss said he was proud of the players. They rose to the occasion, in the sense of being ready to play and in putting forth a solid effort all game long, even if they didn't win. "The best part of playing the game is that you went out there and left your hearts on the field," Voss said.

Speaking of the field, there were no recommendations to have the Valdez field showcased in *Better Homes and Gardens*. After the game Gerke emptied gravel from his shoes and looked over the scrapes on his left elbow.

"The field sucks," Romine said.

What sucked the most was that Sanders was a few blocks away in Providence Valdez Medical Center hospital instead of with the team. Yes, the Whalers missed him during the game. Yes, his absence bothered them. And yes, they were worried about him. "We thought about him, though it sounds as if he just got a little bit of a bump on the noggin," said Denver Enoch.

Fishel's great touchdown catch was the highlight reel play for the Whalers, but he said it still felt like one that got away.

"If we had fought a little bit harder, maybe it would have gone into overtime," Fishel said.

Voss, who had been vocal in his praise of Sanders throughout the year said he thought Sanders' injury took the starch out of the team.

"Me, too," said the coach in an unusual admission. "I'm supposed to be able to get past it, but you don't know what's going to affect you."

As the team packed up to depart Valdez, other aches came to light. Ruckle's knee problem was known, but not the severity. It was hyper-extended, but hopefully nothing worse. Then, in a scary moment, Forrest Ahkiviana began complaining of neck pain and a headache. He too was taken to the hospital briefly. It turned out Ahkiviana had a minor concussion, but was able to join the team for the trip home.

Sanders was another case. The doctors would not allow him to leave without additional observation. While the rest of the squad left, Trent and Colton Blankenship stayed in Valdez with Sanders. A couple of hours later he was cleared to go.

Instead of a scenic drive back to Anchorage with stunning, snow-capped mountains to see, the drive took place in the dark, with the threat of moose stepping into the road. Sanders was heavily medicated and lay across the back seat of the vehicle, barely awake for most of the journey. However, he did recall later that Trent Blankenship was driving pretty darned fast and hit at least one bump that tossed him around like a big wave on the ocean.

That trio survived the superintendent's driving and flew back to Barrow the next day. To everyone's relief, Sanders felt better already. His wound was a red badge of courage, but not long lasting.

CHAPTER 25

# *The Longest and Last Road Trip*

A VISITOR TO BOTH PLACES might have difficulty acknowledging that Barrow and Sitka are two communities in the same country, never mind the same state. They are about as far apart and as different as two places can be and still be connected by statehood.

Barrow, at the top of the world, is situated on tundra, with no trees at all. Sitka, about fourteen hundred miles away near the bottom of the state in Southeast Alaska, is in the 16.8-million-acre Tongass National Forest filled with western hemlock, cedar, and Sitka spruce trees. The Sitka spruce routinely grew to heights of 220 feet.

In the middle of winter, when the temperature plunges to –40°F in Barrow, it could be +40°F on the same day in Sitka. Sitka, a community of about 8,800 people, has a Russian occupation influence dating to the 1700s, and is a seaport, located on a small-boat harbor. Homes built in the 1890s face the water, and lush, intensely green islands brimming with small trees are just a few hundred yards offshore. In Barrow, when residents gaze out at the water of the Arctic Ocean they are viewing a seemingly endless horizon. In Barrow it snows, in Sitka it rains. Barrow has whale bones on the beach, Sitka has totem poles in a park. Barrow operates under the Native influence of Iñupiat Eskimos. Sitka operates under the Native influence of Tlingit Indians.

Given the size of Alaska, even dwarfing Texas, it is apparent that no other high school football team in America experienced as long a road trip during the 2007 season. And given how long it took the bedraggled Whalers to reach Sitka they might have made it faster to Bangkok.

The Barrow players dipped their toes into the swirling tsunami waters of modern air travel at 11:00 A.M. Thursday and landed in Sitka at 11:00 P.M. Friday. A thirty-six-hour journey.

"You can't get to Sitka," said Colton Blankenship as he staggered into the airport lounge.

No one could believe it. Flight from Barrow, layover in Anchorage, stopover in Juneau, and on to Sitka, with delays everywhere in-between.

"Thirty-six hours," Coach Houston said. "There's got to be a better way."

This was the better way. Jet service. What was the alternative? Dog sled? Paddling canoes? When the exhausted Whalers reached Juneau, just a hop down the coast, Houston said the thinking was, "Let's just swim the rest of the way."

There was a small cheering section awaiting the Whalers for their last game of the season, including a couple of elderly transplanted Barrow women, some distant relatives of other Barrow relatives, and most obviously and loudly, Daniel Thomas's sister Deidre, seventeen, a senior at Mount Edgecumbe School, with some of her friends. The plane arriving late did not do much for them; they broke their 11:00 P.M. curfew to sneak out of their dormitories to meet the team, and every minute extra they stayed out enhanced their chances of getting caught.

Daniel's older brother, Josh, attended Mount Edgecumbe, as some other family members had done in the past. Daniel said his mother, Gwen, cried when Josh left home, but by the time he was a senior and by the time Deidre joined him she had become accustomed to their absence. Deidre visited Josh in Sitka and liked the environment. "So I stayed," she explained.

That separated her from Daniel and her parents, but there were maybe a dozen kids from Barrow and the region at Mount Edgecumbe, so it was like a second home. She liked being in a completely different place, with the likelihood of meeting different people rather than seeing the same ones every day. She said she got homesick sometimes, especially when returning to Barrow for three weeks over winter break.

With Josh and Deidre in Sitka, Daniel gave attending Mount Edgecumbe some serious thought, but decided against it. One temptation was the milder weather. Deidre would call home and hear all about the blizzard raging and then go, "Oh, it's in the 30s here."

In the end, though, weather did not play a significant role in Daniel's decision to stay home for high school.

"I didn't want to be known as Josh's brother," said Daniel, who wanted to carve his own path in Barrow. "Having football helped out a lot. My mother's mother went here. It has a good academic reputation."

Just about all of the Whalers' walking wounded were present and accounted for, healed from the hits they took against Valdez. Jason Ruckle said his knee was OK. Forrest Ahkiviana said that after the Valdez game ended, he suddenly got dizzy and his vision went blurry, but that had passed pretty quickly.

"Nothing would keep me from playing," he said.

Justin Sanders felt the same way. By the time Sanders arrived back in Barrow after the Valdez game, word had spread of his injury. He said that everyone he encountered was scared for him, but he bounced back pretty quickly with some rest and his neck was fine.

"I was gonna come even if they said I couldn't play," Sanders said.

Half an hour after bursting into baggage claim, the Whalers had grabbed their oversized luggage, crammed with sleeping bags and pads and the like, and were filing onto a school bus that would take them to their hostel for the night—the floor at Sitka High. Would it be a one-star or two-star gym experience? It didn't matter. As tired as they were they could sleep hard anywhere. Thirty-six hours?

"I wouldn't want to do this trip every week," Coach Arnhart said.

Although Barrow's overall football history had about as many words as the Z section in the encyclopedia, a couple of paragraphs had to be included. The Whalers and the Wolves played twice in 2006, and the Whalers' first win ever came over Sitka, provoking the first Arctic

Ocean victory dip. Some said there was a little bit of bad blood between the two squads because of trash talking, but many of the players on the teams weren't the same in 2007. Sitka was 2–3, Barrow 3–3.

It was a sleep-in morning for the players. "We were exhausted when we got here," Coach Voss said. "Every time you make a trip, it's major logistics."

Food ranks as importantly as sleep, and that was one way the coaches could rev up the guys. One player wanted to go to Subway. It was a luxury opportunity he didn't want to pass up. Since it was the end of the season for Barrow, with no playoffs, the restaurant variety would dry up in another day or so and fast-food outlets would once again become something seen on TV screens or in the imagination.

Joe Burke was the only freshman who traveled. Kept back in school one year, Burke admitted that he hadn't always taken school seriously, but that football had provided focus and motivation to keep his grades up. Without football, who knows? But there were other freshmen who hadn't made a road trip, and with the home schedule ending so early, Voss worried about retention. Would Nathan Snow come out for the team again next year? Would Adrian Paniego try again? Voss hoped so. He wanted the young guys to mesh with the older guys and work their way into more playing time.

"I think they'll probably come back next year," Voss said.

The atmosphere as everyone groaned awake was low-key, ambling even. The players were more focused on feeding their bellies and personal grooming, it seemed, than in clobbering Sitka. As a group the Whalers were good-natured, gregarious. Ornery outlooks were in short supply. They tried to psyche themselves up for some violence, but it wasn't always easy to tell how the talk was going to translate when the tackles and ends collided at the line of scrimmage.

"We're going to jump on some people today, man," Ahkiviana said.

A little bit more than an hour to game time, there was a crisis. Tim Barr was pulling on his uniform piece by piece, but came up short. He frantically ripped through his bag, dumped out the contents, and with panic seizing his chest realized the worst was true. He had left his size 12 cleats in Barrow.

"Right now is a bad time," Voss said.

The Whalers never seemed to get the details part of packing 100 percent right each trip. Sometimes it was a uniform belt missing. Sometimes it was an elbow pad. The players did not make a list and check it twice. If they were Santa Clauses a whole bunch of children would have been disappointed. They packed by grabbing gear and stuffing it into a bag.

"I don't understand how this happens week in and week out," Coach Houston moaned. "Forgetting helmets, jerseys, shoes."

As unfathomable as it seemed to Houston for a player to travel to a game without a major piece of equipment, center Mike Gonzales was sympathetic to Barr.

"I had to play a game in my Adidas last year," he said.

For the time being, Barr put on a pair of low-cut gym shoes, too. A search party was formed. Where could you buy football shoes in Sitka on a Saturday morning? Voss rousted Sitka school personnel to ask for advice. A very stressed Barr began counting out dollar bills from his travel stash.

"Last game and he's got to buy a pair of cleats," Edwards said. He whistled, as if saying, whew, he was glad it was not him and that it was going to be a pricey expenditure.

The players gathered at one end of the gym to hear their coaches' pregame speeches one last time this season. And for some, for the last time, period. This was a young football team. There were only a half-dozen seniors, some of whom had barely had the chance to learn the rules of the game before they had to give it up.

This was the final Barrow football game for Tim Barr, Denver Enoch, Mike Gonzales, Jarid Hope, Zac Rohan, Jason Ruckle, and Big John Lambrecht. Would any of them ever play organized football again? Chances were slim. This appetizer, this short season, and whatever they experienced in 2006, may well have been their only true taste of the game.

"For all of the seniors, this is your last football game," Coach Igou said. "It's something you'll probably remember the rest of your life. We need to come out and play hard for our seniors, our program and our community.

"Let's go out and play four quarters. From the first snap, they need to know we're here and we mean business. Dominate them from the first snap."

Coach Arnhart was looking for a smoother trip for the offense, fewer penalties, sharper execution.

"We should have no mistakes," said a coach dreaming of a perfect game. "Backs, find the hole and explode."

Voss, ever the father figure, the head man in the group, brought up the trashtalking concerns.

"These guys have been known to talk a little bit," Voss said. "Don't get drug into it. Knock 'em down, but help 'em up. Be good sportsmen."

The team gathered in a circle, half dressed, uniform jerseys not all quite tucked in, the players' locker room once again a foreign gym, held hands, and recited the Lord's Prayer. Then Voss dashed out the door, jumped in a rental van, and went shopping, trying to find Barr some new shoes for his final game.

Houston seized on a very good angle for motivation. The season had been shortened by a game when Ketchikan pulled out back in early August, leaving a seven-game schedule.

"Let's go 4–3," Houston said. "Let's not be under .500. We're better than that."

Left unsaid was that finishing with a winning record would be a remarkable effort given the newness of the program, the lack of experience, and the travel rigors.

Houston, as always good at finding a homily, seeking out a minisermon, borrowing someone else's writing to inspire the team, opened a copy of *Season of Life*, and began reading. The author, Jeffrey Marx, had been a Baltimore Colts ballboy as a youth and grew up to be a sportswriter. One of his friends was Colts lineman Joe Ehrman, a team captain, who became a minister and through his work with a high school football team sought to build better men as well as football players.

Marx renewed his acquaintanceship with Ehrman, and spent some time following his team and players to see how the principles of instilling responsibility into teens translated into making better men. Houston read passages aloud from the book, one he had read many times. That was the goal here, he thought, seeing football as more than just a sport, imparting lessons that would stick for life.

So Houston read and the Barrow players listened. And as game time approached, they exited through a side door of the school. The field was not just outside the school, but something like half a mile away. There was no bus.

The school was surrounded by gigantic trees, an environment so different in its lushness from the flat, open landscape of Barrow. The players couldn't see much more than a few hundred feet away in any direction. The coaches just hoped they could see the forest for the trees and execute their overall plan.

In full uniform, the visiting Barrow Whalers football team, prepared to play their last game of the 2007 season, lined up single file or in twos and began a brief march through the neighborhoods of Sitka to the football field.

CHAPTER 26

# *End Game*

IT WAS A BIT OF A PECULIAR PROCESSION, twenty-one fully uniformed Barrow football players walking around the corner of Sitka High School, taking a left into a neighborhood, and another right. The players were on their own, no one leading them in a vehicle, or giving them directions. It was good that someone in the group knew the way, because they couldn't see the field from the school.

There was virtually no traffic in the residential area on a late Saturday morning. And hardly anyone was outside their homes, either. Only a couple of youngsters looked at the team decked out in white jerseys with blue pants hustling past, making small talk, thinking of the game ahead.

It was a typical Southeast Alaska day: the temperature was 50-ish, the sky gray, with a mild breeze and some drizzle. From a distance, looking down from the parking lot, the field appeared to be wet cement. It was gray and flat, the smooth composition of compressed volcanic dirt seemingly aching for someone to roll around in it, or, like a Grauman's Chinese Theatre replica, awaiting hand- or footprints.

During calisthenics, Coach Voss reappeared, empty-handed after his tour of Sitka sporting goods stores, which meant two shopping stops that did not yield results. Voss appealed to the Sitka coach to see if the Wolves had any extra gear lying around, and a bag full of mismatched shoes of all sizes materialized on the Barrow sideline.

Tim Barr began looking for the size twelves. Mike Olson, who did not play as much as the linebacker, offered to loan Barr his game shoes and make do with something from the extras bag. The generous gesture was like giving a buddy the shirt off your back.

"If I go in," Olson said as he sifted through the couple of dozen odd shoes, "I'll deal with it."

The Whalers had a pretty decent-sized cheering section. Daniel Thomas's sister, Deidre, returned with a gaggle of friends to root for Barrow. They were there supporting the entire premise of the Barrow season: "We Believe!"

The first quarter began well for Barrow. Robert Vigo, built more like the backup running back he was rather than the outstanding defensive end he proved to be, somehow again compensated for his lack of bulk with speed and demolished the Sitka quarterback with a sack. Justin Sanders then made like All-Pro Devin Hester on a punt return, giving Barrow good field position. And less than six minutes into the period, Albert Gerke tossed a wobbly pass to Sanders, who plucked it out of the air for a twenty-one-yard touchdown.

The rested Sanders, who felt no ill effects from his scary neck injury the week before, was everywhere on offense and defense. Cody Romine tipped an errant Sitka pass and Sanders intercepted that. The steal led to a second touchdown, this one on a fifteen-yard run by Anthony Edwards. Although both extra point tries missed, Barrow led 12–0 before the end of the first quarter.

At one point, Big John Lambrecht, who still had those little things going wrong, had to leave the game, sit down on the bleachers, and replace a gashed shoestring.

The Wolves came through with a big pass play that gave them the ball first-and-goal at the Barrow 7-yard line. But the Whaler defense stiffened—boy did that make Houston and Igou happy—and Sitka was forced to try a twenty-five-yard field goal. Vigo, his blazing speed once more jumping him around blockers, penetrated the backfield and blocked the kick. Vigo was one of those players who had a knack for making the big defensive play at the right time. From the first game against Seward, when he made key sacks, to the final game against

Sitka, this characteristic was on display all season. And the guy didn't crack 175 pounds soaking wet in the Sitka rain.

At various times during the half, it appeared that Barrow would break out and take a larger lead, but mistakes contributed to the score being stuck on 12–0 at the half.

These types of games were dangerous. One team could dominate, but then a single, ill-timed mistake could turn the game into a one-possession game, fire up the opponent, and change the entire momentum. The idea was for the Whalers to put distance between them and the Wolves, make the Wolves doubt themselves, make the Wolves think it was impossible to win.

"You've just got to play hard-nosed football," Coach Igou said.

They were doing that and it was paying off. After all, if the game ended with a two-touchdown margin nobody would complain. Still, there were twenty-four minutes to play, so there were no guarantees, either.

"You're letting them stay in the game right now," Voss said.

Igou said it firmly, with conviction, and from the heart. "We've got to come out with reckless abandon," he said. It sounded good, but nobody really knew how that applied to the playbook.

Gerke, handing off smoothly, spotting receivers when they were open, and darting out of the pocket when Sitka's defense collapsed on him, led the Whalers deep into Wolves' territory. Then he culminated the drive with an eight-yard touchdown run for an 18–0 lead.

That was a backbreaker, and the Whalers were definitely in control after that. Vigo registered another sack to spoil Sitka comeback thoughts. Before the end of the third quarter, Austin Fishel scored on a thirteen-yard pass from Gerke on the left side and followed it up with a two-point conversion pass. 26–0. Then Sanders returned a weak punt thirty-five yards for a touchdown and Vigo caught a two-point conversion throw. 34–0. Oh yeah, baby, things were humming now.

In the fourth quarter, the Whalers looked crisper than ever. Fishel caught another touchdown pass, this one for twenty-six yards, and Thomas kicked the extra point. It was 41–0 and the scoreboard clock began ticking down with running time.

Vigo had been a defensive spark. As surely as touchdowns lit up the scoreboard, he lit up the defense with his tenacious play. He looked as much like a defensive end as Pee Wee Herman, but proved the famous coaching adage, "speed kills."

"The coaches told me that's what they needed in that position," Vigo said. "They needed somebody fast." He paused and, with his dental-commercial smile, added, "Beautiful season."

The Whalers made more big plays, did more things right, and won as handily as they had in any game all season. The season ended without squeezing into the top two in the Greatland Conference standings, but Barrow was 4–3. A winning record. That was something. As young and inexperienced as the Whalers were, to finish above .500 was an achievement few anticipated. We believe, indeed.

When the team huddled in a circle on the soggy field with the coaches, emotions flowed. There was satisfaction because of the 4–3 record. There was happiness because of the big win. And there was sadness because this group would never be together again in the same circumstances. The season was over and players would go their separate ways. Their Barrow High football career was over for certain seniors.

Leaning on one knee listening to the coaches, absorbing the situation, Big John Lambrecht teared up. His eyes were red and he cried softly. He said nothing and most of his teammates had their backs to him as they faced the coaches. But Brad Igou noticed and he wanted the other Whalers to know how important playing football was for Lambrecht.

"Take a good look at Big John," Coach Igou said. "Because that's what it means. Seniors, it was a pleasure and an honor to work with you." Igou had kept it a secret that he was turning fifty that day, but announced that the victory was a great birthday present and thanked the guys for delivering it. Olson gave him a hug.

Arnhart took a moment.

"You guys should be proud of yourselves," he said. "Good season."

Jarid Hope, who almost missed the entire deal with a broken leg, thought so.

"A winning season," Hope said. "Pretty cool. This team rocks."

Barr went through the process of retrading footwear with Olson and returning the odds-and-ends shoes to Sitka. He lamented that he only got one year to play high school football and now it was over.

"It was great," Barr said softly.

The two-a-days seemed long, but now they seemed to be a long time ago. The practices seemed long, but now they seemed to have passed by awfully quickly. Same with the games. The schedule had a period at the end of it, not a dash.

"Once you've done it, it seems fast," Zac Rohan, another senior, said. "I had a great season. We were still learning."

No one around the Greatland Conference—no sportswriters, no Barrow fans, really—had known what to expect from this bunch of players and this group of coaches. They gained a little bit of experience the year before, and experienced stunning nationwide attention on the trip to Florida and for receiving the gift of the field. Yet none of that specifically predicted that they'd end up 4–3.

"We had a victorious season by one game," Alastair Dunbar said.

The seniors knew they had been part of something special, that they could always say they were part of the start-up of Barrow football. In future years, when the Whalers won the Greatland Conference title, and the state title, too, that they were bound to get if they kept at it long enough, these young men could say that they had played.

"This is it for me," Mike Gonzales said, thinking ahead to graduation and his desire to join the Air Force and fly jet planes instead of continuing his football education on the field. "Barrow football is history for me. I became friends with a lot of people I wasn't close to before."

He smiled. Mr. Social Director was on top of the entertainment schedule for the night. There was a dance in town, and surely members of the victorious football team (even if they were from out of town) might be popular with a certain segment of the female population.

"We will try to meet some ladies," Gonzales said.

The happy walk from the field to the high school reversed the path of the pregame trek, weaving through a couple of side streets. Maybe there was a little bit more strut in the Whalers' steps. The small group of seniors was finished, but the majority of the team—freshmen, sophomores, juniors—was due to return. This was a young team, very much still building, but the skill positions were manned with sophomores likely to bust out. It would be no picnic playing the Whalers during the 2008 season. They definitely had the makings of a playoff team. The next week, Edwards was named first-team all-league on offense and defense and Gerke was chosen second-team all-league for his play in the secondary. Senior Jason Ruckle was named first team all-conference for his work at defensive tackle, and Lambrecht was second-team on offense.

"I'm glad we had a good season, being 4–3," Gerke said. "It's great. Now we just keep going. It's good for the community, too. The kids can watch us practice and learn. They'll be better than we are now."

When the team returned to its Sitka High gym sleeping quarters, some players lay down for a nap. Some took showers. Some pulled out cell phones to inform people back home that they had won.

Keifer Kanayurak and Big John dressed, went outside, and looked at those towering trees. On the walk back from the field Kanayurak had scooped up an enormous, three-foot-wide leaf. Some people pick up loose change from sidewalks. Kanayurak was mesmerized by a chunk of botanical debris the likes of which would never be seen in Barrow. The leaf seemed to be a leftover from the filming of *Mutiny on the Bounty*, or some other Pacific Island movie. He and Big John stared at the leaf, handled the leaf, simply flat-out marveled at the size of the leaf. In the end, they decided not to take it home because it probably would be dented, torn, or otherwise mutilated on a multi-airplane, hopefully-not-thirty-six-hour return journey.

The contrast between the city of Sitka and the city of Barrow couldn't have been clearer.

"It's crazy," Dunbar said as he watched his teammates discard the leaf.

Big John became emotional all over again when he began talking about the end of the season and the end of his Barrow football career. The sadness in his face, the tears welling in his eyes, told the story as eloquently as his words. The win meant so much to him. The players all hugging afterward was something he would remember. All of that came through in a simple summary sentence.

"It's my last year," Lambrecht said.

Lambrecht seemed more than ever like the teddy bear his teammates said he was.

Voss sat down on the concrete stairs at the gym's side, periodically gazing at the tall trees and letting his mind flash back to different moments of the season. He knew nobody expected his team to win four games. But he also silently believed before the start of the season that it would be at least this good. Just because the team had the notoriety of being from Barrow, Alaska—the Top of the World—didn't mean it wasn't all just football. He felt the same things would work and the same things would fail as they would with any other young football team.

"I thought we easily could go .500," Voss said. "You still make second-year mistakes. You've got to have the patience to see it out. You can take the whole bunch of them and put them anywhere in the United States and they'd just be kids."

Maybe so. But these football players weren't from just anywhere in the United States. Players with last names like Ahkiviana, Evikana, Kaleak, or Kanayurak would not be listed on football rosters in South Carolina or Louisiana. They represented an Iñupiat Eskimo community, whose team nickname of Whalers was a symbol of a tradition thousands of years old.

Olson, a thoughtful sophomore, understood this well. Being part of Barrow football at the beginning meant something to him.

"We can look back on this one day and say, 'I did that,'" Olson said. "But the amount of community pride we've gotten out of this, that's been the best thing."

It showed up in so many ways: Price Brower, at a game in his polar bear pants, with the Whalers megaphone in his hands. The words "Go Whalers," painted in yellow on a blue trash bin across the street from the high school. Clancy Itta's twelve-year-old son, Addison, proclaiming, "I want to play football."

At the end of the National Football League 2007–8 season, playoff games contested in Green Bay in a snowstorm one week and in frigid cold the next were the talk of the country. Midweek between those playoff games the mercury tumbled to –45°F in Barrow, with a –75°F windchill factor. If anyone wondered why the Alaska high school football season ended in October, there was a meteorological phenomenon to support the schedule makers.

Whaler football had been over for a couple of months by then. But it had created warm memories.

The Whalers realized they had done something pretty special during their first season in the Greatland Conference. All of Alaska took notice. They put Barrow on the map for people who were geographically challenged. They won more than their share of games. And they stamped their own brand of thunder on the tundra in the sport of football.

BARROW HIGH SCHOOL

# FOOTBALL ROSTER 2007

| Last name | First name | Position | Class |
| --- | --- | --- | --- |
| Ahkiviana | Forrest | Off/Def Line | Sophomore |
| Barr | Tim | Linebacker | Senior |
| Blankenship | Colton | Off/Def Line | Sophomore |
| Burke | Joe | Linebacker | Freshman |
| Dunbar | Alastair | Linebacker | Sophomore |
| Edwards | Anthony | RB/DB | Sophomore |
| Edwardsen | Van | DB | Junior |
| Elbert | Taylor | FB/LB | Junior |
| Enlow II | Forrest | RB/DB | Sophomore |
| Enoch | Dane | Off/Def Line | Junior |
| Enoch | Denver | Off/Def Line | Senior |
| Evikana | Dave | DB/RB | Junior |
| Fishel | Austin | WR/DB | Junior |
| George | Luke | FB/LB | Sophomore |
| Gerke | Albert | QB/DB | Sophomore |
| Gleason | Cody | TE/DE | Sophomore |
| Gonzales | Mike | C/Def Line | Senior |
| Hope | Jarid | FB/LB | Senior |
| Kaleak | Robin | Off/Def Line | Sophomore |

| Last name | First name | Position | Class |
|---|---|---|---|
| Kanayurak | Keifer | Off/Def Line | Junior |
| Lambrecht | John | Off/Def Line | Senior |
| Litera | Trevor | Off/Def Line | Junior |
| Martin | Jim | WR/DB | Junior |
| Olson | Mike | Off/Def Line | Sophomore |
| Panigeo | Adrian | WR/DB | Freshman |
| Pili | Ganina | WR/DB | Junior |
| Rock | Mac | WR/DB | Junior |
| Rohan | Zac | Off/Def Line | Senior |
| Romine | Cody | QB/DB | Junior |
| Ruckle | Jason | Off/Def Line | Senior |
| Sanders | Justin | WR/DB | Junior |
| Snow | Nathaniel | WR/DB | Freshman |
| Stotts | Mikey | RB/DB | Sophomore |
| Thomas | Daniel | QB/P/K/DB | Sophomore |
| Vigo | Robert | RB/LB | Sophomore |
| Wilson III | John | Off/Def Line | Junior |

**Head Coach:** Mark Voss.

**Assistant Coaches:** Brad Igou, Brian Houston, and Jeremy Arnhart.

# About the Author

LEW FREEDMAN IS A CHICAGO-BASED SPORTSWRITER who lived in Alaska for seventeen years. A prizewinning journalist, the former sports editor of the *Anchorage Daily News* is a graduate of Boston University and earned a master's degree from Alaska Pacific University. The author of thirty books about Alaska and sports, Freedman lives in Bolingbrook, Illinois, with his wife, Debra.

12108